HO NCE

BODY BOOK

BLOOD, BONES AND BODY BITS

DISGUSTING DIGESTION

BULGING BRAINS

Three Horrible Books in One

NICK ARNOLD TONY DE SAULLES

SCHOLASTIC

Scholastic Children's Books,
Commonwealth House, 1-19 New Oxford Street,
London WC1A 1NU, UK

A division of Scholastic Ltd
London ~ New York ~ Toronto ~ Sydney ~ Auckland
Mexico City ~ New Delhi ~ Hong Kong

Published in this edition by Scholastic Ltd, 2000

Blood, Bones and Body Bits
First published in the UK by Scholastic Ltd, 1996

Disgusting Digestion
First published in the UK by Scholastic Ltd, 1998

Bulging Brains
First published in the UK by Scholastic Ltd, 1999

ISBN 0 439 99954 5

Printed by The Bath Press, Bath

10 9 8 7 6 5 4 3 2 1

Contents

Blood, Bones and Body Bits

Disgusting Digestion

Bulging Brains

BLOOD, BONES AND BODY BITS

Nick Arnold has been writing stories and books since he was a youngster, but never dreamt he'd find fame writing about Horrible Science. His research involved inspecting sick, battling with threadworms and volunteering for brain surgery and he enjoyed every minute of it.

Nick's hobbies include eating pizza, riding his bike and thinking up corny jokes (though not all at the same time).

Tony De Saulles picked up his crayons when he was still in nappies and has been doodling ever since. He takes Horrible Science very seriously and even agreed to investigate what happens in an operating theatre and where school dinners go. Fortunately, he has made a full recovery.

When he's not out with his sketchpad, Tony likes to write poetry and play squash, though he hasn't written any poetry about squash yet.

INTRODUCTION

Science is sickening! Extra science homework is really rotten – but one of the most horribly sickening science subjects is the science of the body. I mean, doesn't the thought of all that blood and all those guts and bones turn your legs into jelly?

Doctors and teachers use a sickening selection of tongue-twisting names for bits you didn't even know you had. By the way – did you know that medical students have to learn 10,000 new words? And you thought English lessons were tough!

But science doesn't just belong to the experts – it belongs to everybody, because everybody's got a body – and you've got every right to know what's going on in yours. Why it gurgles and creaks and squelches and other tantalising topics.

And that's what this book is about. The things YOU really want to know about YOUR body. The horrible bits. The horribly interesting bits. Here's your chance to find out what billions of germs are doing lurking in your guts. What happens when you cut a brain in half, and why doctors once covered their patients in slimy leeches. So if you find science a closed book – here's a chance to change your mind.

And once you've boned up on bones and got the inside story on your insides – who knows? You might even find the body horribly amazing. Then you could teach your doctor a thing or two. Or even blind your teachers with some really sickening scientific facts. (That doesn't mean doing nasty things to their eyeballs!) One thing is certain. Science will never be the same again!

BITS OF BODY

A disgusting discovery

It was past midnight and the rain was splattering against the window-pane of the lonely attic room. By the dim light of a candle Baron Frankenstein gazed in horror at the creature that he had just put together from bits of chopped-up dead bodies. The monster was unbelievably, hideously ugly. Suddenly a shudder seemed to run through the creature's body and it stirred like a heavy sleeper about to wake. . .

DON'T PANIC! It's only a story. Frankenstein was written by Mary Shelley nearly 200 years ago and no one has succeeded in making an entire human being out of bits of body . . . yet. But just supposing you wanted to have a go, here's a bit of advice. . .

If this sounds too gruesome to be true, remember that in the Baron's time there was a serious shortage of bodies to cut up. In many countries this grisly practice was against the law. This was a problem because scientists could only probe the secrets of the human body by the dissection – cutting up – of dead bodies. In desperation, some scientists turned to crime.

The Baron's guide to body-snatching

Body-snatchers were people who went about stealing bodies. The body-snatchers knew that doctors would pay handsomely for a nice fresh corpse to cut up. Here's how to get hold of one yourself (and make some extra pocket money).

Method 1 – execute a robbery. This was the method used by Andreas Versalius, a famous 16th-century scientist, when he was living in the old town of Louvain in Belgium.

1 Wait until dark.

2 Go to a nearby place of execution and remove the corpses of any criminals you find.

3 Cut up the body and hide bits of it under your cloak. That way you can smuggle it all past the guards on the city gates without anyone asking awkward questions.

4 You can hide the bits of body in your bedroom and put them together later.

If you can't find any bodies lying around things get a tiny bit more difficult.

Method 2 – rob a grave. This method was used in both Britain and America in the 19th century.

1 Wait until dark. You will need a wooden spade for silent digging, a lantern, a canvas sheet, some ropes with hooks attached, a crowbar and a sack.

2 Go to a graveyard. Make sure you keep an eye out for angry relatives, vicars, etc. who might just try to stop you digging up the bodies.
3 Dig up the grave. Spread the dug earth on the sheet ready for you to shovel it all back again afterwards. This avoids making a mess that might give you away.

4 Lift the coffin with the hooks, then lever open the coffin using the crowbar. Sssh! Keep it quiet!
5 Put the body in the sack. Fill in the hole and run for it. You should be able to do all this in an hour. Oh, and don't forget the sheet!

Body jigsaws

Let's imagine that by hook or by crook you managed to get hold of some bits of body. Now you can start putting them all together to make your very own Frankenstein's monster! Unlike a normal jigsaw, you have to start with the middle bits, not the edge (the skin!). Make sure you put all the pieces in the right places and don't forget any vital parts or it won't work. If you make a mistake you will have to cut the body open and take a few bits out in order to fit the missing bit in its proper place. Here's a list of body bits to help you know what's what in your body.

Stretchy skin

A huge waterproof, germ-proof outer covering. It's better than any other kind of clothing because it actually repairs itself when it gets damaged. It also has its own heating and cooling systems. Skin wraps round the rest of the body bits to keep them in position.

Fabulous fat

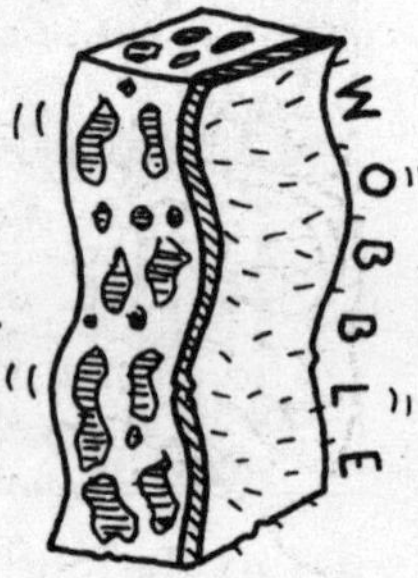

Fit a layer of fat snugly underneath the skin. Slabs of fat also slop and wobble around the tummy and hips area. Fat keeps out the cold. It acts as a convenient place for storing spare sugar from all those sweets your monster eats. Your monster will use up some of the sugar when it goes for its morning jog.

Eyeballs, ears and snotty nose

Very important for seeing, hearing and sniffing (in that order). In fact the really important bits of these body parts are the bits you can't see. These form the high-tech gadgetry that converts the information picked up from the senses into signals for the brain to de-code. So make sure those nerves are all properly wired up.

Other items you will need . . .

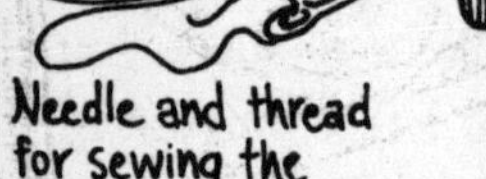

Needle and thread for sewing the body together

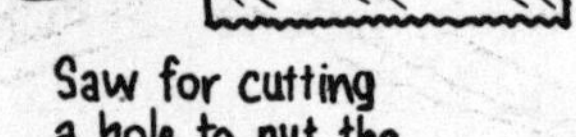

Saw for cutting a hole to put the brain in

Funnel for pouring blood into the body

Delicate nerves

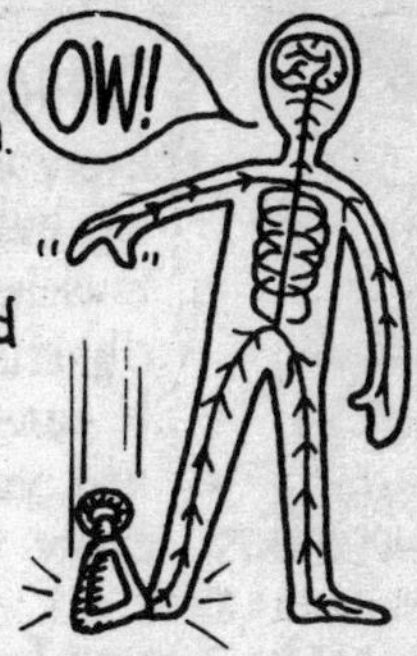

These are the monster's signalling system. They tell the brain what's going on and transmit orders from the brain to get those lazy muscles moving. Nerves extend into every part of the body - from the top of the head to the tips of the toes. But the main nerves all join up in the spinal cord inside the backbone.

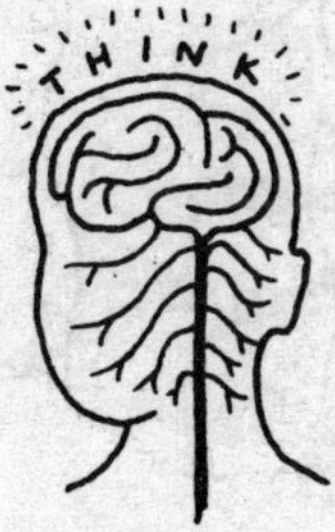

Brilliant brain

This bit acts as the boss of the monster's body. Gently plop it inside the top part of the skull, nicely protected from the outside world. It contains all your monster's memories and personality so don't bash it around too much.

Sturdy skeleton

There are 206 bones - give or take a few extra ones that some people have. Bones are very important to keep the body upright and stop it collapsing like a deflated balloon. Make sure you get the bones in the right order. This is very tricky, especially when you get to the 26 bones that make up a single foot.

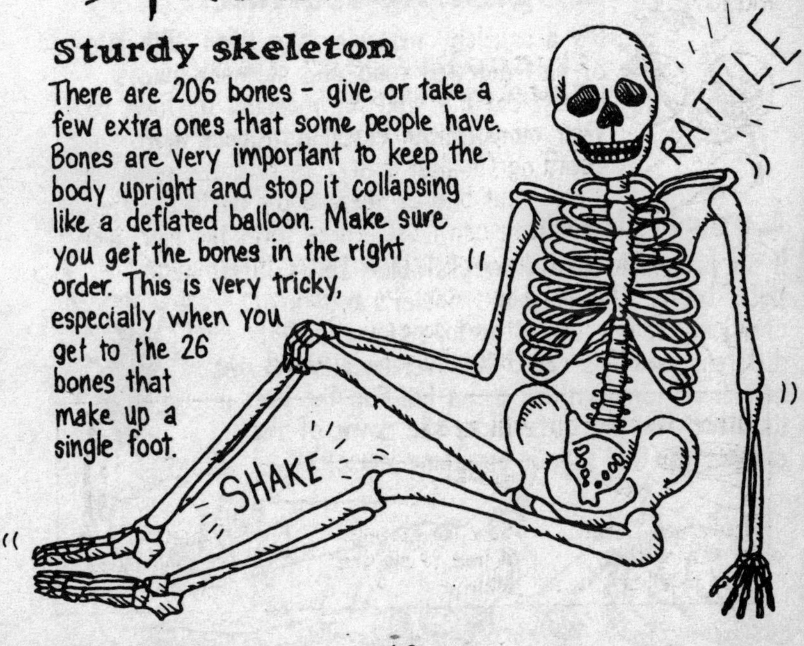

Mighty muscles

Everyone's got muscles even if they're not big bulgy ones. There are hundreds of muscles and they need to be put in their rightful places or they won't work properly. In each hand there are twenty muscles – and your monster will use 200 muscles every time it takes a step.

Tough teeth

These are the hardest parts of the body – guaranteed to tackle those rubbery school dinners. Make sure you put the teeth in their correct positions and teach your monster how to brush them regularly.

Disgusting stomach

It's a squelchy muscular bag filled with bits of half-digested food and stomach juices. Lovely! But it's vital for mashing up food so your monster can digest its dinner more easily.

Lovely liver

It's a brownish/purplish/reddish blob about 15cm thick. Lovely. This is your monster's built-in chemical factory and it performs over 500 different jobs. It's called the liver because no-one can 'liver' long without it, ha ha. Pop the liver in its place over the guts under the dome of the diaphragm (that's your breathing muscle).

Clever kidneys

These filter the blood and take out the waste products from your monster's body. It's got two kidneys and the one on the left-hand side of the body is always higher up than the right one.

Beautiful blood

It's the body's transport system, and it carries oxygen gas breathed in through the lungs and little bits of food to nourish the body. And that's just for starters. There are also white cells that fight germs and platelets that help the body heal itself. Yes - blood's got the lot. Your monster will need about 5 -5½ litres (9-10 pints) of the gloopy red stuff.

Hardworking heart

This lump of muscle is vital for pumping the blood around the body. Make sure you put the heart in its correct place - nearer the right side of the chest. Also make sure you get it the correct way round - the left-hand side of the heart pumps the blood round the body, but the right side only pumps it round the lungs.

Foamy lungs

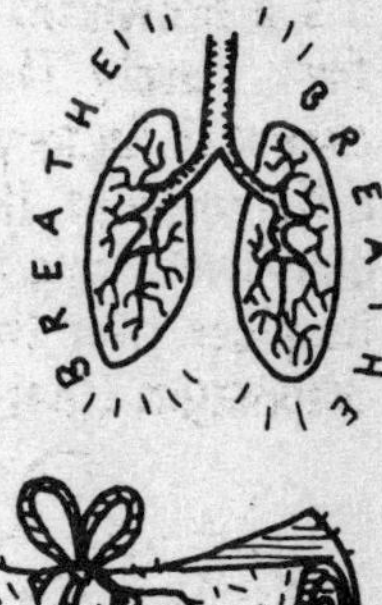

These are like a big spongy pair of bellows in the chest that can hold up to six litres of air. Your monster needs to breathe in order to get the oxygen from the air to keep its body cells alive.

Weird bits 'n' pieces

Some bits of the body are well known. We've all heard about the brain and we've all heard from the stomach when it starts rumbling. But what about the not-so-well-known bits? Which of these bits are just too weird to be true? (You get double the score if you can work out where any of them fit in!)

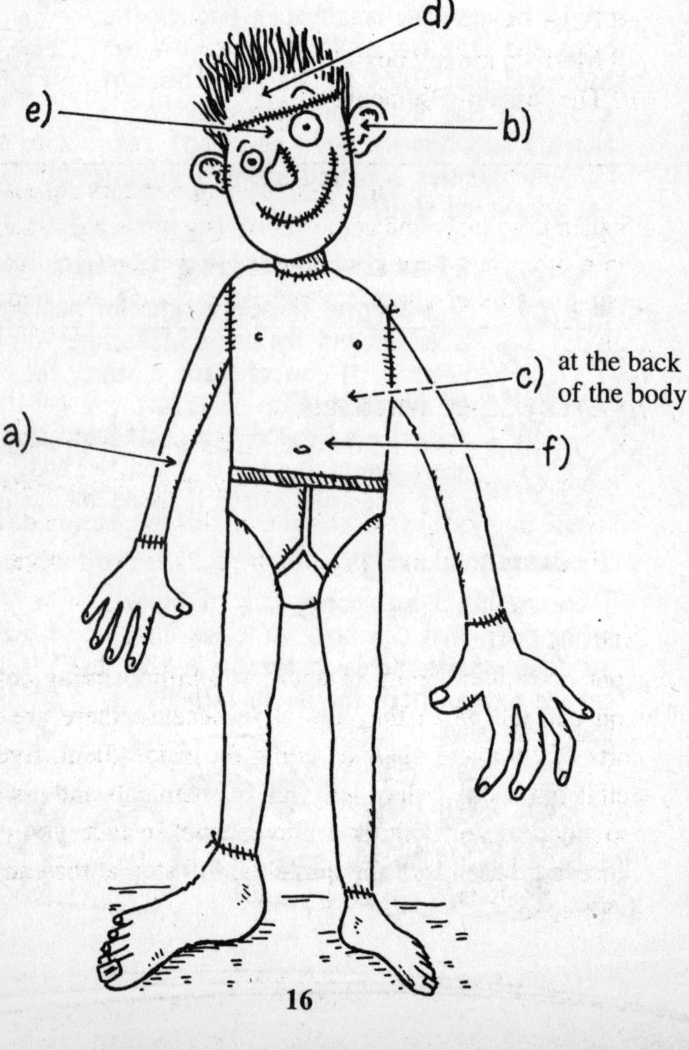

1 The oval window
2 The funny bone
3 The innominate canal of Arnold
4 The wish bone
5 The boomerang bone
6 Fabricus's ship
7 The bicycle tendon
8 Lane's kinks
9 Morris's kidney box
10 The fossa of Blumenbach

Answers: True 1 b) Inside the head - it's part of the hearing system, **2 a)** In the arm, **3 d)** In the skull, **6 e)** Part of the skull, **8 f)** Twists in the guts, **9 c)** Skin marks over the kidneys, **False 4, 5, 7, 10.**

Is everything working?

Whilst you are assembling your Frankenstein's monster, it's always a good idea to occasionally check that the bits of body are in good shape. You can do this by peering down a microscope and making sure the cells are still alive. . .

Secret cells

Your body is made up of about 100 billion living cells. You can tell when they are alive because there are all sorts of chemical changes going on inside them. Every cell is like a tiny ball of jelly full of chemicals and it's far too small to see without a microscope. In fact, you can squeeze thousands of them into the full stop at the end of this sentence.

Inside the cell is a secret world. There are tiny objects called mitochondria (mito-con-dre-a) that produce energy, and there are pathways and little storage areas. And each cell has a nucleus that stores the information to make new cells. Sometimes the cell reproduces by pulling itself into two pieces.

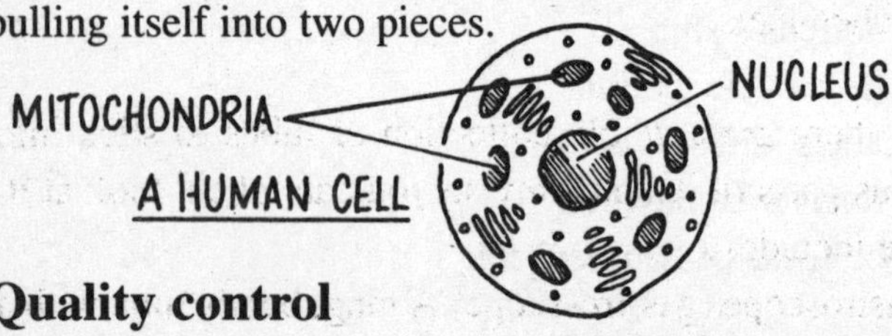

Quality control

Once your Frankenstein's monster is assembled you'll need a collection of amazing but slightly gruesome tools to check whether everything is in working order inside.

X-rays

Some of the devices below use X-rays. These are a special kind of light ray that you can't actually see. X-rays can pass through the body's skin, muscles and fat but not solid bone. This is why an X-ray picture can check out whether the bones are in good shape.

CAT – computerised axial tomography scanner. This amazing machine scans a slice of your monster's brain using X-rays and shows the result on a computer screen.
Angiogram (An-gy-o-gram) An X-ray picture of your monster's blood vessels after they have been injected with chemicals.

Then there are a whole collection of tubes to stick into various parts of its anatomy so you can take a look at it. These include. . .

Gastroscope (gas-tro-scope) A long, bendy tube with a light on the end. Ideal for poking down its throat to see into its stomach and guts.

Ophthalmoscope (op-thal-mo-scope) A bright light and viewer to see what the inside of its eyeball looks like.

Arthroscope (ar-throw-scope) A tube a bit like a telescope for peering inside your creature's joints.

Otoscope (ot-o-scope) A light a bit like a torch for shining in your monster's ear-holes.

All these bits of equipment are useful because without them it's horribly hard to see what's going on inside the body. There's usually a layer of sweaty skin in the way. Let's take a longer look at it. . .

SWEATY SKIN

Poke around in the darker corners of your house and you may find a lovely collection of fingernails, hair and bits of skin. Bits of skin? Well – you know those pretty bits of dust that dance in the sunlight on a summer's morning? Most of them are bits of flaked-off skin – just some of the ten billion bits of skin you lose every day!

Skin fact file

Name of body part: Skin

Where found: All over the outside of the body

Useful things it does: It helps to keep you at the right temperature and keep out germs.

Grisly details: It suffers from a disgusting array of skin diseases such as boils, carbuncles, etc.

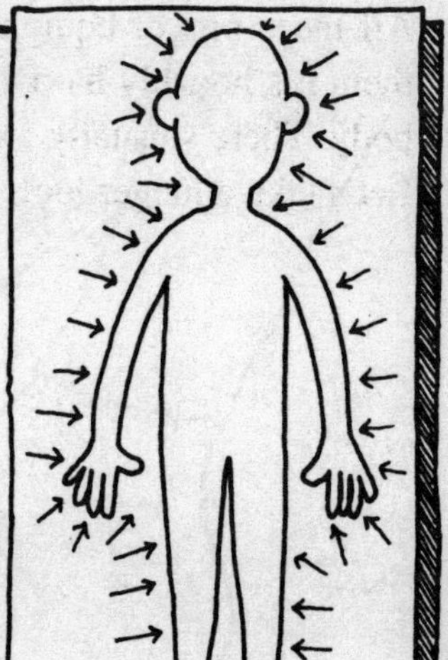

Amazing features: If you removed an adult's skin it would cover about 2 square metres (2.4 square yards). A child's skin covers about 1.5 square metres. Skin is the heaviest part of your body and weighs a whopping 2.5-4.5kg (5-10lbs), depending on your size.

Disgusting skin diseases

Doctors like nothing better than reading at mealtimes. And their favourite reading matter? Colourful medical magazines with pictures of skin diseases. Gulp! Here's your chance to check whether you could be a doctor. Try matching the picture to the disease:

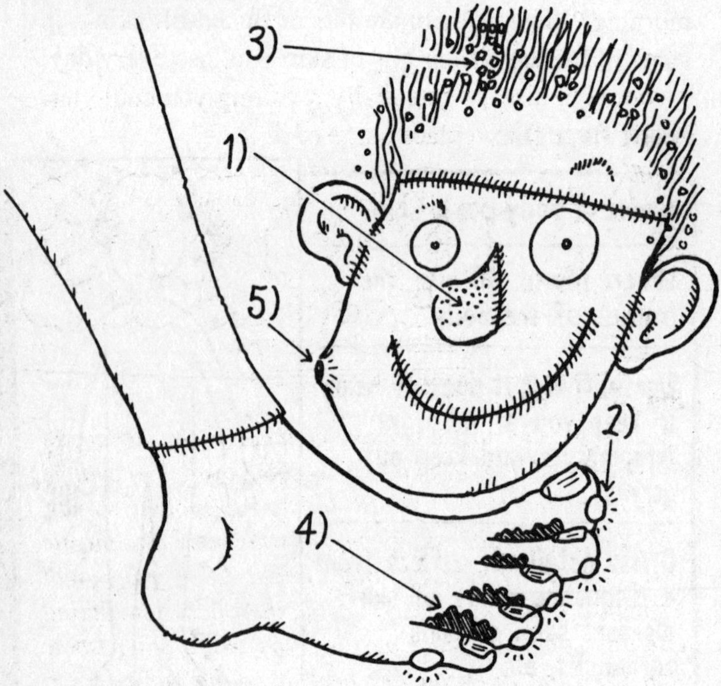

a) A fungus that grows between the toes and makes the skin peel.
b) A gland-opening that's been blocked with sweat or grease – it swells until it bursts, spraying pus everywhere.
c) Painful, itchy blotches on your toes caused by the blood supply cutting off in cold weather.
d) A build up of dead skin cells stuck together with grease.

e) Greasy dead skin cells that turn black when they come in contact with the air.

Answers: 1e) Blackheads 2c) Chilblains 3d) Dandruff 4a) Athlete's Foot 5b) Boils

Nasty nose jobs

If your skin disease gets really revolting you could have plastic surgery to replace some of it.

Bet you never knew!

Modern plastic surgeons make changes to the surface of the body – adding or taking away skin in order to change what someone looks like. If you've got enough money, you can change almost any part of your body. But plastic surgery actually began in India about 2,000 years ago! Criminals were punished by having their noses cut off but one day someone found out that you could stitch some skin from the forehead or cheek over the wound so it didn't look so bad. In Sicily, Italy, they took the idea one stage further. A sinister surgeon named Branca cut off a slave's nose and sewed it onto one of his patients who had lost his own nose in a battle! Modern plastic surgeons make changes to the surface of the body – adding or taking away skin in order to change someone's appearance. These operations are called "skin grafts".

But if skin can be amazingly horrible on the outside – on the inside it's also horribly AMAZING.

Getting under your skin

If you removed an adult's skin (a very messy job) it would cover about two square metres (2.4 square yards). A child's skin covers about 1.5 square metres (1.8 square yards). Skin is the heaviest part of your body and weighs a whopping 2.5-4.5 kg (5-10 lbs) depending on your size. That's as heavy as a bag stuffed with food from a supermarket! But the outer layer of your skin is less than 1 mm thick. Even so, it's packed with sensors for hot and cold, and blood vessels and fat and cells for producing sweat and so on. Confusing isn't it? Try imagining your skin as an incredible high-tech, high-fashion space suit. Would you dare to wear it?

The Birthday Suit

Have YOU ever wished to slip into something more comfortable? Something that's cool in hot weather and warm in cold weather. Try the new birthday suit. But guess what - you've got it on already! Yes, it's that suit you got for your birthday – that's the day you were born!

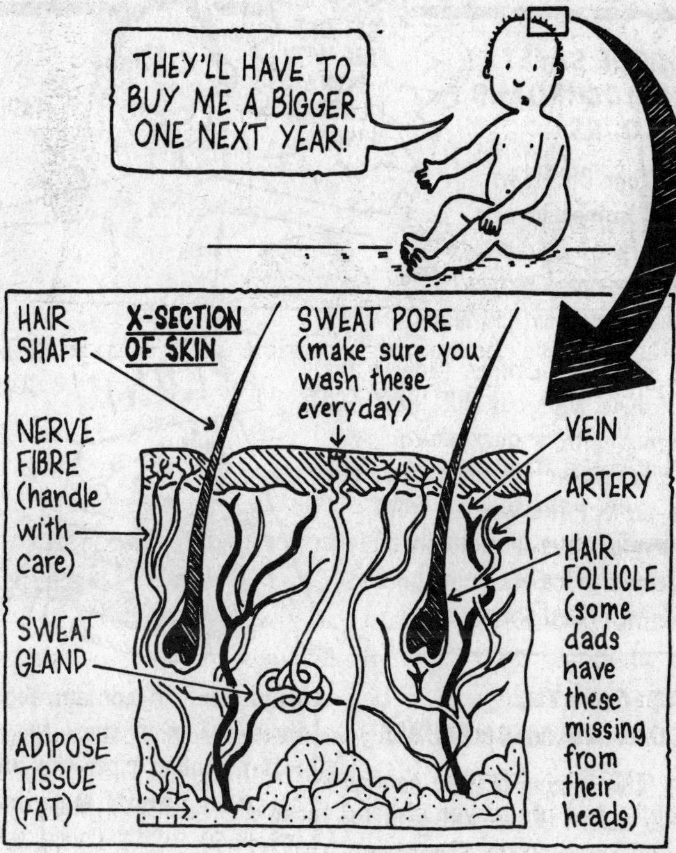

Marvel at these incredible features. Amaze your friends with THE BIRTHDAY SUIT's unique technical wizardry!

The amazing BIRTHDAY SUIT

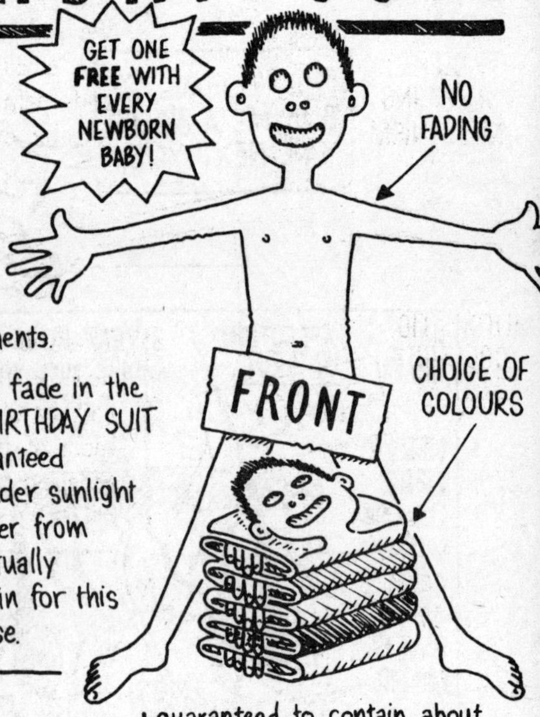

UNIQUE SAFETY PHOTOCHROMIC COLOURS

1. Your BIRTHDAY SUIT comes in a variety of colours all provided by its unique melanin pigments.

2. Ordinary clothes fade in the sunshine but your BIRTHDAY SUIT comes with a guaranteed darkening action under sunlight to protect the wearer from harmful rays. It actually creates extra melanin for this all-important purpose.

AUTOMATIC COOLING MECHANISM

3. This unique feature springs into action if the suit gets too hot. The water-cooling pipes produce sweat to cool the outside of the BIRTHDAY SUIT.

4. Every BIRTHDAY SUIT is guaranteed to contain about three million of these tiny water-cooling pipes (known as sweat glands) and each one is so tightly coiled that if you pulled it out it would be over a metre long! The total length of your pipe system is 50km (31 miles)!

MANUFACTURER'S WARNING

5. The automatic cooling systems can easily lose 1.7 litres (quarter of a gallon) of sweat every hour in hot weather, so make sure it's well supplied with water.

6. The sweat under the arms and between the legs contains chemicals that germs like to eat. Yum! The germs make the stale sweat all yucky and smelly. (Please see Care and maintenance instruction 9 – for everybody's sake.)

7. Some people use deodorants to tackle the little problem above. These work by blocking the holes in the cooling systems. Fortunately they don't stop most of the sweat from escaping otherwise the BIRTHDAY SUIT would overheat.

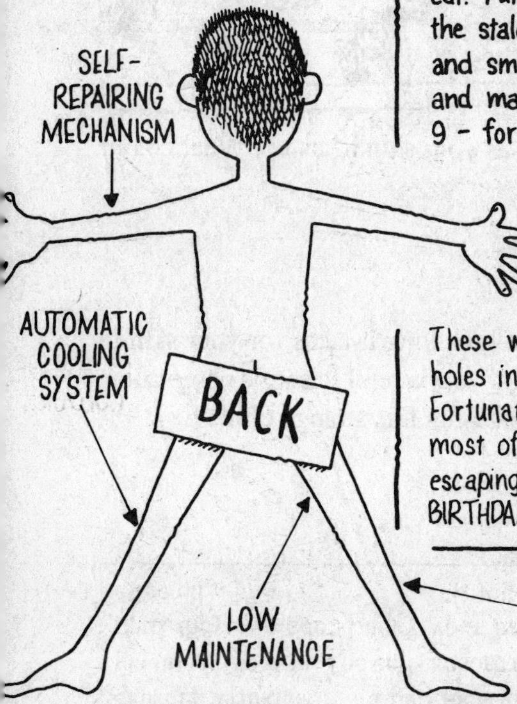

CARE & MAINTENANCE INSTRUCTIONS

8. Your BIRTHDAY SUIT needs very little maintenance because of its unique self-repair mechanism. If it gets torn or damaged it will simply re-grow!

9. All you need to do is to gently wash the outer layer in soap and water to remove any dirt and flaky bits. Don't worry if bits drop off – the BIRTHDAY SUIT will always grow some more underneath!

Dare you find out for yourself . . . how your skin works?

For this experiment you will have to take a hot bath. It's OK – all the great scientists had to make sacrifices.

1 Note what happens as your skin heats up. What colour does it go?

a) Red

b) Blue

c) White

2 Using a watch, time how long it takes for your skin to wrinkle up. As a result of your careful scientific observation, what do you think is causing this strange effect?

a) The heat

b) Old age

c) The water

Answers 1 a) The colour is due to the blood vessels that run under the skin widening to allow more blood in. This helps release heat through the skin and cools your over-heating body! **2 c)** Your skin is covered by a layer of oily grease called sebum that keeps the water out. But after a while some of the water seeps through and makes the under layer waterlogged. This crumples up the top layer causing wrinkles. It's a bad idea to let too much water get under the skin. The cells absorb all the water they can until they explode! Lucky your hair and nails are not affected.

HORRIBLE HAIR AND NASTY NAILS

What's the point of hair and nails? Hairs always seem to end up blocking the bathroom plug hole and nails get nasty black grime stuck underneath them. But then they're also interesting in a disgusting kind of way.

Hair and nails fact file

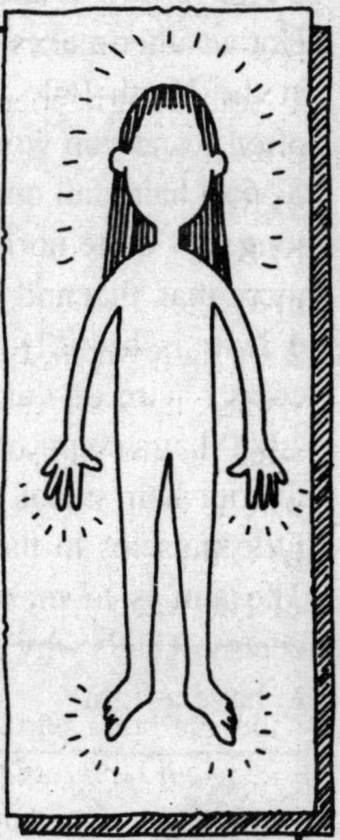

Name of body part: Hair and nails

Where found: Your body is covered by five million little hairs but your longest hairs are on your head (surprisingly!). Nails are found on your fingers and toes, but you knew that.

Useful things they do: Hair keeps you warm. Your nails stop your fingers and toes squashing up every time you touch something.

Grisly details: Hair and nails are said to continue to grow for a while on dead bodies.

Amazing features: Hair and nails are both made out of a hard substance called keratin. It's the same stuff that makes feathers and dinosaur claws.

Hair-raising hair

Here's your chance to hoodwink your hairdresser with a few hair-raising facts.

1 Most people have about 100,000 hairs on their heads. Fair-haired people can have 150,000 and red-haired people have to make do with about 90,000. (I wonder who counted them all!)

2 Hair grows at about 1 cm a month or 0.33 mm a day. Hot weather makes your hair grow faster. So if you lived at the North Pole you wouldn't need your hair cut so often – and you wouldn't want it cut so often.

3 Most hairs fall out before they reach 90 cm (35 inches) long. It's quite normal to lose up to 60 hairs a day. Any more than that and you might start going bald!

4 Hair is horribly strong. One hair is stronger than a copper wire of the same thickness. A rope made from 1,000 hairs could lift a well-built man.

5 Your hair stands on end when you're scared because little muscles in the skin pull on the roots of the hairs. The aim is to make you look big and fearsome to an enemy. That's why cats fluff their fur when they're going to have a fight!

Nail-biting notes

Now mystify your manicurist with these nails' tales.

1 Your nails grow from an area underneath the skin called the nail bed. (This is nothing to do with the bed of nails that Indian fakirs sometimes sleep on.)

2 If you trap a nail in the door it will stop growing and drop off. With a bit of luck a lovely brand new nail will grow underneath. That's OK then!

3 Sometimes toenails start burrowing into the surrounding flesh. This horribly hurtful condition is caused by not cutting the nail straight across. But cutting nails is better than biting them!

4 Nail biting doesn't exactly kill you – but it looks revolting and makes your nails sore, and it helps lots of germs leap into your mouth. It also tends to put people off their soup in posh restaurants. Especially when you chew your toenails as well!

5 If you didn't cut your nails for a year they would be 2.5 cm (one inch) long.

But that's nothing compared to some people!

Record-breakers

Longest finger nails Shridhar Chillal of Pune Maharashtra in India stopped cutting his finger nails in

1952. By 1995 the nails on his left hand had reached 574 cm (226 inches) long.

Longest hair Mata Jagdamba of India has hair 4.23 m long. This is amazing because, as we've already said, normally a hair will stop growing and drop out by the time it reaches 90 cm (35 inches).

Longest beard Hans N. Langseth of the USA grew a 533 cm (209 inches) long beard. Sadly, Hans is no longer with us – he died in 1927. But you'll be relieved to know that the famous beard is now a museum exhibit.

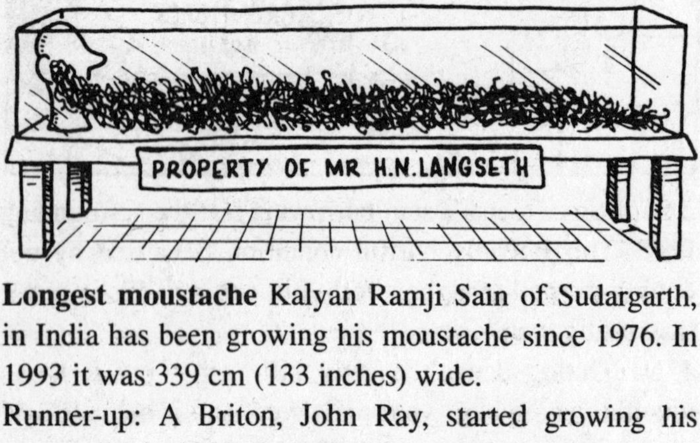

Longest moustache Kalyan Ramji Sain of Sudargarth, in India has been growing his moustache since 1976. In 1993 it was 339 cm (133 inches) wide.

Runner-up: A Briton, John Ray, started growing his moustache in 1939. By 1976 his moustache was 189 cm (74 inches) wide. But then he sat on one side of it in the bath and 42 cm (16 inches) of hair split off the end.

Bet You Never Knew!

Even with hair all over it, your skin can sense things that touch it. Oh, so you DID know that! Well, bet you never knew that the human fingertips are so sensitive that they can feel an object move even if it only stirs a thousandth of a millimetre. Sounds like a really touchy subject! And touch is just ONE of your five sense-sational senses.

SENSATIONAL SENSES

Congratulations! You're a sensitive person – how could you be anything else with your super-sensitive touch, sight, taste, smell and hearing? And whether your view of the world is happy or sad, your senses help make sense of what's going on around you. But they're also horribly incredible in their own right – in fact they're SENSE-ATIONAL!

Sensitive senses quiz

Which senses are too sensationally sensitive to be true?

1 Your senses are so sensitive that they only take a quarter of a second to let you know when something is happening. TRUE/FALSE

2 Your eyes can tell the difference between eight million colours. TRUE/FALSE

3 Your eyes are 1,000 times more sensitive to light than the most light-sensitive film. TRUE/FALSE

4 Some people can see ultra-violet rays produced by the sun. TRUE/FALSE

5 Your tongue can taste a single drop of lemon juice even if it's mixed up with 129,000 drops of water. TRUE/FALSE

6 Your nose can detect a cheesy old pair of socks 200 metres (219 yards) away. TRUE/FALSE

7 Your ears can tell the difference between two sounds even if they are only ten-millionths of a second apart. TRUE/FALSE

8 Your ears can identify 1,500 levels of sound from high-pitched squeaks to deep booms. TRUE/FALSE

9 Some people can hear air whooshing around in the upper atmosphere. TRUE/FALSE

10 Your body can tell what time it is even if you're in a room without windows. TRUE/FALSE

Answers: 1 FALSE – your senses work much faster than that! **2** TRUE. **3** TRUE. **4** FALSE and don't try it. Looking at the sun can harm your eyes! **5** TRUE. **6** FALSE – but I suppose it depends on how strong the socks pong! **7** TRUE – if the sounds come through separate ears. **8** TRUE. **9** Supposedly TRUE but unproven – half a mark for this answer! **10** TRUE.

Your touchy senses

You've heard about the sensitive sensors under your skin? Well, did you know that they too come in no less than FIVE sensational varieties? Each one keeps you in touch in a different way.

To show you how, we need a brave volunteer. Can you

spot which sensor is doing the sensing in the five tests below?

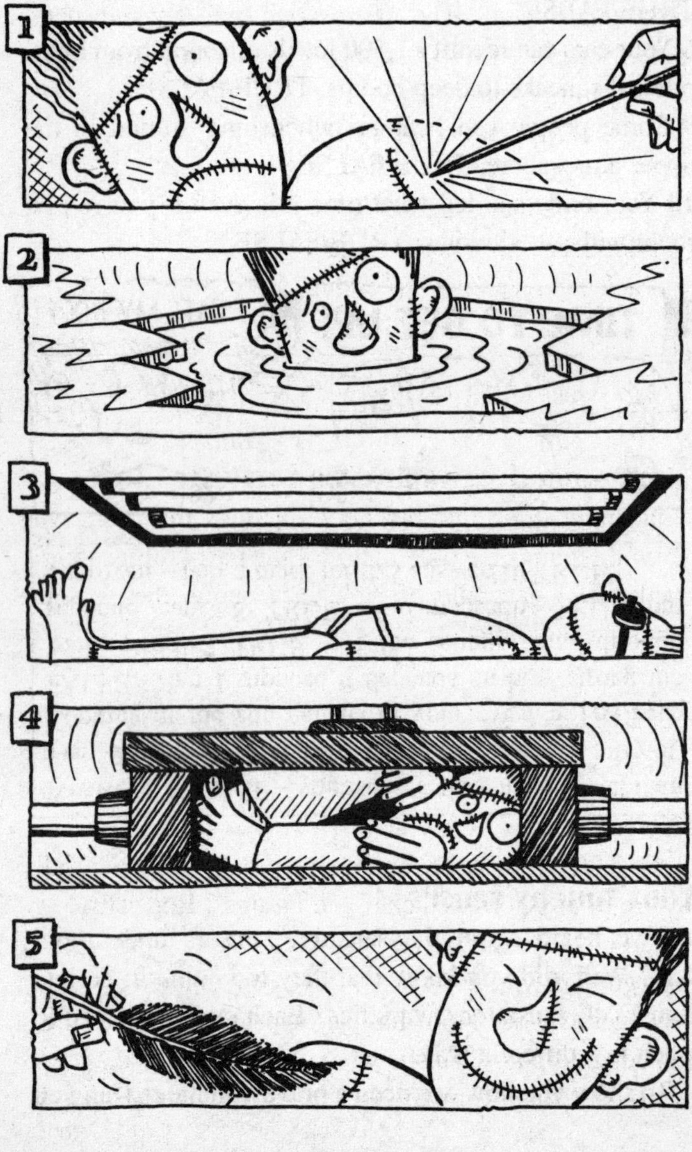

These are the sensors that you must match with the pictures. Some are named in honour of the scientists who discovered them. The person who discovered nerve endings deserves a special mention – it must have been a very painful experience.

a) Ruffini's receptors – for heat

b) Krause's receptors – cold

c) Nerve endings – pain

d) Meissner's receptors – touch

e) Pacinean receptors – pressure

Answers: 1 c) 2 b) 3 a) 4 e) 5 d)

Pain – good news and bad news!

You might think that the nerve endings that bring you painful feelings are only there for the nasty things in life. And you'd generally be right. But surely there's some good in everything?

The good news – 1

You have 500,000 sensors to keep you in touch with the outside world. Hooray!

The bad news – 1

And 2,800,000 nerve endings to make you painfully aware of any horrible aches and twinges. Boo! Hiss!

The good news – 2

But luckily your brain has its own built-in pain-killers called endorphins. This is why a soldier can lose a leg in battle and hop along without feeling any pain! Hurray!

The bad news – 2
Afterwards it hurts A LOT – and not only that. People who lose arms and legs often feel their missing limbs itching even when they're not there! Shame!

The painful truth

Pain is there to warn us that we're getting hurt. "Stop!" say your nerve endings. "And try to be more careful next time!" It's a sensible message. So you see, a bit of pain is good for you! Sounds a bit like the sort of thing your teacher might say, doesn't it? But is that good news?

A sensational sight

Your most sensational sense is sight. After all, without it we'd all be in the dark! But did you know that your eyeballs are like tiny little video cameras full of watery jelly? Is this the sort of camera that you'd like to discover in your Christmas stocking?

The eyeball camera

Seeing really is believing with the incredible EYEBALL CAMERA. Now you can keep up with the speediest sporting action even at night! Just point your camera in the right direction. Wherever you go, your EYEBALL

CAMERA goes too! In fact, it's so useful it's worth you using the two that you've already got – you know, those gloopy blobs that sit snugly in your eyeball sockets!

THE EYEBALL CAMERA

High-tech gadgets

1 Just behind the iris is a self-adjusting lens for focusing on objects near and far.

2 Your **Eyeball Camera** has no less than 130 million light-sensitive cells squeezed into an area the size of a postage stamp.

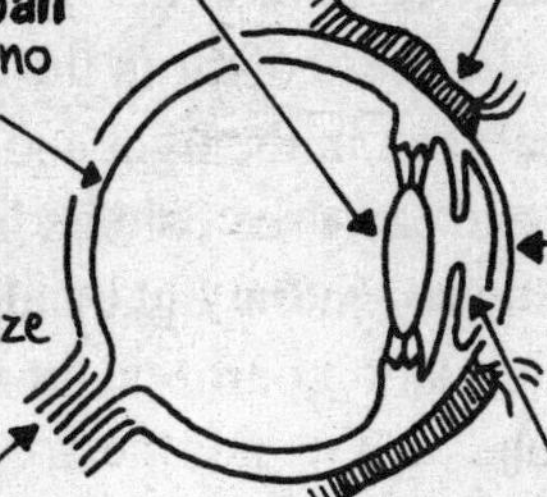

3 Nerves carry the picture to your computer screen (or brain)!

Unique protection features

1 A self-closing eyelid dust cap protects your **Eyeball Camera** when not in use.

2 Your **Eyeball Camera** lens is protected with a clear disk. No more nasty little flies spoiling your lovely clear pictures.

3 The lens of your **Eyeball Camera** is further protected by an iris ring. (lovely choice of colours!) Automatic iris hole-shrink mechanism stops you getting dazzled by bright lights!

FREE MOVING PARTS

1 Your **Eyeball Camera** is the only camera in the world that's full of water! It's got wobble-free jelly in the front section for a really clear view of life!

2 **An incredible extra.** Six slim muscle handles hold your **Eyeball Camera** securely and allow it to swing about without falling on the floor!

Dare you find out for yourself . . . how your eyeballs work?

Naturally you'll want to try out your sensational eyeball camera as soon as possible. So here are a few tests to try.

Test 1: Seeing in the dark

You will need a darkened room, a torch and a tomato. Shine the torch at the tomato and then away from it. What happens to the colour of the tomato as you shift the light away from it? Any idea why?

a) The tomato appears red both in the light and out of it. This is because the eye sees colour in the dark.

b) The tomato appears red in the light and grey out of it. This is because the eye can't see colours in the dark.

c) The tomato appears red in the light and blue out of it. This is because the dark confuses those little light-sensitive eyeball cells.

Test 2: Test your pupils*

You will need a darkened room and a mirror with a light over it. Wait in the room until your eyes are used to the dark. Cover your left eye with one hand and switch on the light over the mirror. Your uncovered pupil suddenly goes smaller. What's happened to your other pupil?

a) It's still large.

b) It's also gone small.

c) It's got even bigger.

* Or you might prefer to test your teacher's pupils – you'll be getting your own back!

Test 3: The vanishing eyeball mystery

Hold the book close to your face and close your left eye. Focus your right eye on the left eyeball. Now slowly move the book away from your face. Why does the right eyeball vanish?

a) The eye can't focus at a certain distance.

b) There's a gap in the light-sensitive cells.

c) The light-sensitive cells get tired and stop noticing things.

Answers: 1 b) There are seven million light-sensitive cone cells inside each eyeball that can see colour (either red, green or blue). But these only work in good light conditions. There are 124 million rod cells that work in dim lighting but they can only see in black and white. **2 b)** The pupils have to work together – it's a bit like being at school! **3 b)** There is a blind spot and when you look at things with it they seem to disappear. This spot is where the optic nerve connects with the inside of the eyeball.

Caring for your eyeballs – eight things you should know

1 You don't need to care for your eyeballs at all! Your body does it all for you.

2 Eyeballs come complete with their own windscreen-washing service – it's called "crying".
3 Fortunately you don't have to be sad to cry. You can produce tears whilst being sick, coughing, or by getting something in your eye or, preferably by laughing!

4 Tears are also spread over your eyeball when you blink. Every blink takes 0.3-0.4 seconds – that's half an hour each day, or five years of your life. What a blinking waste of time!
5 Any tears you don't use dry up in the drainage tube that leads from the corners of your eyes to the inside of your nose. These dried-up tears form the sleepy dust you rub from your eyes every morning!
6 Each of your eyes is protected by about 200 eyelashes. Each eyelash lasts three to five months before it falls out and another grows in its place.
7 Tiny mites live in the base of your eyelashes. They have eight legs each and look like alligators! But don't worry – they won't do you any harm. In fact they are doing you quite a favour by gobbling up harmful germs!
8 If, despite all this care and attention, your eyes don't see very well – you may need glasses.

> ***Bet You Never Knew!***
> *Do you wear glasses? If you're short-sighted you may have difficulty focusing on far-away objects. Being long-sighted means, well you can probably guess. These problems happen because your eyeballs aren't perfectly round. A pair of glasses are like extra lenses for your eyes. Well, cheer up – it's easier than taking the eyeballs out and squashing them into shape!*

Savage spectacles

One of the first people to wear "glasses" was the rotten old Roman Emperor Nero. He used a curved piece of emerald to help him enjoy the savage spectacle of lions tearing people apart at the Roman games. That sounds like really bad taste. . .

Terrible tastes and sickening smells

Here's the problem with taste and smell. They're sensational senses all right. They bring you some sensational sensations like your favourite foods and the smell of roses. But they also bring you foul bitter tastes and sickening stinks!

Terrible tastes

To find out more about taste you've got to peer into your

wet drooling mouth. Better take a look now before you chicken out!

Look closely at your tongue. Say Aghhhhhh! Can you see those little bumps and lines? The little lines are crammed with 8,000 or so taste buds linked to the brain by nerves. Different buds handle sweet, sour, salty and bitter tastes.

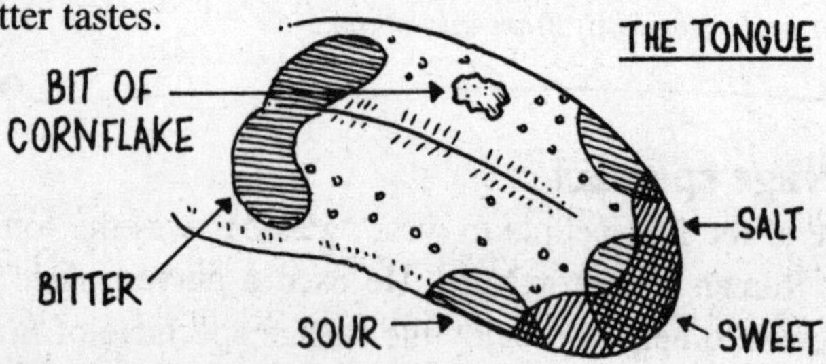

The really tasteless question is – why are you supposed to taste bitter things at all? I mean – how many bitter-tasting foods do you actually like enough to eat? Well, you're not actually meant to eat most of them – spitting them out would be a lot better for you. This is because most poisons taste bitter, so the bitter-sensitive taste buds are there to tell you that you're just about to eat some vile POISON.

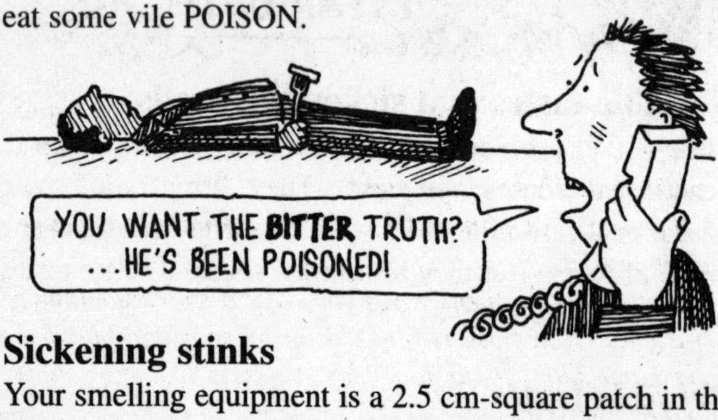

Sickening stinks

Your smelling equipment is a 2.5 cm-square patch in the top part of the area behind your nostrils. This patch has over 500 million tiny thread-like sticking-out bits called cilia (silly-ah).

Cilia have a really sickening job – they hang around in groups of eight from rod-like trunks buried in snot. (Yuck!) Smells take the form of tiny bits (called molecules) that float about in the air. When a smelly molecule lands on one of the cilia it triggers a chemical change that's passed on as a signal to the nerves.

Sensationally sensitive

Your sense of smell is sensationally sensitive. It's actually 10,000 times more sensitive than taste! That's OK when there's something nice to be sniffed but there are some really revolting odours around. And did you know your nose can sniff one molecule of the stinky juice squirted by a skunk even when it's mixed with 30,000,0000,000 molecules of fresh air?! Yeuch!

Bet you never knew!

People lump taste and smell together because. . .

1 They work together to help you appreciate the delicious flavour of your favourite foods.

2 In fact when you're eating your favourite fries and thinking, These are sensationally scrummy-tasting chips, *you're actually smelling them!*

3 If you couldn't smell them they'd probably taste like cardboard!

4 That's what happens when you have a snorting stinker of a cold. Your nose is blocked up by snot and because you can't smell, your food doesn't taste like it should! Sounds horrible!

Silly sound detectors

Ears are eerie things. After all, just think how odd some people's ears look. And guess what? They're even odder on the inside! Just listen to this. . .

How the ears work

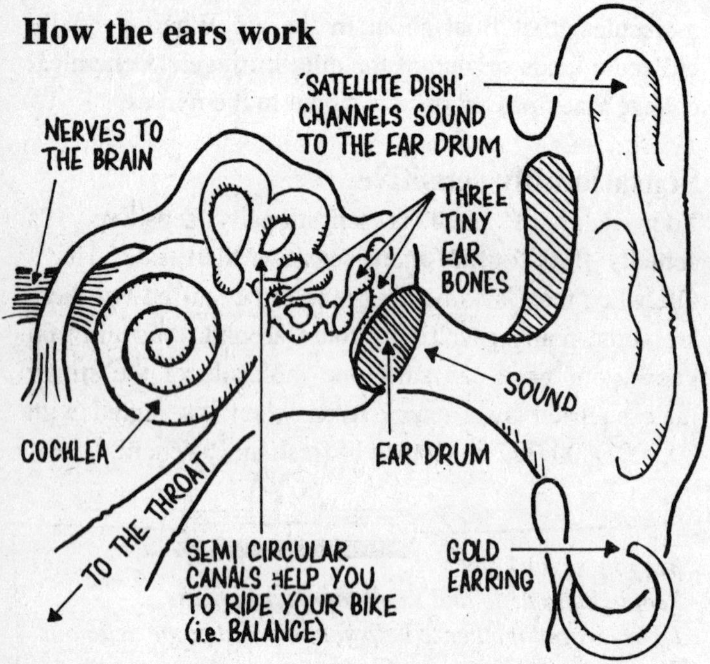

The ears work like a couple of satellite dishes linked up to a drum, linked up to a triangle and stick linked up to a microphone with a carpenter's level attached! Simple, isn't it?

1 Like satellite dishes, your ears pick up signals in the air and bounce them into the central hole. With your ears, the signals in question are sounds.

2 The eardrum's a bit like a real drum. It trembles when sounds hit it.

3 The trembling eardrum makes the tiny ear bones jangle just like a triangle hit by a stick.

4 The cochlea picks up the sounds and makes them into nerve signals that go to the brain. It's a bit like a microphone picking up sounds and sending them down a wire.

5 Like a carpenter's level, the semi-circular canals are full of liquid that sloshes around as your head moves. Sensors in the canals stop you losing your balance. This is good news for tight-rope walkers!

An urgent horrible health warning

Dear Reader

Are you reading this page in a car or a ship? Well – DON'T! If you try to concentrate on something that keeps moving (like now) – your semi-circular canals end up getting confused. Your brain is baffled by the confusing signals and (according to one theory) produces chemicals that make you violently travel sick!

P.S. If you already feel a bit queasy try to avoid being sick over this book. The pages might stick together.

P.P.S. Oh dear, too late.

Dare you find out for yourself . . . why your ears go POP?

Try listening to yourself yawning. You may hear a few tiny tingling pops at the start of the yawn – keep trying if you don't hear them at first! So what causes them? Clue: it's something to do with your eustachian (you-station) tube – a useful little tunnel linking your mouth with the inner parts of each ear.

1 The tube is closing up to protect the insides of your ear from being yawned out of your head.
2 The tube contains little poppers that sound off when air goes past them.
3 The tube is opening up to allow the extra yawned-in air to reach the inside of your ear.

Answer: Normally the tube is closed but it opens if the air pressure increases at either end. Examples might include when you suddenly go down or up a steep hill or when you breathe in deeply.

Taking leave of your senses

Each one of your senses is unique and sensational in its own way. But they all have one thing in common. They all need someone or something to talk to and give them a quick answer. So they send all their information to the same place – your very baffling BRAIN.

THE BAFFLING BRAIN

Your brain is baffling. Baffling, bemusing, bewildering and brain-bogglingly bamboozling. For instance, how can this 1.5 kg (3 lbs) of pinkish-grey blob be more powerful than the most powerful computer in the entire known universe? Everything it does is baffling – including its mystifying memory and strange sleeping habits.

What does the brain do all day?

Now there's a baffling question. Unlike other parts of the body it doesn't seem to do anything exciting like squirt blood, leap about or fight germs. It just sits there wobbling nervously. It looks like a watery blancmange and it even squelches if you poke a finger in it and waggle it about.

But the brain is always busy. Even when it doesn't seem to be doing much your brain is crackling with the electrical force of millions of nerves – just tell that to your teacher next time she accuses you of daydreaming! Your brain fires off signals, feelings, orders and thoughts at incredible speed. And in order to perform at such baffling speed your brain needs some strong nerves . . . lots of them.

Nerves fact file

Name of body part: Nerves

Where found: Form a network throughout the body but mainly in the spine and connecting to the brain

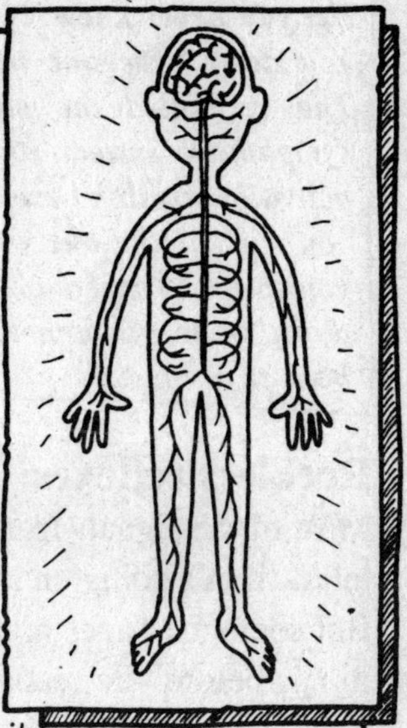

Useful things they do: Take info from your senses to your brain. Bring orders from your brain to the rest of your body.

Grisly details: You can wire a battery to nerves in a chopped-off finger and make it twitch. There's one for the school science lab!

Amazing features: Nerves can carry signals at 100 metres (109 yards) a second – that's one of their slower speeds!

Speedy signals

Nerve messages are electrical signals zipping down the nerve cells and leaping from cell to cell. Phew – sounds tiring! The nerve cells don't actually touch one another. Signals are passed on by chemicals that leap the gap between cells and spark an electrical pulse on the other side.

Bet you never knew!

You don't have one nervous system. You've got two! They're called the parasympathetic system and the sympathetic system, and they both deal with all those activities you don't ever think about. For example, when you run for the bus your parasympathetic system tells your heart to speed up. And when you have chance to sit down, your sympathetic system brings your heartbeat back to normal.

Reckless reflexes

Most of the signals from your nerves go to your brain to tell it what's going on in the different parts of your body. But some messages move so fast that they make you do things before you realise it and control it. Sounds like a good excuse for doing something really reckless – like breaking things!

But if reflexes are moves you make without thinking, which of these aren't reflexes?

1 Snatching a hand away from the heat

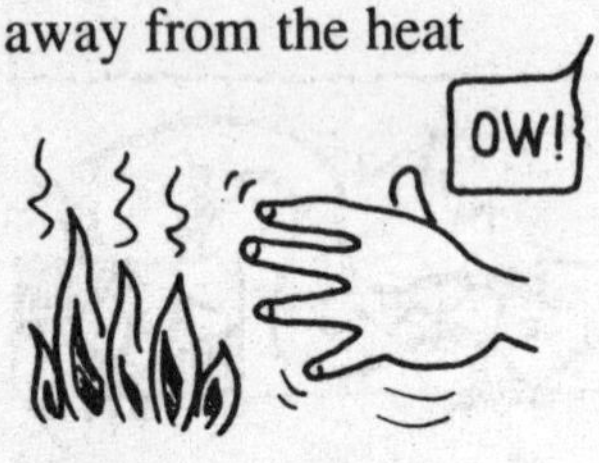

2 Blinking

3 Riding a bicycle

4 Sneezing

5 Getting washed in the morning

6 Hair standing on end when scared

7 Rolling the eyes

8 Eating breakfast

Answers: Reflexes – 1 2 4 6 7 Non-reflexes – 3 5 8

Dare you find out for yourself . . . how to test your reflexes?

Have you been hit below the kneecap by a doctor wielding a small rubber hammer? If so – it was probably to test the nerves that cause a reflex that works when you're walking. Here's how to do it yourself.

1 Rest one leg loosely over the other.

2 Lightly tap the upper leg just below the kneecap. What happens next?

a) The leg jerks forwards.

b) The leg jerks backwards.

c) A small purple patch appears on the lower leg.

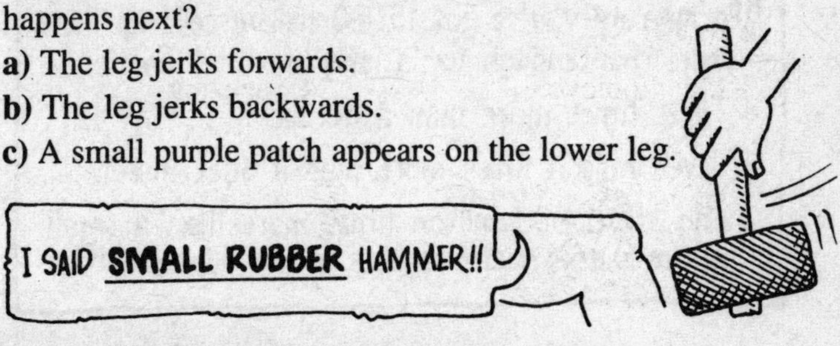

Answer: a) If you got c) you were probably bashing the wrong bit of leg.

Reflexes are alright as far as they go. But to do anything interesting you need to ask your baffling brain.

Baffling brain fact file

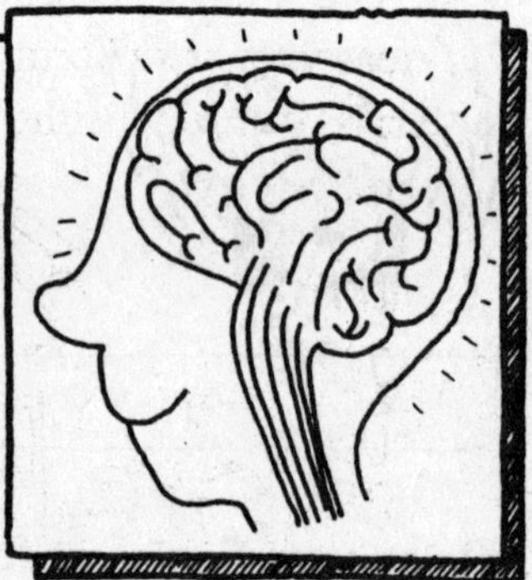

Name of body part: Brain

Where found: Inside the top part of your skull.

Useful things it does: Bosses the rest of your body about. In charge of your memories, thoughts, dreams, etc.

Grisly details: Your brain cells started dying off as soon as you were born. And they aren't getting replaced.*

Amazing features: The brain is more than 80 per cent water!

*Fortunately you've got 15,000 million cells up there ~ more than enough for a long life-time! That's:

- Three times more than a gorilla.
- Seven million times more than a stick insect.
- And about 900 million times more than a small worm that sometimes lives in the human gut.

Teacher's brain tour

If the brain is incredibly baffling on the outside – the inside is even more baffling. It's like a big office building (even your teacher's is quite big) with lots of rooms filled with people doing things you don't understand. Well, here's a guided tour of your teacher's office block – I mean – brain.

Note: Don't touch anything on the tour as it might give your teacher a brainstorm! And don't remove any of your teacher's brain cells either – he or she hasn't got enough to spare!

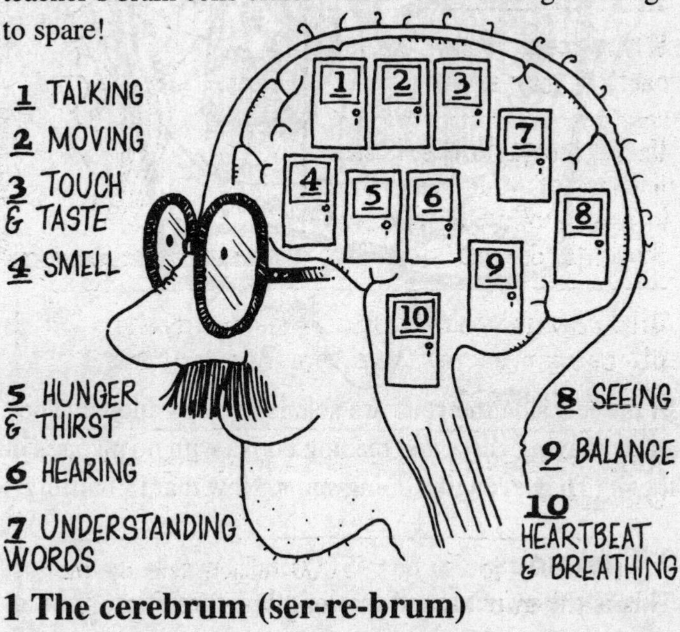

1 The cerebrum (ser-re-brum)

Includes your teacher's library where his or her murky memories are stored. Also the boss's office where decisions are made, and offices for the speech, hearing, moving, touch, sight, understanding and feelings (probably a very small office in this case) departments.

2 Two separate halves

Many of these offices are split into two halves linked by communication cables. In the right half the staff are artistic and emotional. They enjoy painting and arranging flowers.

In the left side the staff are scientific and rational. They enjoy playing chess and reading books with no pictures in them. (They even like doing sums. Now that IS baffling!)

3 Thalamus

This is the switchboard that relays information from all your senses to the brain.

4 Limbic (lim-bick) system

This is where your teacher's feelings are checked to make sure he or she can feel anger, fear, sadness – and even happiness. (Yes – teachers do occasionally experience this emotion.) The staff make sure your teacher doesn't get so happy he walks around with a silly great grin all day.

5 Cerebellum (serry-bell-um)

Staff here control your teacher's more skilful movements. OK – there aren't too many of these.

6 Under-brain

This is another switchboard for transferring news about reflexes happening elsewhere in your teacher's body.

7 Hypothalamus (hi-po-thal-a-muss)

In this broom cupboard are the controls for your teacher's sweating, growing, sleeping and waking, thirst and hunger control systems. There's also the control panel for the autonomic nervous system. It's a big job for a little office!

8 The pineal (pi-knee-al) body

No one knows what goes on here. Perhaps it's your teacher's time-control system. It may tell your teacher to wake up in the morning and to stay awake through your science lesson! No – DON'T reset these controls!

Be a brain scientist

Can you use your knowledge of how the brain works to predict the results of these baffling brain experiments?

Experiment 1 In the 19th century, French scientist Paul Broca weighed 292 male brains and 140 female brains. He concluded that on average female brains weighed 200 g (7 ounces) less than male brains. How would you explain this result?

a) Men are cleverer than women.

b) Boys are more big-headed than girls.

c) Men have bigger heads than women.

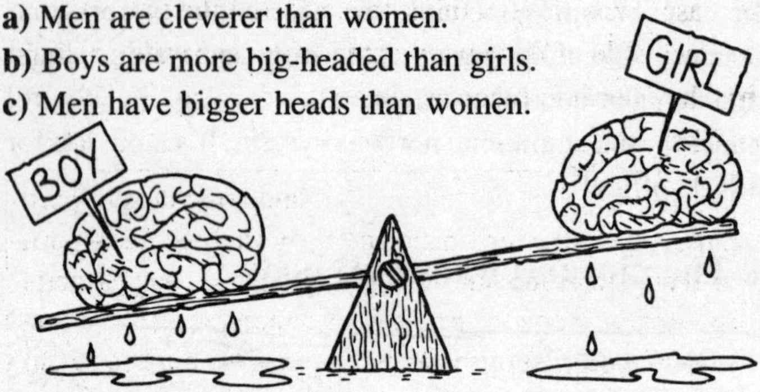

Experiment 2 In 1864, two French doctors were discussing what happens to the brain after the head is cut off. As luck would have it one of the doctors was due to have his head chopped off shortly. So the condemned doctor bravely agreed to try winking his right eye three times in response to a shout from his friend. But what was the result of this grisly experiment?

a) The head stuck its tongue out.

b) Nothing – because the brain was dead.

c) The head winked once.

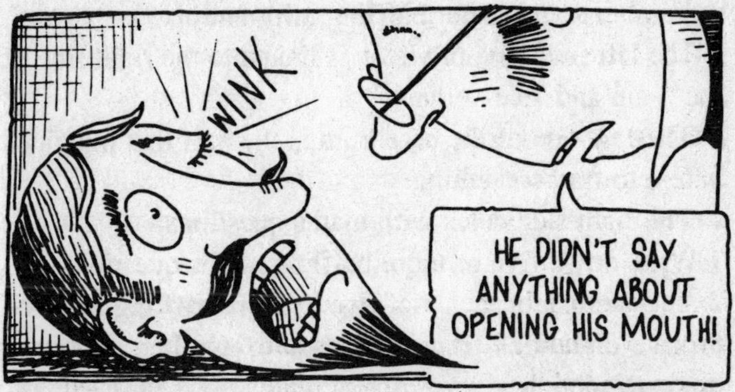

Experiment 3 Some surgeons cut the nerves connecting the two halves of the cerebrum in order to combat brain disease. How do you think this affected the patients?

a) Each side of their body acted like a separate person.

b) They became twice as clever.

c) They died.

Answers: 1 c) Men and women and boys and girls are equally clever. Women have a similar number of brain cells squashed into a smaller head. But scientists have discovered that men and women use different parts of their brains to answer the same questions. **2 b)** Scientists believe that the brain can only live for about 11 seconds after the head is cut off. **3 a)** Amazing but true! One man tried to hit his wife with one hand whilst the other hand tried to stop him doing it!

Dare you find out for yourself . . . how your friend's brain works?

Reassure your friend that this experiment does not

involve any pain. And they won't need to have their head cut off either. Absolutely not. But you do need to remember some rather baffling information.

- The left side of your vision is linked to the right side of the brain and vice-versa.
- The left side of the cerebrum is the half that imagines where to find something.
- The right side deals with maths questions.

1 Write down five or more baffling maths questions.
2 And write another list of five or more baffling requests to give directions from one place to another, e.g. from home to school.
3 Don't tell your friend the aim of the experiment. Stand facing them about three paces away.
4 Ask your friend a maths question followed by a whereabouts question until you have completed both lists.
5 Watch their eye movements. What happens?

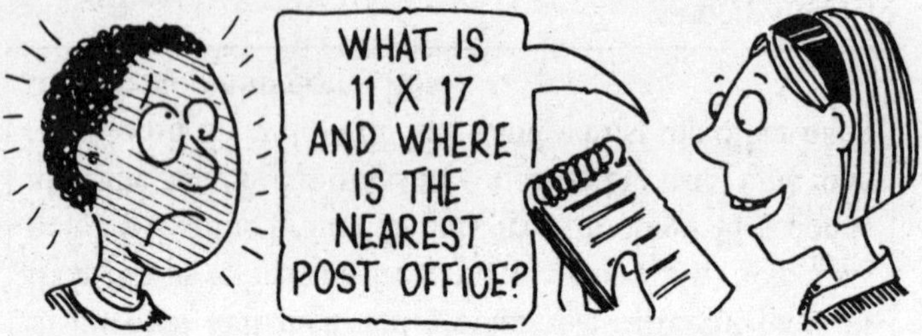

a) Their eyes roll upward before they answer the whereabouts questions and go cross-eyed with the maths questions.
b) Their eyes go right for the maths questions and left for the whereabouts questions.
c) Their eyes go left for the maths questions and right for the whereabouts questions.

Answer b) This allows the side of the brain that is answering the question to get on with the job without having to see things at the same time.

How to baffle your teacher

Here's how to baffle your maths teacher with your amazing brain power.

1 Ask your maths teacher the answer to the sum 4 divided by 47. Try to sound rather casual as if you've just thought up the question.

2 Make sure your teacher doesn't cheat by using a calculator.

3 After a lengthy pause for thought your teacher should be able to come up with something like 0.08 or even 0.085.

4 Smile sweetly and say,

"I don't think that's quite right. I think it's 0.08 510638297872340425531914893617021276594468."

5 Pause to savour the expression of shock on your teacher's face.

6 Hopefully your teacher won't realise that this incredible feat of mental arithmetic has already been performed by Professor A.C. Aitken of Edinburgh University.

7 Of course, if you don't happen to be a mathematical genius you'll have to learn the answer off by heart. (Tip: it's easier if you learn the numbers in groups of three or four and then string them together.)

Baffling learning

One of the most baffling things your brain does is

learning. It's incredible how they expect you to learn so much. Children at school have to learn on average TEN new words every day! But that's nothing! For example, Bhanddanta Vicittabi Vumsa of Burma learnt 16,000 pages of religious text off by heart.

Russian journalist Solomon Veniaminoff never forgot anything he learnt in his entire life!

Learning is all about remembering things. But the really baffling thing about learning is that scientists don't quite understand how memory works! Or maybe they can but they can't remember. But it's thought to involve electrical and then chemical changes within the brain cells. Or something like that. It's all very vague . . . and very baffling.

The baffled brain

The baffling brain is easily baffled. Just take a look at the picture below – is it a vase or are they two heads? See what I mean? Your brain just can't make up its mind.

Bet you never knew!

Brain bafflement can easily result from a bash on the head. For the brain this can be a deeply baffling experience involving loss of memory or even loss of consciousness. The damage is caused by the violent movement sloshing the poor old brain about. When one girl banged her head she started writing backwards ... and was only cured when she banged her head again cheering her favourite football team on the telly!

No laughing matter

Chemicals such as pain-killers can also baffle the brain. Some just deaden pain without knocking you out, but the more powerful pain-killers actually cause the brain to lose consciousness. So who invented these powerful drugs? Well, it's a painful story.

Once upon a time surgeons performed operations without any pain-killers. They would cut off your leg or whip out vital portions of your anatomy and all you got was a gag to stop you screaming too loudly! But that was before Mr Horace Wells got in on the act.

Connecticut, United States, 1844

Horace Wells was deeply in on the act. And he wished he wasn't. The act in question was a display showing the effects of laughing-gas and Horace was in the audience. But Horace Wells wasn't really watching the show at all because he was busy being in agony. The plump, smartly dressed dentist was suffering from the most embarrassing ailment for anyone in his profession . . . toothache. It was so annoying – that he, the great Horace Wells – the inventor of a wonderful new solder for fixing false teeth should have to endure this awful indignity.

He made another effort to concentrate on the entertainment. Laughing-gas, or nitrous oxide, as scientists called it had been discovered about 70 years before. And it didn't just make you laugh. A few whiffs had even the most outwardly boring person singing, dancing, fighting, talking nonsense or even passing out. The hugely popular laughing-gas shows employed bouncers to protect the audience from the crazy antics of volunteers who breathed the gas.

Suddenly, one of the volunteers went berserk. There was a struggle and the man got injured – but he didn't seem to feel any pain!

Lucky you, thought Horace Wells nursing his aching jaw. Then a little light bulb flashed inside his head and for the first time that evening he smiled. (Just a bit – you can't smile too easily with toothache.) If laughing-gas could deaden pain and knock you out . . . then perhaps . . . perhaps just maybe. . .

After the show Horace Wells approached the organiser with a somewhat baffling request.

"Could you lend me some laughing-gas?"

Wells hoped to knock himself out whilst another dentist removed the aching tooth. In those days pulling out a tooth was a painful and rather bloody job involving a huge pair of tongs and a great deal of tugging. But Horace Wells breathed in the gas and didn't feel a thing!

"It's a new era for tooth-pulling!" he exclaimed in triumph as the effects of the laughing-gas wore off. Or that's what he meant to say but since his mouth was still sore the words probably came out as,

Yes, he, Horace Wells was about to sell the pain-killing secret of laughing-gas and become rich and famous. Seriously rich.

But the pain-killing project came to a rather painful conclusion. The first public use of laughing-gas by a dentist ended in disaster when the patient woke too soon. He had received too little gas. During a later operation another patient died after receiving too much gas. A few years later Horace Wells himself came to a painful end. He went mad as a result of breathing too much pain-killing gas and in 1848 he took his own life. But he didn't die in vain. Today the idea of using a pain-killing gas (not laughing-gas!) for operations is well-established.

Fortunately you don't need to rely on gas to send you to sleep.

Your brain's baffling bedtime

Every night at about the same time your brain does something remarkable – and quite baffling. It winds down its operations, pulls down the shutters and more or less switches itself off. Yes, that's right, it goes to sleep. Altogether your brain will spend at least 20 years in this odd condition. Why? Well, the really baffling bit is that no one really knows!

All you need to know about sleep – in three easy lessons

In order to make sleep less baffling here is a course of sleep lessons. It's taught at night school, of course, and unlike ordinary school, the teachers don't mind if you nod off!

Lesson 1 – falling asleep

1 Make sure you are neither too hot nor too cold. It helps if you go to bed at the same time each night.

2 Lie very still with your eyes closed. Try counting backwards from 1,000 or imagining yourself on a lovely relaxing holiday.

3 You'll notice that you can't pin-point the moment when you fall asleep. Some people feel they are falling and twitch violently at this point so they have to start all over again!

Lesson 2 – what happens when you're asleep?

1 Here are a few things you ought to know before you fall asleep. Whilst you are sleeping. . .

- Your body temperature starts falling.
- Your weight drops by 28-42 g (1-1.5 ounces) each hour.
- You can change position up to 40 times a night.
- You can wake up for less than three minutes at a time

and you probably won't remember it in the morning.
2 Don't worry about listening out for danger whilst you're asleep – your brain does this job automatically.
3 Here are some things you shouldn't do whilst asleep.

- Try not to sleep walk – about one in 20 children do this.
- Try not to snore too loudly. This disgusting din is made by someone sleeping on their back with their mouth open. As they breathe in, the wobbly bits at the back of their mouth start rattling noisily.

4 You can stop snorers by putting something hard and prickly (such as an old hair-brush or hedgehog) into the bed. The snorer rolls onto his back and the prickles wake him up!

5 After about 90 minutes of sleep your eyeballs start twitching but the nerves to most of your muscles shut down so you can't move. You are about to enter the most baffling part of your sleep – the DREAM ZONE.

Lesson 3 – exploring the dream zone

1 Welcome to a strange world where time and space have no meaning and where nothing is impossible.
2 Dreams are caused by signals fired towards your brain by nerves underneath it. When you are awake this area screens out boring sounds – that's why you don't notice

traffic or your teacher droning on and on and on. Zzzzzzzzzz.

3 Most dreams take 6-10 minutes but the record for the longest dream is 150 minutes! During your 20 years asleep you can look forward to watching 300,000 dreams!
4 Every night you make several trips to the dream zone.
5 Some good and bad dream news. THE GOOD NEWS: Happy dreams are three times more common than sad dreams. THE BAD NEWS: As it gets towards morning you are more likely to encounter nightmares. If you're reading this in bed you'd better save the next chapter till morning – you don't want to dream about ghastly groaning skeletons now, do you?

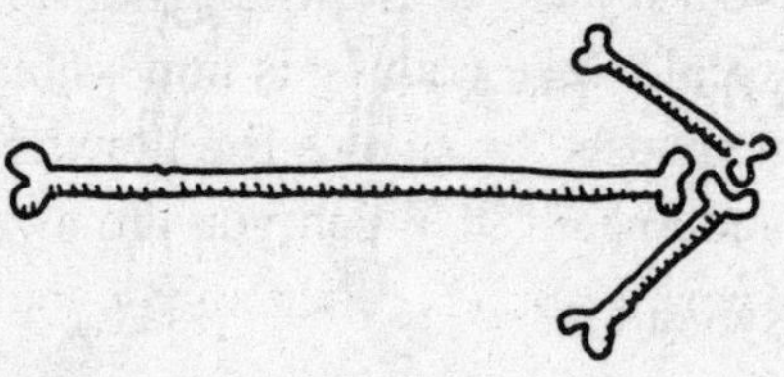

BONES AND GROANS

Bone up on bones

Spooky stories are full of groaning skeletons. But skeletons don't groan for the fun of it. No. They're groaning because that's what bones do to you. They ache and they break and if you happen to have muscles attached to your bones they ache even more! Funnily enough, bones make some scientists groan too. Well – imagine having to remember all 206 bones in the human body! Here are a few of the more memorable groans – er, I mean bones.

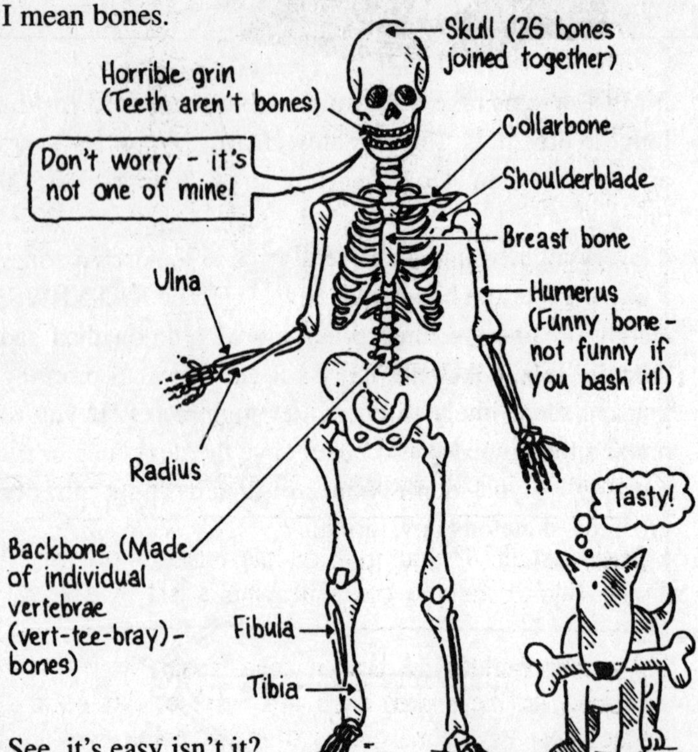

See, it's easy isn't it?

Bet you never knew!
Some people have more than 206 bones. People who spend most of their time riding horses often develop extra bones in their thighs. Some people have an extra pair of ribs and a few people even have extra fingers and toes!

Bones fact file

Name of body part: Bones

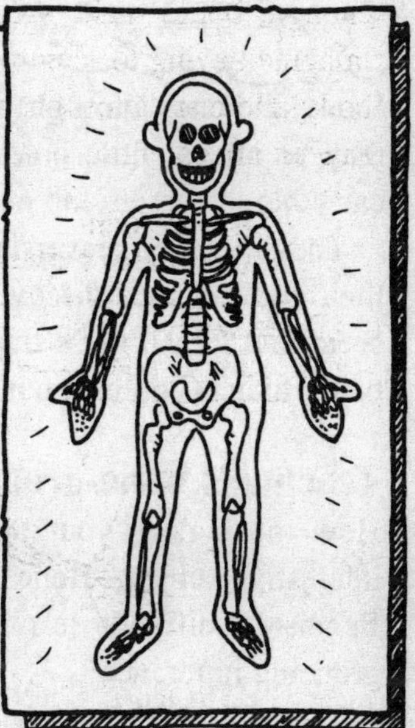

Where found: Your bones form the skeleton that makes up about 25 per cent of your weight. Bones are made from a tough stringy substance called collagen (collar-gen), and strengthened with a mixture of hard materials.

Useful things they do: They hold your body upright and give your muscles something to pull against.

Grisly details: If you took all the minerals out of your thigh bone you could tie what's left in a knot.

Amazing features: A broken bone repairs itself. As long as the broken ends are "set" or put back together - new bone grows over the break.

Bones – the inside story!

Some bones are solid with an area of spongy bone on the inside, others are long and hollow and their empty centres are filled with juicy jelly-like red marrow. Dogs love marrow because it's full of meaty goodness. So should you. Your marvellous marrow makes you 173 BILLION brand new blood cells every day.

Look at bones through a microscope and you'll see they've all got little holes in them. These tiny tunnels carry blood vessels and nerves.

They're called Haversian canals (Have-er-shun) after their oddly-named discoverer – Clopton Havers. It may seem odd to call these tiny tubes "canals" but it sounds better than ' Clopton's bone-holes" at least.

Teacher's bone-groan test

How much does your teacher really know about this interesting subject? Bone up on the answers to this ultra-fiendishly difficult test and show up your teacher's groaning ignorance!

1 You will only find one of these bones in the human skeleton. Which one?

a) The tail bone

b) The elbow bone

c) The nose bone

2 If you wanted to hold up a heavy weight what would be the strongest thing to use?

a) A stone pillar

b) A concrete pillar

c) A leg bone

3 A giraffe has seven bones in its neck. How many neck bones has a human got?

a) 3

b) 7

c) 12

4 How many bones does a baby have?

a) 206, just like a grown-up person.

b) 86

c) More than 350

5 Some Tibetan priests use the skull as a drinking cup. How much liquid do these creepy cups hold?

a) 500 ml

b) 1.5 litres

c) None – it trickles out through the eye-sockets.

6 What bone forms the sticking-out bit of your ankle?

a) The bottom of the tibia

b) The ankle bone

c) The top of the heel bone

7 What is a wormian bone?

a) A wiggley little bone in the little toe.

b) An extra bone sometimes found in a baby's skull.

c) A bone infested by worms.

Answers: 1 a) Yes – that's right! We've all got tails! The coccyx (cox-sicks) is a mass of three to five joined-up bones at the end of the backbone. Fortunately it's not long enough to poke outside the body! **2 c) 3 b)** The giraffe bones are much longer! **4 c)** Lots of these extra bones join up as the baby grows up. **5 b) 6 a) 7 b)**

What your teacher's score means:

0-3 Make no bones about it – your teacher is a bone-head!

4-5 Your teacher can teach you a few facts but only knows the bare bones of the subject.

6-7 Your teacher is probably an osteologist* (ost-tee-ol-o-gist). He or she may even have a real human skeleton at home for study purposes.

* An expert on bones.

Bet You Never Knew!

An osteologist studies bones looking for clues that can identify the person to whom the skeleton belonged. Do you think you could do this? Here's your chance to use your skills to solve a truly horrible true mystery.

The wandering bones

It was 7 December 1976, Long Beach, California. The TV cameraman was in for a nasty shock. He was in a haunted house side-show filming a TV series. As he moved a gruesome dummy away from the rest of the film crew – its arm fell off! The arm was real. And there was bone underneath!

The police were called but it soon became clear that this was no ordinary dummy – it had once been alive! The police discovered three fiendish facts. The body had been pickled in the deadly poison arsenic. It had been shot by an old-fashioned type of bullet dating from before 1914. In the body's mouth was a coin dated 1924.

The police then traced a series of former owners of the

body. The former owners (who had all thought the body was a dummy) were colourful showmen who scraped a living exhibiting the gruesome specimen at funfairs. The oldest showman thought he could remember buying the body in Oklahoma. Then local history buffs dredged up a possible identity for the butchered body – Elmer McCurdy, cowboy and outlaw.

Elmer McCurdy's luck had run out at dawn on 7 October 1911. When the sheriff's men came for him he was drunk with stolen whiskey and exhausted after a night spent hiding in a hayloft. A young lad was sent up to the hiding place.

"The boys want you to surrender, Mister!" he cried.

"I'll see them in hell first!" roared the outlaw.

McCurdy died with his boots on after slugging out a desperate gun battle until his six-gun was empty. After the outlaw's death an undertaker had preserved the body and charged people to see it propped against his parlour wall!

Many people tried to buy the body but all offers were refused. Then the undertaker gave the body away to a nice man who said he was Elmer's long-lost brother.

Three months later the body appeared in a street-show in Texas.

But could the police bone experts prove that the body actually belonged to McCurdy? Here is a description of the outlaw dating from 1911. Which of the following features might you be able to check by examining the bones inside the body?

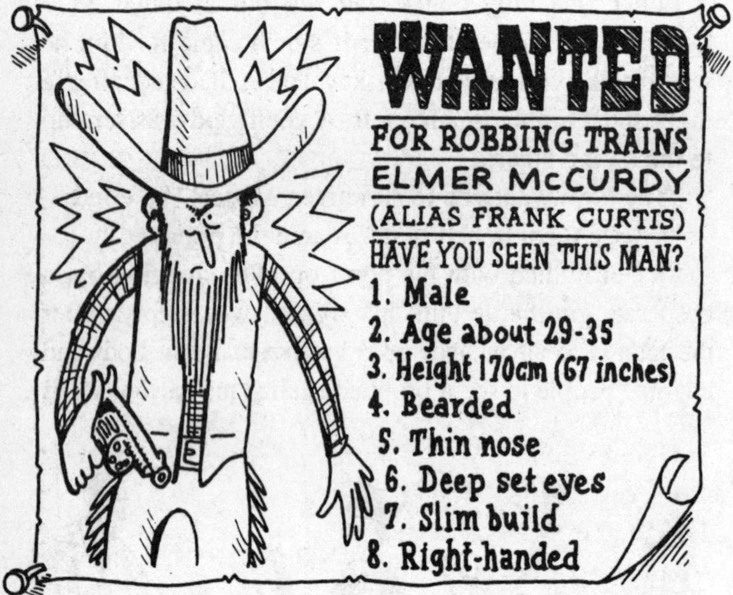

Answers: 1 Yes, females have wider pelvic bones. **2** Yes, as he grew older some of his bones joined together. **3** Yes, by the length of the thigh bones. **4 5 6** No. **7** Yes, by looking at the build of the skeleton. **8** Yes, marks on the right arm bones showed traces of more developed muscles than on the left side.

After studying the bones the scientists were certain they

had the right man. The final proof came when they found that an old photo of the outlaw's head perfectly matched the shape of the skull. And so, at long last, Elmer McCurdy's body was given a decent burial – nearly 66 years after he was killed!

Join up the joints

Could you be a bone expert? If so you'd need to know how to fit a skeleton together. The bones in a skeleton fit together to form joints and the trick is to assemble the joints correctly. But it's not easy – there are over 200 joints to join up!

Here are the main types of joints.

1 Hinge joint. Joints such as the knee work like door hinges, allowing the bones to move backwards and forwards. But they don't move so easily from side to side.

2 Gliding joint. The ankle bones can easily slide up and down and from side to side.

3 Ball and socket joint. As the name implies this is a ball and socket that allows arm and thigh bones to move in most directions.

4 Swivel joint. This joint allows the bone on top to move up and down and from side to side.

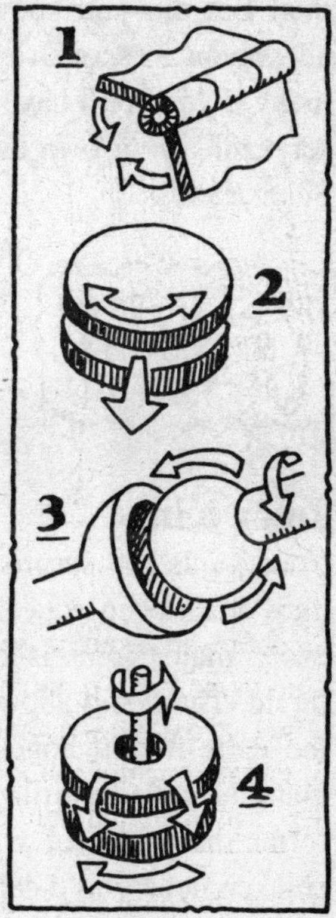

5 Saddle joint. The bone on top is like a jockey on a saddle. So it sways about and leans in all directions – without falling off!

Lucky ligaments

Imagine if your arm fell off every time you threw a ball! This doesn't happen because tough cords called ligaments hold your bones together over the joint. Contortionists stretch their ligaments as they bend their bodies into horrible positions. You'd groan if you tried this! But did you know that your ligaments and joints allow you to scratch every part of your body? This is lucky if you don't have anyone to scratch your back. Try scratching your own back some time – but NOT during Science class.

Juicy joints

Your joints are surprisingly quiet. They don't groan – they don't even squeak. You can tiptoe softly because every major joint is cushioned in a bag of squelchy liquid. The liquid allows the joint to move smoothly and the ends of the bones are also padded with a softer material called cartilage (karta-lidge). The same stuff forms the bridge of your nose – but if you saw it in a chicken bone you'd call it "gristle".

Moaning muscles

No matter how supple your joints are – you can't make a move without using your muscles. THE GOOD NEWS is that you've got over 600 of them. THE BAD NEWS is that they can make you moan in aching agony!

Groaning muscles fact file

Name of body part: Muscles

Where found: Under the skin and surrounding various body bits.

Useful things they do: They're ALWAYS hard at work squeezing the food through your guts, pumping blood and so on.

Grisly details: Muscles can squeeze so strongly that they break your bones! But they have sensors to stop them squeezing that much!

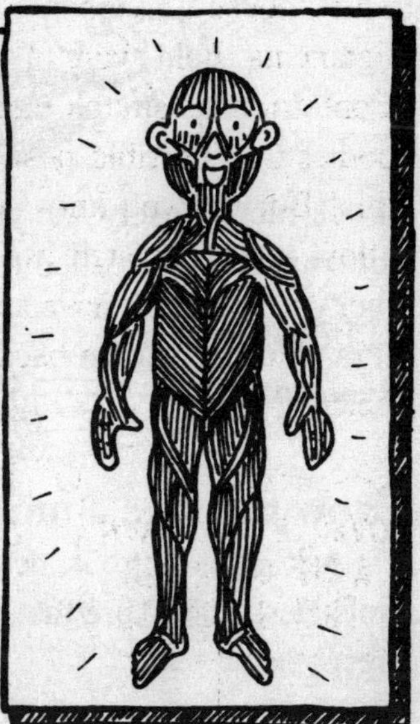

Amazing features: Muscles are anchored to bones by tough tendons. A tendon won't go Twaang! unless you hang a 58-tonne weight from it!

Getting to grips with muscles

To get to grips with your muscles you need to take a closer look. A much closer look. . .

If you cut a muscle in half you can see that it's made of thick bundles of stringy fibres.

Look more closely and you'll see that a fibre is made up of smaller fibres called fibrils.

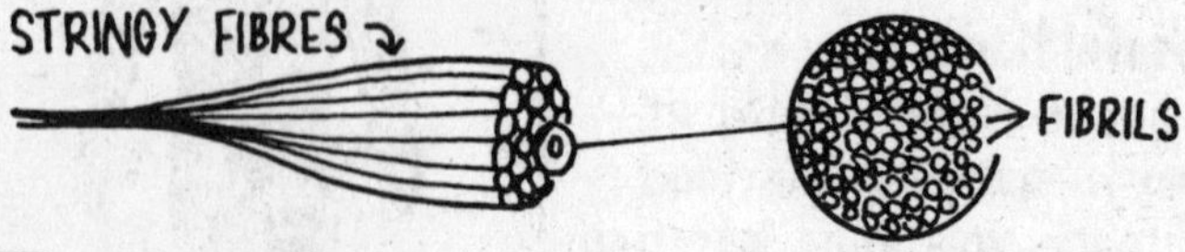

How to make a move

1 Ask one of your nerves to send a signal to your muscles. Make sure that the tiny fibrils are shortening in response.
2 Check that your blood contains enough sugars to provide the energy to power the muscle.
3 The muscle contains chemicals that produce energy by breaking up the molecules of sugar.

But before you move a muscle there are few more things you should know. . .

Groaning muscle facts

1 Muscles have complicated, instantly forgettable Latin names. See if you can remember these.

a) Gluteus maximus – bottom. Makes a nice cushion for sitting on.

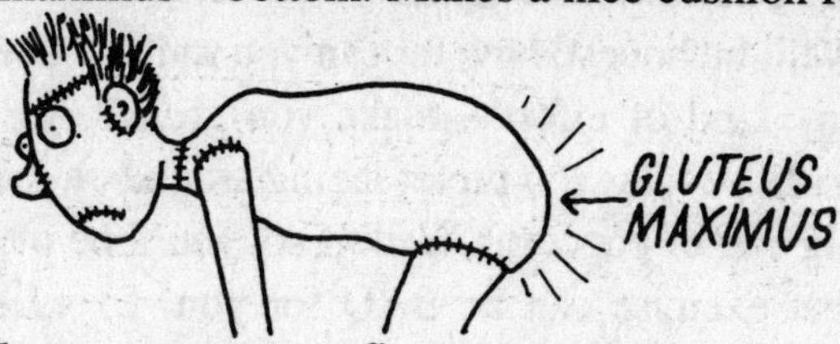

b) Digital flexor – wags your finger at people.

c) Levator labii superior – helps you to snarl. Just say the word and you'll be snarling!

2 Muscles can pull but they can't push. That's why muscles work in pairs. One muscle pulls one way and the other muscle pulls in the opposite direction!

3 You can watch the tendons pulling your muscles. Just spread your fingers and waggle them up and down.

4 When you stick your tongue out there's no muscle doing the pushing from behind. A muscle pulls across the tongue and this pushes the tongue forward.

5 As people get older tough stretchy fibres build up inside the muscles. That's why giants and monsters don't like eating stringy old grandparents. They prefer a succulent tender CHILD! Help!

Groans at the gym

Well, be honest, how far can you run? Or does exercise – any kind of effort – make you groan? Are you one of those people who prefer lazing around on the sofa with a big bag of popcorn? Well, if so, you'll be pleased to hear that exercise can be BAD for you! Every sport should carry a Government Health Warning.

Horrible Health Warning 1 Getting off the sofa is dangerous! Your heart suddenly has to pump blood up to your brain and not along a level. Sometimes your brain doesn't get enough blood and you feel dizzy. That's why aircraft pilots sometimes faint on a sudden turn.

Horrible Health Warning 2 Even when you're up-and-running it's horribly hard work for your body. Your poor feet and ankles have to put up with a pressure of SIX times your body weight. The arches of your feet flop down as they hit the ground. Your fat wobbles, your brain squelches and even your eyeballs bounce slightly in their sockets!

Horrible Health Warning 3 Violent exercise is especially bad for you . . . it can cause some especially groan-worthy pains.

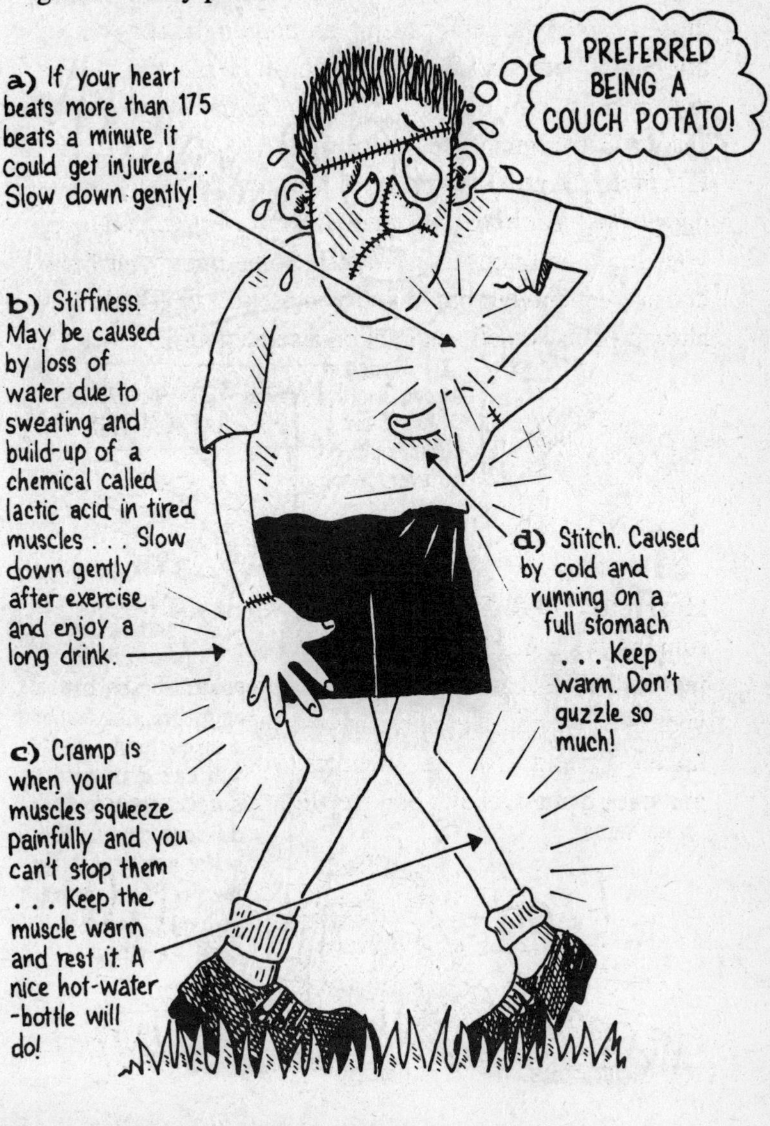

But if there's one thing worse than taking exercise it's NOT taking exercise. Look what you miss out on.

DISGUSTING DIGESTION

Could you murder a rich chocolate cake dripping with cream and icing? Does the hint of jam roly-poly and extra-thick custard make your tummy thunder? If so – you're going to find this chapter horribly tasteless. Imagine your food being chewed and squashed and squelched as it's taken into your body. It's all due to your disgusting digestive juices.

Disgusting digestive glands

A gland is a body bit that produces juices. At different points in your guts, glands lurk – just waiting to spray your food with digestive juices. But can you believe the horribly huge amounts of juice they produce? We're not talking little squirts here. . .

Glands	Daily Squirt
Saliva	2 litres *
Stomach	1-2 litres
Pancreas	1-1.5 litres
Liver	1 litre

That's a total of over six litres every day!

* You end up gulping most of this down! Yes, that's 50,000 litres (5,500 gallons) of spit in a lifetime! Or enough to fill 100 baths!

Digestive juices contain chemicals called enzymes. The enzymes work horribly hard to break up the food molecules into smaller molecules that your body can absorb more easily. The hotter the body gets the faster these changes happen, until at 60°C they suddenly stop. Mind you, if you ever got that hot you'd be cooked anyway!

Dare you find out for yourself . . . how enzymes work?

Rennet is a sloppy substance that contains rennin – an enzyme also found in the human stomach. Make sure it's OK for you to use the ingredients below and get someone to help you use the hob.

852 millilitres (1.5 pints) of fresh full cream milk
Sugar
Rennet – available from supermarkets
Saucepan
Bowl
Tablespoon

1 Heat the milk in the saucepan and stir well until it's warm but not hot. DON'T BOIL IT!
2 Pour the milk into the bowl and stir in one tablespoon of sugar.

3 Place the bowl in a warm place.
4 Very gently stir in one tablespoon of rennet. Don't touch the bowl for ten minutes.

5 Ten minutes later . . . what's happened to the milk?
HORRIBLE HINT: If your experiment has worked, the rennin will have digested the milk.

a) It's turned into a disgusting smelly yellow mixture with soggy white lumps in it.

b) It's turned into a solid wobbly mass.

c) Nothing

Answer: b) And it's delicious served cold with cream! (If you can bear to eat it.) If **c)**, then the milk was too hot for the enzyme to work.

A horribly healthy diet

Are you a fussy eater? Your body is! To stay healthy your body has to digest a balanced diet. That means all the types of food shown below and NOT just the ones you like!

1 Fibre helps your guts grip your food and keep it moving on its long trek to the toilet.

2 Proteins help your body build and repair its cells. Ten per cent of your body is made of this stuff.

3 Carbohydrates (car-bo-hi-drates) are found in starchy foods. Once they're digested they become sugars that your cells turn into energy.

4 Sugars provide your body with easy energy. Your lazy body feeds the sugars straight to the cells.

5 Fat is a useful store of energy and it helps build body cells – often in a wobbly layer around your tummy.

A sickening sandwich

Could you combine foods that contain fibre, proteins, carbohydrates, sugars and fat in a ONE sandwich snack?

Here are some possibilities.

1 A ham and jam sandwich with a fizzy drink.

2 An egg and baked beans wholemeal-bread sandwich (yuck!) and a mug of hot chocolate.

3 A chip sandwich with white bread followed by treacle pudding washed down with loads of lemonade (burp!).

4 A healthy wholemeal lettuce sandwich followed by a sugar-free nut bar and a glass of mineral water.

Answers: 1 Yes, but it sounds horrible. **2** Yes, but it sounds equally horrible. **3** No, worse luck! **4** No, it lacks sugar and protein. Could YOU invent something less sickening?

A horribly unhealthy diet

As if digestion isn't horrible enough just look at the horribly unhealthy things that some people eat.

1 Some people eat earth. This is horribly unhealthy because it's teeming with germs and tastes disgusting.

2 In 1927 a woman complained of stomach pains. She was rushed to hospital in Ontario, Canada. There, doctors found that she'd swallowed 2,533 objects including 947 bent pins.

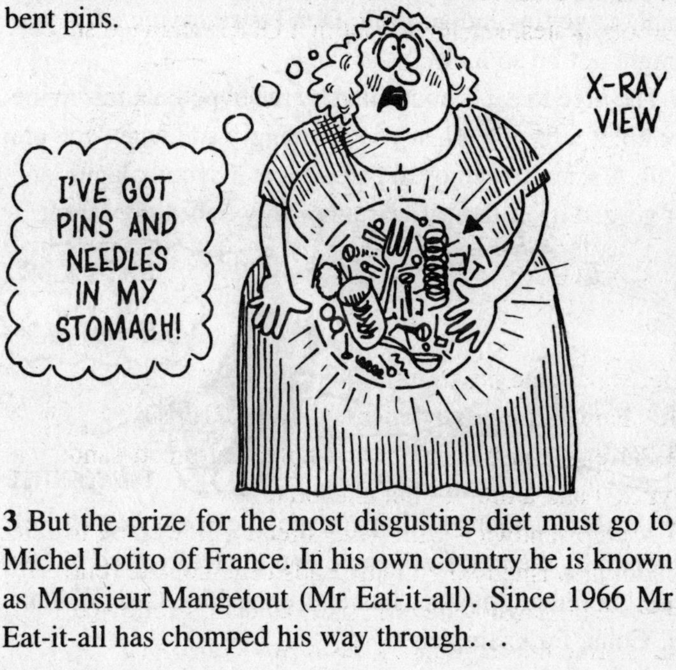

3 But the prize for the most disgusting diet must go to Michel Lotito of France. In his own country he is known as Monsieur Mangetout (Mr Eat-it-all). Since 1966 Mr Eat-it-all has chomped his way through. . .

He generally eats 900 g (31 ounces) of metal a day. All without getting indigestion. (Don't try this yourself – you might not be so lucky!)

4 The urge to eat is controlled by the hypothalamus in the brain. It tells you when you are hungry and when you are full. A scientist removed part of a rat's hypothalamus and it gorged itself until it was a horribly unhealthy fat rat.

5 At this moment millions of people are trying to lose weight by dieting. But people don't actually need to lose weight unless they are horribly unhealthy. Like William J. Cobb, for example.

In 1962 William J. Cobb weighed 364 kg (57 stone). He was so round that he could only roll like a barrel. Not surprising – considering he was carrying 91 kg (14 stone) of fat! So William decided to go on a diet and within a year or two he was down to 106 kg (16 stone, 7 lbs). He had lost the weight of three large men!

6 Most people can only lose about half their normal body weight. This takes about three weeks if the person doesn't eat. Then they die – and that's a really unhealthy thing to happen!

Horribly healthy diet complications

To stay horribly healthy you need more than a balanced diet. You've got to eat things that you can't see or taste – like minerals for example. Luckily you don't have to go around looking for minerals to eat. Ordinary food contains minerals in tiny amounts – and that's all your body needs! For example, slurp a milk shake and you're doing your bones a favour. Milk contains the bone-building minerals calcium and phosphate. Then there are other chemicals called vitamins and they're really VITAL.

Vital vitamins

Vitamins are vital because if you don't get enough of them in your diet you become horribly unhealthy. Feel more like gobbling up those greens now?

Vitamin	Found in:	Not enough causes:
A	Milk, butter, eggs, fish oil, liver.	Lots of illnesses and you can't even see in the dark.
B1 and 9 other B vits.	Yeast and wholemeal bread. Also found in milk, nuts and fresh vegetables.	Victim loses energy and can't get out of bed – sounds worse than a Monday morning.
C	Oranges and lemons. Fresh fruit and vegetables.	Loss of teeth, bleeding gums, dark spots on body. Bad breath. Yuck!
D	Oily fish, dairy products.	Bent bones and bandy legs. Bad news for footballers.
E	Wholewheat bread, brown rice and butter.	Scientists aren't quite sure about this one.
K	Green veg, liver	Blood doesn't clot properly – very messy!

It took scientists a great deal of trial and error to discover the disgusting effects of lack of vitamins. But solving these medical mysteries gave them something to crow about.

The sick chickens mystery

Eijkman Christianson was at his wit's end.

In 1884 he had gone to Indonesia to study a mystery disease. The locals called it, "I can't."

He injected animals with germs thought to cause the disease. The animals stayed healthy!

Then his pet chickens went down with the disease.

He moved them to another place and they got better! But why?

Maybe they just needed some fresh air.

Or maybe it was due to a change in diet? In their first home the birds were eating boiled rice.

Now they were eating brown rice.

It turned out that the brown outer layer of the rice grains was rich in Vitamin B. This prevented, "I can't" or as we call it, beri-beri.

Mind you, it took Eijkman many years of experiments to prove that eating the wrong rice had made the chickens sick. As for the chickens themselves – things could have been worse. Imagine if something had gone wrong with their digestive bits and pieces. They'd have been sick as parrots then! Yes, we're talking about the gruesome guts!

THE GRUESOME GUTS

Guts are gruesome. Gobsmackingly, grossly, stomach-churningly sickening. In fact – if you thought too much about where your food went you wouldn't feel like eating it! But if there's one thing even more gruesome than guts, it's the scientists who find guts fascinating. Oh yes, and then there's the smelly stuff that pours out the other end. Yuck!

Gruesome guts fact file

Name of body part: Guts

Where found: Mostly under the chest area in the lower part of the body. (See below.)

Useful things they do: Absorb your food once it has been digested.

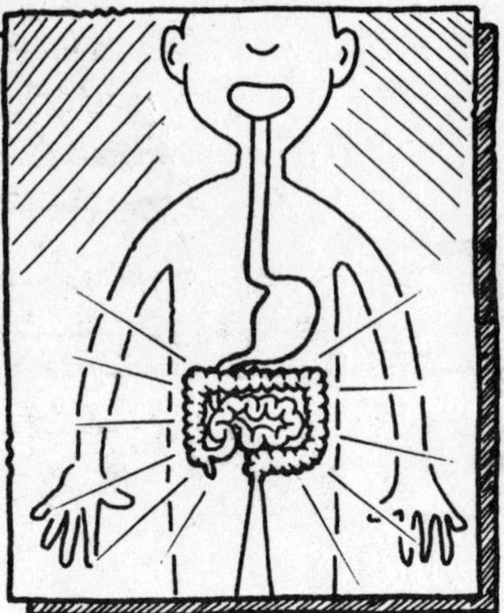

Grisly details: The guts form a continuous tube up to 8m (8·7 yards) long. That's longer than a huge slithery snake!

Amazing features: Your guts are held in place by the mesentery (mes-en-terry). This stops the guts slopping about and tying themselves in knots!

Dare you find out for yourself . . . what's inside your mouth?

Open wide! Here's where it all begins. The gobbling, munching mouth – grinding up the goodies before they hit the guts. Imagine what it's like to be a bit of food!

Tooth truths

The first thing you'll have to worry about are those gigantic spit-dripping jaws. They're made from enamel and they're so tough you need a diamond to drill into them. Inside each tooth there are nerves and blood vessels just like any body part. Not all teeth are the same – there are different-shaped teeth for different jobs. Here are a few that we picked up from a dentist's floor.

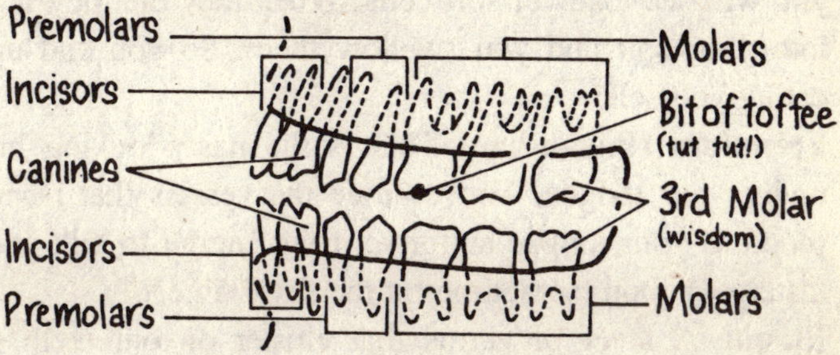

So how many teeth have you got? It depends on how old you are. You started off with 20 teeth that appeared when you were very young. As you get older these fall out and new teeth push through your gums. Here are some tooth totals – which is closest to your own number of teeth?

1 Incisors a) 2 b) 8 c) 4
2 Canines a) 2 b) 4 c) 8
3 Pre-molars a) 4 b) 8 c) 12
4 Molars a) 4 b) 8 c) 12

Answers: 1 b) 2 b) 3 b) or **c)** Younger children have four pre-molar teeth and adults have eight. **4 b)** or **c)** Younger children have eight molar teeth but adults often have 12.

Can you spot any of these in your mouth?

Uvula (You've-yer-la) This horrible little wobbly bit spends its time hanging around in your mouth. The name means "little grape" – can you see why? No one knows exactly why it's there but it does help you swallow.

Mouth lining If you look at this through a microscope you will see loads of soft cells. When they die they fall into your spit and you swallow them. So you end up eating yourself!

Frenulum (Fren-u-lum) This is the nasty-looking bit under your tongue. You can see the vessels that bring blood to your tongue and give it the energy to talk and taste your food (sometimes at the same time!).

Plaque A layer of germs that cluster on our teeth – they're responsible for tooth decay and bad breath! (If you find any, brush it off!)

Gruesome gobbling

Once you've checked your mouth – get ready to swallow. Oddly enough most of us manage to do this without thinking. This is probably because swallowing is a reflex action. But it's also a horribly complex operation – see if you can do it by following these instructions. (NOTE: try not to dribble all over your nice clean book.)

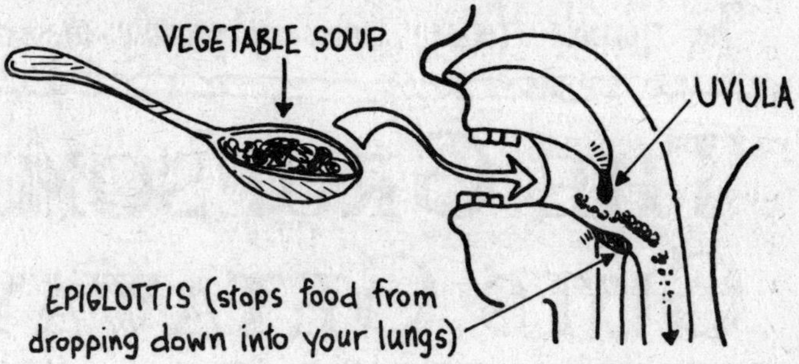

1 Using your tongue press some food you chewed earlier on to the roof of your mouth.

2 Force the food towards the back of your throat.

3 Swing up your uvula to prevent the food making a dash for freedom up your nose. On second thoughts don't worry about doing this – it happens automatically.

- NOTE 1: Try not to laugh when you eat. When you laugh your uvula swings DOWN – so you could find that the soup you've just slurped up is dribbling out of your nostrils!
- NOTE 2: Try not to breathe whilst you're swallowing. If you do your food goes down your windpipe and you have to cough it up! You've got a little lid called the epiglottis (eppy-glot-tis) that closes off the top of your windpipe to prevent this happening.

Wouldn't you like to know what really happens to your food after you swallow it? No? Go on – it's REALLY horrible.

A gruesome guts tour

Here's a gruesomely thrilling alternative to the usual boring tourist trip. Just imagine being shrunk down to the size of a pinhead and boarding a coach the size of a pea. Then imagine going on a guided tour of someone else's guts! And guess what? Your dinner's thrown in! That's if you feel like eating any . . .

The Horrible Holiday Company proudly present...

THE GRUESOME GUTS GETAWAY!

EMBARK ON THE TRIP OF A LUNCHTIME.

THE SMALL PRINT

1. If you get digested and turned into a chemical soup it's not our fault – OK?
2. There will be <u>no</u> toilet stops until the end of the tour.

<u>**1.00 pm**</u> Enter the mouth. Fasten your safety belts and close the windows securely. It's wet outside and we're about to dive down the gullet waterfall. Splosh!

1.01 pm
Amazing 9 to 13-second free-fall as we're squeezed 25cm (10 inches) down the gullet!

1.02-6 pm Five hour stopover in the stomach. Plenty of time to admire the slimy stomach walls with their 35 million digestive juice-producing pits.

- Enjoy the beautiful sunset effect as a red hot pepper makes the stomach glow.
- Listen to the mighty roar of the rumbling stomach as trapped gases squelch around amongst the food.
- Experience the gut-churning thrill of the stomach big dipper as it churns and churns again every 20 seconds. (If you feel a bit queasy, sick-bags are provided.)

6.00 pm A sudden lurch takes us from the stomach into the intestine. Then what better than a relaxing 6m (6.5 yards) cruise down the scenic small intestine? (Speed 2.5cm (1 inch) per minute.)

- Feel the lovely smooth gliding motion as we're squeezed along. The slimy gut walls help to stop the guts from digesting themselves.
- Marvel at the velvety insides of the intestines made up of five million tiny projections called villi.

- Gasp as we are covered in enzyme-rich digestive juices squirting down from the pancreas and liver.
- Wonder as the food chemicals are sucked into the villi.
- Puzzle over the mystery of the appendix. Everyone's got one of these finger-like things sticking out of their intestines. But no-one knows what it's for!

10.00 pm Spend the night in the comfortable and spacious large intestines. Here the surroundings are peaceful, lie back and listen for the

relaxing gurgling of the water as it's taken out of the remains of the food and back into the body.

7.30 am (Give or take a few hours). Put on your life jacket and parachute. It's time for splash down in the toilet!

Some sickening scientists

Of course, the first scientists who investigated the guts had to learn the hard way. That's by gruesome guesswork, sickening speculation and some awful emetic* experiments.

* WARNING TO READERS: An emetic is something that makes you throw up. Vomiting is a reflex action caused by strong squeezing of the muscles around the stomach. It could even be triggered by reading this chapter. Don't try any of these experiments at home – or at school!

Emetic experiments

If you thought that science is all about spotless white coats and squeaky-clean labs . . . THINK AGAIN! Here are some sickening experiments you shouldn't try.

1 René Réamur (1683–1757)

Claim to fame: Famous French scientist. Expert on just about everything, including technology and industry.

Emetic experiment: Trained a kite – (that's a bird not the thing on a string) to sick up its food. Then he pored over the vile vomit to see what the half-digested food looked like.

Disgusting discovery: The meat didn't go rotten inside the bird's guts. This was because the chemicals in the bird's stomach killed the germs that made things rot.

2 Lazzaro Spallanzani (1729-1799)

Claim to fame: Famous Italian scientist. Expert on volcanoes, electric fish, thunderclouds and how a snail grows its head back after you cut it off.

Revolting research included:

- Forcing animals to swallow tubes of food and then making them sick so he could study how the food had changed. The animals included cats, dogs, oxen, newts, sheep, a horse and some sinister-looking snakes.
- Doing the same experiment on himself. Eating his own sicked-up food. He ate one bit of food three times just to see how it had changed!
- Making himself sick again so that he could study his own stomach juices.

Emetic experiment: Kept a container of sick in a warm place for a few hours.

Disgusting discovery: The food continued to be digested. (This was because the enzymes produced by the stomach didn't stop working.)

3 Claude Bernard (1813-1878)

Claim to fame: French scientist. Cut up loads of human bodies and made disgusting discoveries about blood and nerves.

Revolting research: Kidnapped dogs (or should this be "dognapped"?) for his experiments. Poked tubes into the poor pooches' stomachs to find out what was going on

Emetic experiment: Added juice from a dog's pancreas to fatty foods.

Disgusting discovery: The fats were digested and made a greasy mess. (This was because digestive juices produced by the pancreas digest fats.)

Could you perform experiments like these? Would you want to? If your answer is "YUGGGHHH!" or "WHICH WAY TO THE BATHROOM?!" then you don't have the stomach for the job. So you wouldn't want to be at Fort Mackinac, United States in 1822. . .

The stomach for the job

The young man moaned in agony. A carelessly loaded shotgun had exploded – blasting a 15 cm (6 inch) hole in Alexis St. Martin's side . . . you could see all his insides. The young Canadian hunter had two broken ribs, a damaged lung and . . . a hole in his stomach.

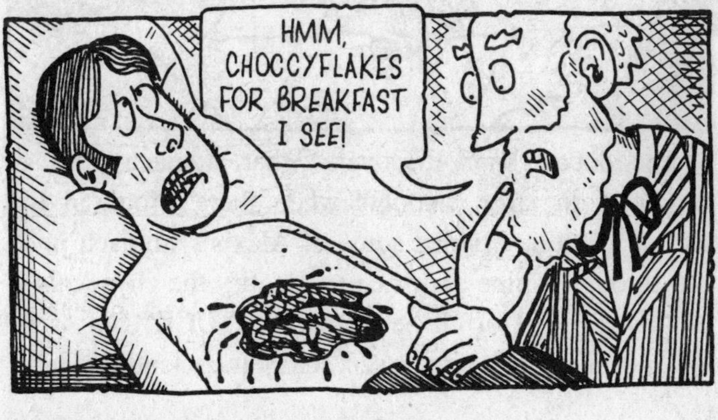

Dr William Beaumont looked at these injuries and shook his head sadly. The patient would die soon. Very soon. In those days the only treatment for this type of wound was to slap on a bandage and arrange the funeral. But against all expectations, Alexis survived the night. Weeks became months and the young man even started to get better! But he had an embarrassing problem.

The stomach hole refused to heal. So whenever he felt peckish Alexis had to bandage his tum to stop its gruesome contents from slopping out!

Oddly enough the young man cheerfully put up with this appalling arrangement. So the devious doctor seized the opportunity to perform some gruesome gut experiments. One day he asked Alexis to swallow a bit of raw meat on a thread. Later he pulled it up again to see how it had changed. On another occasion Dr Beaumont poked a thermometer through the hole and watched it leap about as the stomach churned!

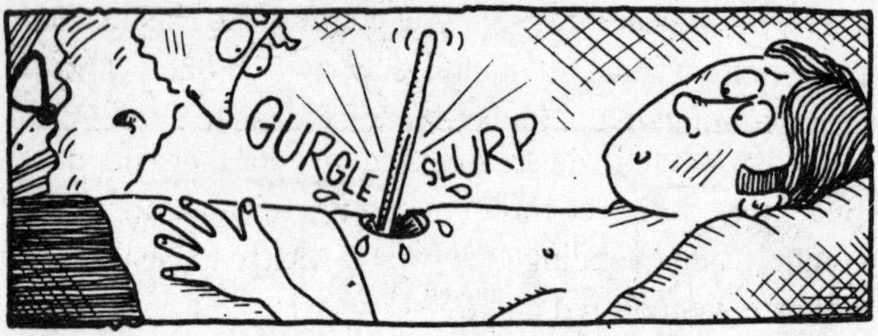

The doctor soon discovered that stomach juice is produced in large amounts when there's food in the stomach. So he drained some of Alexis's stomach juice out through a pipe and tried to identify the chemicals it contained. First of all he tasted it – YUCK! But as he wasn't sure what it was he sent it to some scientist friends.

They discovered the juice contained hydrochloric acid – a powerful dissolving chemical. This is useful for breaking down food and killing germs.

Sometimes the doctor and his patient would have a row. You've got to see it from Alexis' point of view. For two years Dr Beaumont had nursed him. But on the other hand . . . well, if there's one thing worse than having a hole in your body – it's being chased around by a meddlesome medic trying to terrorise your tummy. And over the next few years Dr Beaumont took to following Alexis so he could perform even more horrible experiments!

Oddly enough these shouting matches provided Dr Beaumont with yet more sickening scientific data. He couldn't help noticing that when Alexis got cross, his stomach went all red and quivery!

At last in 1833 Dr Beaumont published his findings. It had taken 11 years of tests and tantrums. Packed full of stomach-churning pictures, the book was an overnight success. The doctor achieved fame and fortune. Yet he owed his entire achievement to one gruesome fact . . . he'd had the stomach for the job!

A weighty matter

Three hundred years ago an Italian scientist named Santorio Sanctorius decided to build an incredible weighing machine. It swung from the ceiling and was big enough for his chair, desk and bed! There was even room for his prized silver chamber pot. Every day Santorio sat in the machine and recorded his weight.

For 30 years he weighed himself. He weighed himself before meals, after meals and during meals. He even weighed all his waste products.

But he still couldn't figure it out. Why did his food weigh more than the contents of his silver chamber pot?

Here's the answer. Much of the missing food turns into energy to power the body. Digested food molecules go from the guts to the blood and then off to feed billions of hungry body cells. Spare sugar and fats get carted off by a useful blood vessel to the storage place in the liver.

Liver fact file

Name of body part: Liver

Where found: On top of the guts and under the diaphragm.

Useful things it does: What doesn't it do? (See below.)

Grisly details: If the liver doesn't work, waste body products build up in the skin.

Amazing features: You can lose 90 per cent of your liver and survive. That little bit of liver grows into a lovely new liver!

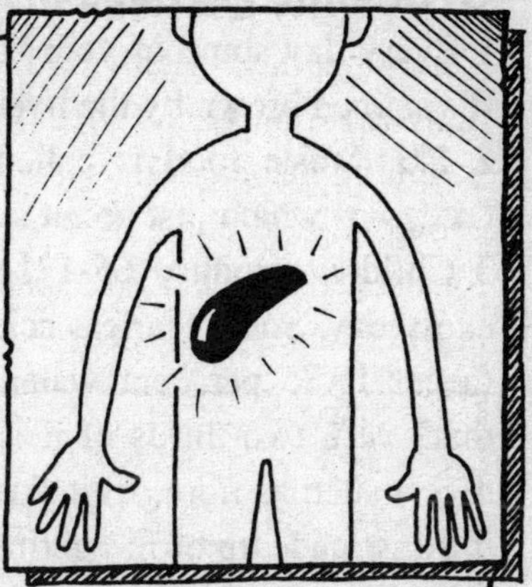

The lively liver

Yes – your liver certainly has a good time – scientists know of 500 jobs it tackles. There may be even more that haven't yet been discovered! The liver. . .

- Controls the amount of sugar in the blood. This is done with the aid of a substance called insulin produced by the pancreas. Too little insulin causes a disease called diabetes.
- Stores spare fat and carbohydrates.
- Makes Vitamin A.
- Gets rid of old red blood cells.
- Produces digestive juices.
- Keeps you warm – all these activities produce heat!

But not all your food is used by the body. Some of it just isn't needed – so the body chucks it out!

Gruesome garbage disposal 1 – waste food

1 Every day some of your food puts in a reappearance. It's stained brown by the liver's digestive juices – lovely.

2 This waste food is called faeces – that's Latin for "dregs" – which just about sums it up.

3 Children produce 65-171g (2-6 ounces) of the stuff every day. Some fearless scientists have discovered that faeces is 75 per cent water, and of the solid material that's left, two thirds of it is food that your body can't digest such as fibre, fruit skins and seeds. And the other third is made up of . . . germs!

4 Yes! Your guts swarm with billions of germs that have somehow managed to get past the acid in the stomach. Ugh! Fortunately, few of them do much harm.

5 UNFORTUNATELY, they do produce gases which, added to the gases from food and drink, can reappear at either end of the body – with hilarious or embarrassing but always noisy (and sometimes smelly) results.

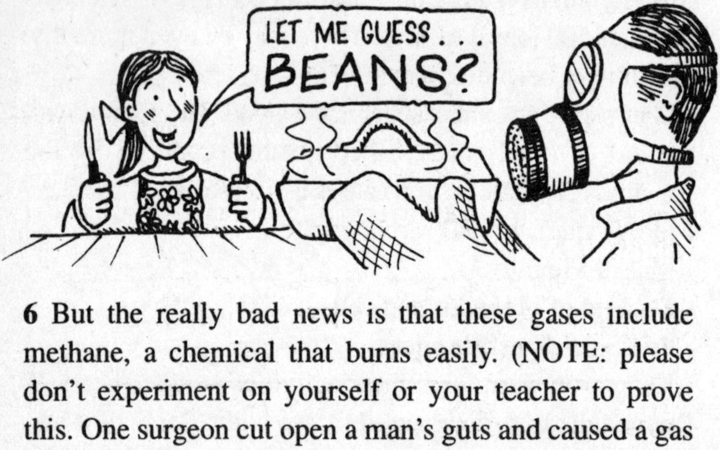

6 But the really bad news is that these gases include methane, a chemical that burns easily. (NOTE: please don't experiment on yourself or your teacher to prove this. One surgeon cut open a man's guts and caused a gas explosion!)

Gruesome garbage disposal 2 – waste water

Much of your food is made up of water. Cucumbers, for example, are 90 per cent water and ten per cent vegetable. Your body is over two-thirds water and water is very useful for making lots of gruesome body fluids such as tears, runny snot and digestive juices. But spare water just isn't needed so it's filtered out by your kidneys.

Kidneys fact file

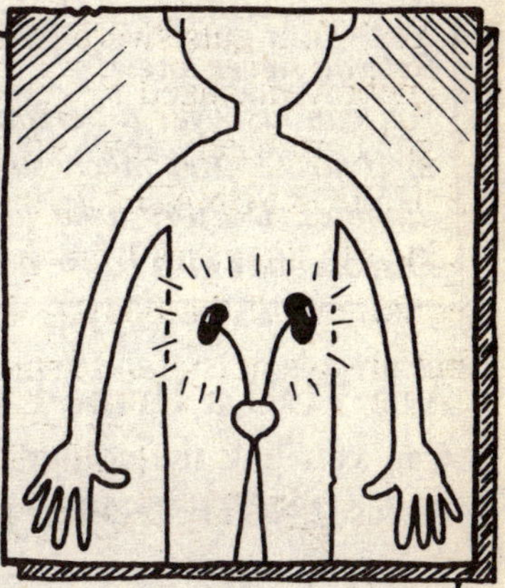

Name of body part: Kidneys

Where found: You've got two at the back of your body just below your lowest ribs.

Useful things it does: Remove spare water, unwanted salt and waste chemicals from the blood.

Grisly details: If not enough water passes through the kidneys the waste forms agonisingly painful stones.

Amazing features: Your kidneys filter 1 litre (1.76 pints) of blood every minute.

How the kidneys work

The kidneys are like millions of tiny coffee filters linked

up to a drainpipe.

1 Each filter takes the form of a tiny tube.

2 A little capsule at the start of each tube takes in fluid from the blood.

3 As the fluid runs down the tuoe, all the really useful stuff such as molecules of food escape back into the blood.

4 All the useless unwanted water plus any extra salts and poisonous wastes trickle down the drainpipe into the bladder.

5 This watery waste is urine.

Bet you never knew!

You can discover a person's state of health by studying their urine. Too much sugar in the urine is a sign of diabetes. Doctors used to taste urine to discover this! Disease may also cause a change in the colour of urine.

Are YOU a Urine Expert?

Can you link the colour of these urine samples to the disease? NOTE: feel free to colour in the urine yourself!

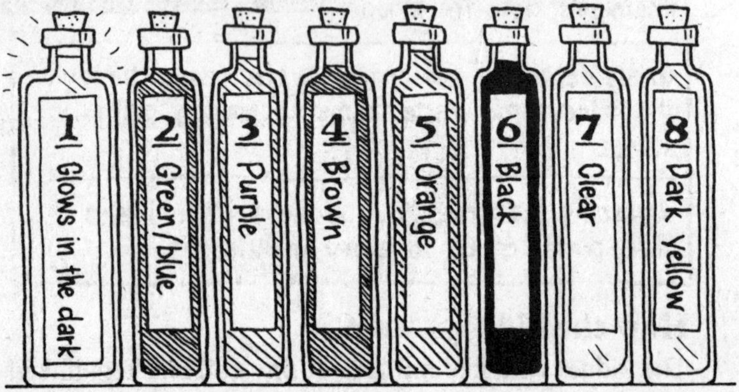

Cause of the colour. . .

a) The patient has been injected with blood from an animal.

b) Blackwater fever – a nasty tropical disease.

c) Cholera or typhus (both deadly diseases).

d) The patient has been drinking a lot of liquid.

e) The patient has been eating too much beetroot or blackberries.

f) The patient is feverish and has lost a lot of water by sweating.

g) The patient has been eating a high protein diet.

h) The patient is a space monster.

Answers: 1 h) 2 c) 3 e) 4 b) 5 f) 6 a) 7 d) 8 g)

Of course, your kidneys couldn't work if your blood wasn't doing its job. That's rushing round your body as fast as your heaving heart can pump it out! Warning. If the sight of buckets of blood makes you wobble at the knees it's wise to put on a blindfold before reading the next chapter.

THE BLOODY BITS

You may think that EVERYTHING to do with the body is blood-curdling. But some bits are bloodier than others. Take, for example, blood itself and the heart that keeps it moving. But blood is also vital for life – here's why. . .

Blood fact file

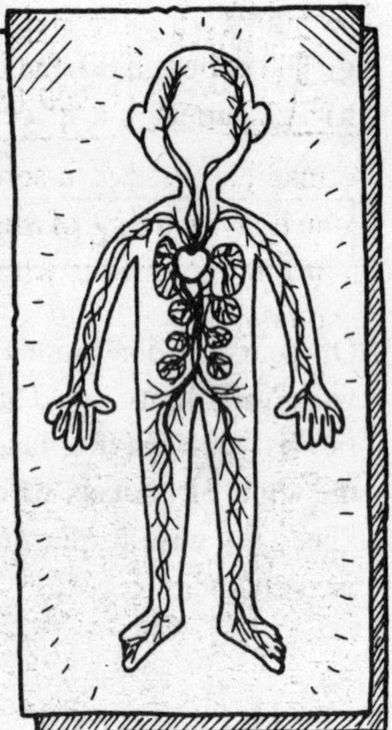

Name of body part: Blood

Where found: Throughout the body in a network of blood vessels. You've got about five litres of the red stuff.

Useful things it does: Delivers food and oxygen and other useful things your cells need to keep going.

Grisly details: You can lose one third of your blood without harm. But if you lose half – it's FATAL!

Amazing features: Blood is so full of things that it's amazing they all fit in – see below.

Blood – what's in it for me?

1 Your blood is yellow! Yes, it's true. If you leave a test tube full of blood for a few hours the blood cells sink to the bottom and you're left with a clear yellow fluid.

2 The yellow stuff is called plasma – it's 90 per cent water and 10 per cent chemicals such as those tasty molecules and minerals that your cells need to grow and stay healthy. Scientists have discovered how to dry plasma to a powder and turn it back into a liquid by adding water.

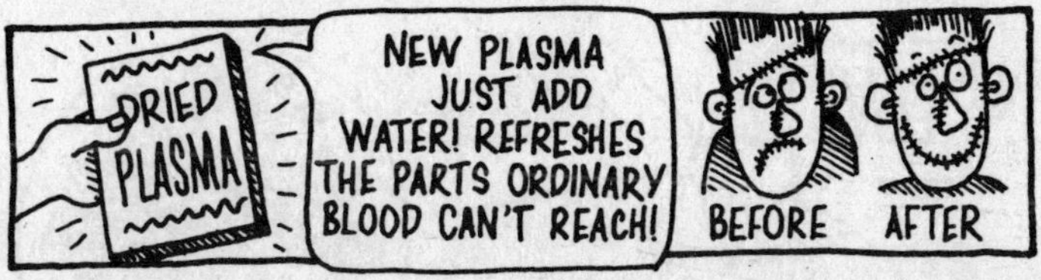

3 Imagine blood as a sort of hot soup squirting through your body. It's full of sugars and other molecules from your food – which is why vampires and mosquitoes find it so tasty.

4 Blood is thicker than water. In fact, it's THREE TIMES thicker. That's not surprising considering that blood is swarming with cells . . . here's what you get in one teeny little millimetre-sized drop!

- 7,000 white blood cells
- 500,000 platelets – (these are little bits of bone-marrow cell that help your blood to clot).

• 5 million red blood cells
Impressive isn't it? But that's nothing. . .
5 In all, your body contains. . .
• 35,000,000,000 (35,000 million) white cells,
• 500,000,000,000 (500,000 million) platelets and
• 25,000,000,000,000 (25 trillion) red blood cells.

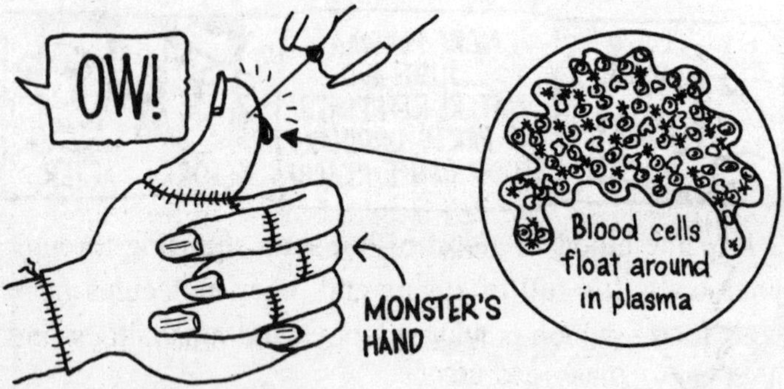

Or so the scientists say. . .
6 But this is only guess-work because it's impossible to count all those cells.
7 The problem isn't just the huge numbers. Every second, three million new red blood cells are made in your bone marrow and three million others die. So by the time you've finally finished counting – you've got to start all over again!
8 There's plenty of room for all these blood cells. Your body contains about 96,558 km (59,962 miles) of blood vessels. If you took someone's blood vessels and laid them end to end they'd go twice round the world. Just imagine a motorway like that!

But if you want to zoom along the blood superhighway in your very own nippy little red blood cell you'll have to learn the rules of the road.

The blood Highway Code

RULE 1: Understand the one way system. Arteries go AWAY from the heart and veins go TOWARDS the heart. NOT THE OTHER WAY ROUND!

RULE 2: No "U" turns allowed. Valves in the veins form bottle necks that stop you reversing.

RULE 3: Red blood cells travel in the centre and white cells creep along the edges.

RULE 4: Make sure you can identify these other road users.

RULE 5: Make sure you don't go over the speed limits. In the big arteries over the heart it's one metre every two seconds. In the capillaries – that's the very tiny blood vessels – it's one metre every half-an-hour!

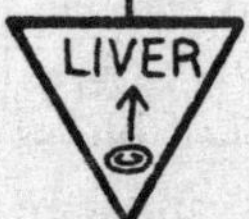

RULE 6: After four months all the red blood cells must report to the liver scrap yard to be broken up. All platelets to be broken up after two weeks.

RULE 7: Beware of blood clots around wounds! All the platelets stick together and produce chemicals that make the plasma sticky. Other road users steer clear – unless you're a real clot!

If you ever get a bit short of blood you might need a blood transfusion. That's when you're given someone else's blood instead of your own. Luckily you don't have to give it back.

A blood-curdling story

Three centuries ago scientists began to wonder whether it was possible to inject blood into humans. But would it work? There was only one way to find out!

One day in 1667 an audience of top British scientists gathered to watch a terrifying trial transfusion. At the centre of attention was a man who had bravely volunteered to have an extra 340 g (12 ounces) of blood injected into his veins. The red stuff had been kindly donated by – a sheep!

1 Can you guess what happened?

a) The volunteer survived.

b) The volunteer's hair turned woolly and he died.

c) The volunteer went mad.

Answer: c) He was described as a bit "cracked in the head". But the scientists reckoned the test worth repeating and more blood transfusions were performed.

But then disaster struck. A man died after another blood transfusion in France. No one knew why! The doctor who performed the operation was accused of murder and although he was found not guilty, the French government banned all transfusions.

Meanwhile the Brits carried on. In those days the technology was rather primitive. One day a doctor offered a sick old man the chance of a blood transfusion. Here's what the doctor planned to do. . .

- Fix a silver pipe to each end of a length of chicken gut.
- Wash the chicken gut out with warm water.
- Stick one silver pipe in the arm of a healthy volunteer.
- Stick the other pipe in the old man's veins.
- Allow the blood to flow into the old man.

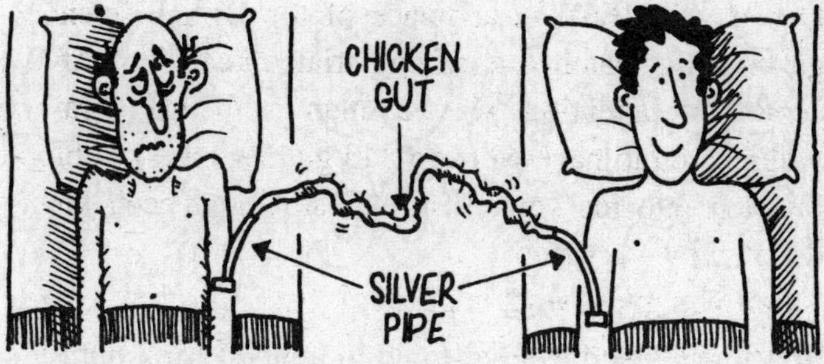

2 What do you think happened next?

a) The old man said "YUCK – NOT ON YOUR LIFE!" and died soon afterwards.

b) The old man said "YES" but the transfusion bumped him off.

c) The old man said "YES" – he got better but the volunteer died!

Answer: a)

During a transfusion there was a risk of blood clots forming and blocking vital blood vessels. But what caused these killer clots? The answer emerged in 1900 when Austrian scientist, Karl Landsteiner, discovered that blood was divided into groups. Your blood group depends on the type of chemicals carried by your red blood cells. When red blood cells from different blood groups collide they mistake one another for germs! Germ-zapping chemicals on the outside of each cell zip into action and the cells end up glued together.

Nowadays blood can be stored in a blood bank until it's needed by someone with the same group. Blood banks don't save money but they do save lives. But sadly Karl's was not one of them. In 1943 he died of a heart attack caused by . . . a blood clot.

Oddly enough, whilst some doctors were trying to give their patients extra blood, others were trying to take it away again. These doctors thought that too much blood was bad for you.

Blood-thirsty bleeders

Yes – 200 years ago your local friendly doctor would do more than give you nasty cough medicine! He'd also try to open your veins to remove all that nasty bad blood! In those days doctors had a selection of vicious-looking knives especially designed for this gruesome job.

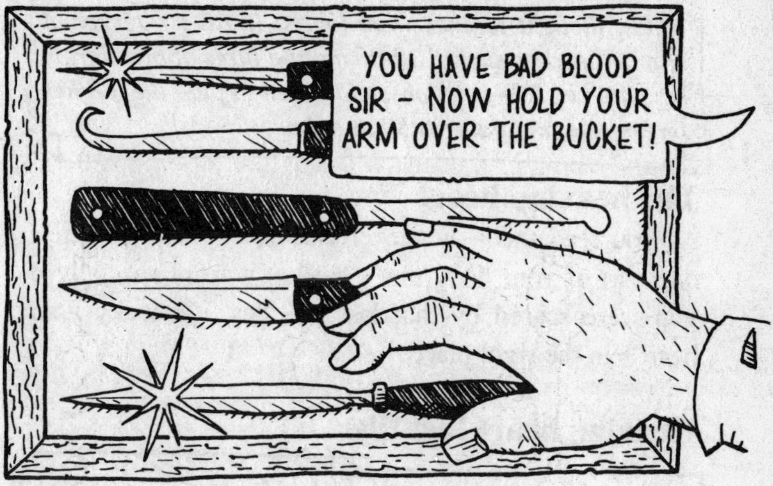

So you don't like the look of them? Well, don't worry – you do have another choice. Can you guess what it is?

A rotten riddle

What's green and yellow and dripping with slime, got ten stomachs, has three stabbing teeth at the front end and by the time it's finished with you it's 15 cm (6 inches) long and GORGED WITH ALL YOUR BLOOD?!

Answer: It's a LOATHSOME leech!!!

And here's the really BAD news! Surgeons were particularly keen on using leeches to take blood from children. They reckoned it was kinder than cutting the kids with the knives!

Bet you never knew!
French doctor, Francois-Joseph-Victor Broussais (1772-1838), thought leeches were lovely. In all it's reckoned that his leeches sucked 20-30 million litres of blood from his patients. The potty physician used to plop the leeches on his cringing patients 50 at a time.

The heaving heart

As you read this – whatever else you're doing, there's one part of your body that's hard at work. Especially if you were scared by that last bit. Yes, it's lucky your heart's in the right place.

Heaving heart fact file

Name of body part: Heart

Where found: The top of your heart is about 8cm (3 inches) to the left of your breast bone.

Useful things it does: Keeps your blood moving.

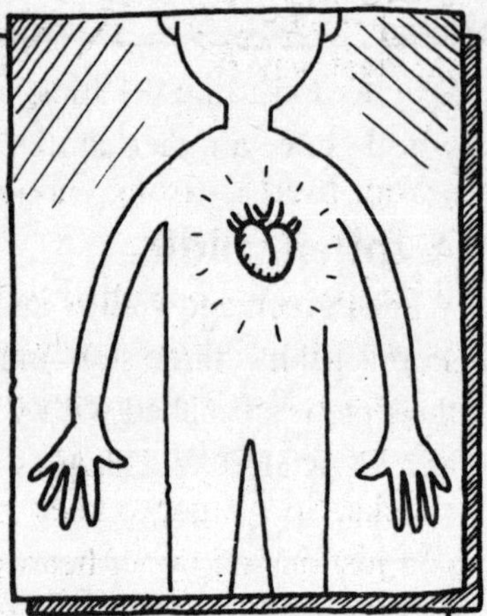

Grisly details: Your heart isn't heart-shaped – it's blob-shaped with a tangle of blood vessels on top. It's about 12cm (5 inches) high and weighs 250-300g (9-10 ounces).

Amazing features: It's horribly hard-working (see opposite page).

The horribly hard-working heart

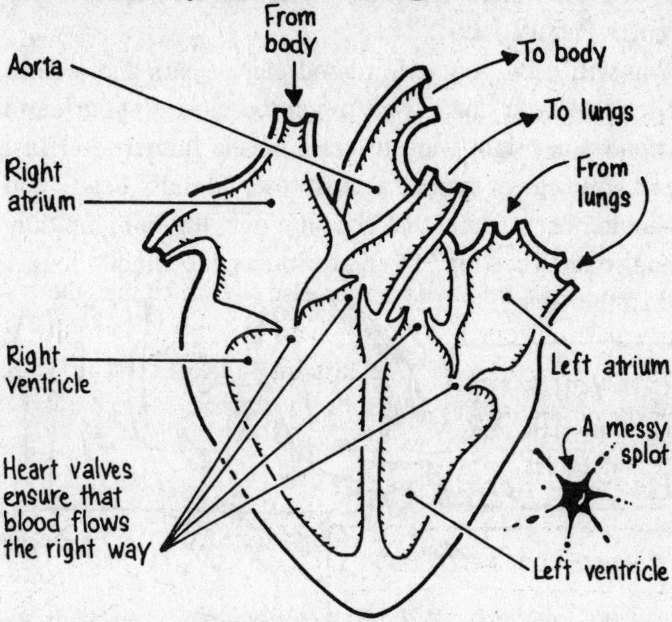

- Your heart is strong enough to pump blood round your body in one minute.
- Its speed is controlled by the brain and influenced by your feelings – this is why your heart beats faster before a science test. But the heart itself is powered by a built-in pacemaker that triggers the heartbeat with tiny electric shocks. So it's got to keep going!
- In just one day your heart pumps enough blood to fill a 10,000 litre (2,200 gallon) tanker.
- In an average lifetime it beats 4,000,000,000 times.
- And pumps over 300 million litres of blood. That's enough to fill 5,500 large swimming pools!
- And in all that time your heart doesn't stop once, not even when you're asleep.

Dare you find out for yourself . . . how your heart beats?

You will need yourself, a good pair of ears and a close friend. (If you don't want to get too close to your close friend you might want to get a plastic funnel too.) Just put your ear or funnel against your friend's heart. You should hear a sound that goes lup-dub, lup-dub, lup-dub, and so on. The "lup" should be louder and slightly longer than the "dub".

Look at the heart diagram on page 123. Each of the four chambers pumps blood in the direction shown. The "lup" sound is the valves at the opening of the ventricles slamming shut. Then the ventricles squeeze the blood out and the "dub" sound you can hear is the closing of the heart valves to prevent the blood squirting backwards.

Your heart isn't the only part of your body that beats. You can feel the blood pulsing in places such as the side of your wrist just under your thumb and on the sides of your neck. What causes these pulses?

a) The arteries pumping the blood forward.

b) The arteries bulging out as a surge of blood from the heart passes by.

c) A bulge in the veins caused by the blood stopping for a moment.

Answer: b)

You might wonder why half your heart is squirting blood to your lungs. Well, your lungs are more than a couple of wheezy wind-bags. They're needed to supply your body with oxygen and the blood takes the oxygen round your body. And without this gas you'd be gasping!

THE GASPING LUNGS

You need your lungs like a breath of fresh air. Literally. Day after day, year after year, your lungs keep puffing away – about 600 million puffs in a lifetime. And you never need to remind them to do their job. But it's a difficult job and the facts that follow about breathing will leave you gasping.

Gasping lungs fact file

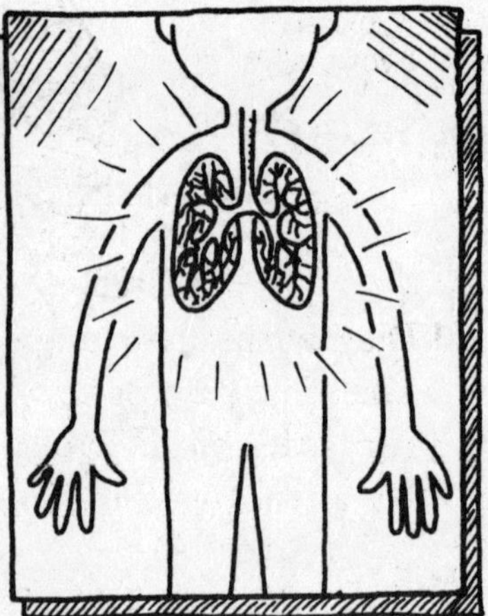

Name of body part: Lungs

Where found: In the chest on either side of the heart. The heart fits into a snug little hollow against the left lung.

Useful things they do: Breathe in air so that oxygen can get into your blood and supply your cells.

Grisly details: Once smokers get ash into their lungs they NEVER get it out again. Heavy smokers' lungs end up like tacky old tar buckets.

Amazing features: Your lungs contain 750 million little tubes and capsules. If these were laid out flat they could cover a tennis court.

Breathing: the inside story

"As easy as breathing" – or so they say. But in fact there's nothing easy about breathing. Here's what happens when you try.

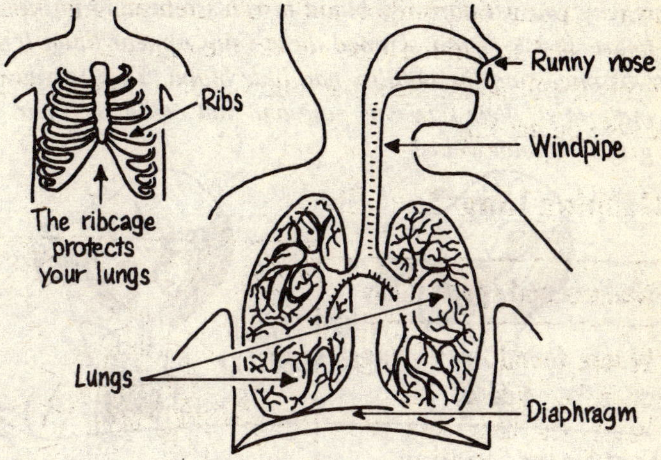

1 Diaphragm (dia-fram) pulls down.
2 Your rib cage rises up.
3 Air is breathed in through your nose and mouth.
4 The air ends up in little capsules called alveoli (al-ve-ol-i).

Your breathing space

The alveoli are the places where breathing actually takes place. Oxygen gas from the air passes into the blood and hops aboard red blood cells for a free ride round the body. Meanwhile the carbon dioxide gas (produced as a waste product by your cells and dissolved in the blood) is rushing the other way. All this takes just one third of a second. Then, the breathing steps 1-4 go into reverse as the air is puffed out again. Yes, it all happens with breathless speed.

Bet you never knew!

Have you got blue blood in your veins? When red blood cells take oxygen from the lungs they're bright red. But after the cells give up their oxygen they're dark red. This is why you get dark red blood in veins returning to the heart. If you're fair-skinned these veins appear blue! It was once said the nobility had blue blood. They stayed indoors so their skin was pale and you could see their gruesome blue veins!

Test your teacher

Is your teacher full of hot air? This tricky test will leave him or her breathless. Here's a clue to start him or her off. An adult breathes about six litres of air a minute.

1 A man stands in a telephone box to make a phone call. The telephone box contains about 270 litres (59 gallons) of air and once the door is closed no more air can get in. How long can the man speak on the phone before he faints from lack of air?

a) 45 minutes

b) 4 hours

c) 45 hours

2 A woman goes to sleep in a room 1.8 x 1.8 x 1.5 metres (2 x 2 x 1.5 yards). The room contains about 1,300 litres (286 gallons) of air. Would she have enough air to survive the night? (Clue: you only need about half the normal amount of air when you're asleep.)

a) Yes – and the following day too!

b) No – she'd die of suffocation.

c) Yes – just about!

3 Think about the size of the room in question 2. How much air do you need to last a lifetime?

a) Enough to fill two large airships.

b) Enough to fill a small hot-air balloon.

c) Enough to fill 339,174 hot-air balloons.

4 Why would someone die if they tried to hide in a lake and breathe through a hollow reed?

a) The lungs can't work in very cold water.

b) The water pressing against the body stops the lungs from breathing out.

c) The water gets in though the ears and drowning follows.

5 A woman has an attack of hiccuping. What part of her breathing equipment is making her hiccup?

a) Her diaphragm

b) Her ribs

c) Her lungs

Answers: 1 a) This really was a problem in old-fashioned phone boxes! **2 c) 3 a)** That's 368,000 cubic metres of air. **4 b)** You cannot do this more than 23 cm (9 inches) below the surface. **5 a)** It's generally caused by eating and drinking too quickly.

Horrible hiccups

What do you think caused this dramatic cure?

a) A massive electric shock

b) A faith healer

c) She had an operation

Answer: c) One of the nerves controlling her diaphragm was destroyed. The hiccups stopped but Lucy couldn't breathe so easily.

Dare you find out for yourself . . . how you talk?

TALKING. Some people never seem to stop. This sad affliction is particularly common amongst teachers. Naturally YOU know how to talk (and when to stop). But can you say what part your lungs play?

Half-way up your windpipe is a triangular opening. It's behind the little bump in your throat that some people call the "Adam's apple". On two sides of this opening, folds of skin stretch as you speak and wobble as air puffs past from the lungs. They're your vocal chords. The larger the chords, the deeper the sounds you can make (this is why most children have squeaky voices).

The basic sounds produced by your vibrating vocal chords are altered by the position of your tongue, lower lip and jaw. You can see how important these bits are when you try this unspeakable speech challenge.

1 Say the word "she" whilst keeping your tongue in your cheek (so you can't move it!).

2 Say the word "pie" without your lips touching one another.

3 Put your hand under your chin and try to talk without your lower jaw moving down.

Which of the above were. . .

a) Possible

b) Just possible but it sounded funny.

c) Impossible

Enjoy endless fun watching your friends attempt the same challenge!

Answers: 1 b) 2 c) 3 b)

Gasping lungs sound-effects

Here are a few other sounds your gasping lungs can make. . .

Yawning

This happens when not enough air is getting to your lungs. So you suddenly take a deep gulp of air. It can also be triggered by boring science lessons.

Laughing

This happens when deep breaths, caused by movements of the diaphragm, are followed by a few short puffs of air from your lungs. This can be triggered by watching your teacher fall off his bicycle.

Crying

Your breathing is exactly the same as when you laugh. Only your feelings are different. Crying may occur as a direct result of having laughed at the wrong moment.

But whatever you do with your lungs there is something you ought to know first. And it's no laughing matter . . . here's the bad news.

Breathing is bad for you

The air you breathe isn't always as pure as it could be. Especially if you live in a big city. Yes – every day you breathe in 20,000,000,000 (20,000 million) tiny bits of pollution, dust and dirt! THE GOOD NEWS . . . your body has ways of dealing with unwelcome visitors.

1 Inside your nose, windpipe and lung tubes there are tiny hairs called cilia (silly-er). Their job is to waft all that nasty stuff back into your mouth and nostrils.

2 The snot in your nose and windpipe is a deadly dust trap. Once stuck in the snot there's no escape for the

grimy gatecrashers. Have you ever noticed that when you work in a dirty place your snot turns black?!

The better news

You can actually cough up dirt . . . this involves closing the top of your windpipe and then suddenly releasing it to allow a blast of puff out at the speed of 150 metres (164 yards) a second!

And sneeze out snot. . . Something tickles the inside of your nose. You close and then open your throat. The air trapped in your lungs blasts its way out. Your tongue blocks the way into your mouth so the dirty, snotty mini-hurricane shoots out of your nose at over 160 km (99 miles) an hour!

The really bad news

It's not just dirt and debris that make you cough and sneeze. The air we breathe is laden with billions and billions of germs. And their whole aim in life is to invade your body and cause disgusting diseases! Atishooooooooo!

DEADLY DISEASES

Remember that sneeze at the end of the previous chapter? It was more than just a puff of air. It was a million droplets of snotty spit and countless germs zooming through the air in search of a victim. And causing disgusting or even deadly diseases. So welcome to the war zone right inside your body! Amazingly, most of the time you don't even know a war's going on!

Little monsters

There are thousands of different types of germs but they fall into two main groups. The brutal bacteria and the vicious viruses – but they're all little monsters.

Brutal bacteria

Bacteria come in a variety of sinister shapes and sizes. Some look like octopuses, others are like sausages and others still have little whip-like tails so they can swim around. They double their numbers every 20 minutes and increase their numbers eight times in one hour. In eight hours a single bacterium can make 16 million copies of itself!

There's something nasty in the garden shed. Something dark and invisible hiding in the corners of your school. And it's waiting to pounce. Many bacteria lurk in shadows because they're destroyed by sunlight. In gloomy weather they float on the wind as high as the clouds. And some are armed with poisonous toxins 100,000 times more powerful than the deadly poison strychnine!

Rogue's gallery

The brutal bacteria include microbes that cause boils, tetanus and upset stomachs. Vicious viruses include colds, chickenpox and measles. There are hundreds of other disease-causing germs – these are just a few of the more sinister specimens!

Botulinus (*Bot-tu-line-us*)

HABITS: Lurks in half-cooked potted meat, soil and rotting leaves.

DAMAGE REPORT: Deadly toxins. Cause double vision, sickness and death!

KNOWN CRIMES: Killed eight fishermen in Scotland in 1922. They had all eaten botulinus-infected sandwiches.

DANGER RATING: Deadly. It makes school dinners look healthy. (But don't worry, this disease is extremely rare!)

Leprosy

HABITS: You can only catch it from prolonged contact with people who already have the disease (and not everyone with leprosy has the catching sort anyway). Slow to develop. It can take years but in the worst cases it makes fingers and toes drop off.

DAMAGE REPORT: Attacks the nerves and skin.

KNOWN CRIMES: Affects several million people in hot countries.

DANGER RATING: Not so dangerous because it's difficult to catch - but very, very nasty if you've got it!

Vicious viruses

To a virus one of your body cells looks like a little planet. That's not surprising because viruses are thousands of times smaller even than bacteria. The virus touches down onto a body cell like a spacecraft landing on the moon. Then the vicious virus injects chemicals to make the cell produce hundreds more viruses. Within half-an-hour all the viruses fly off to seek more victims and the poor old cell splits like a pea pod. It's died from over-work!

Influenza

HABITS: Changes its form every year so your body's defences can't recognise it easily.

DAMAGE REPORT: Fever, aches and pains, runny nose - a few days off school.

KNOWN CRIMES: In 1918 a world-wide 'flu epidemic killed 25 million people.

DANGER RATING: No known cure. Luckily most types of influenza don't kill you - otherwise you'd need more than a few days off school.

Typhus

HABITS: Lives inside lice that scratch their disgusting droppings into the human skin. Ugh!

DAMAGE REPORT: Causes a red rash, fever and death. Kills the louse too by the way - but who cares?

KNOWN CRIMES: Unlike most criminals, typhus germs actually enjoy prison. In 1750 infected lice jumped from criminals to the judges and jurors at a London trial. Three judges and eight jurymen suffered the death penalty.

DANGER RATING: Still common in many parts of the world but can be treated by drugs.

Bet you never knew!
Bacteria don't have it all their own way. Most of the time they enjoy good health – but they are sometimes invaded by tiny tadpole-like viruses and suffer deadly diseases themselves. Serves 'em right!

The body strikes back

Now for the good news. Your body is ready and waiting to bash germs – even if you're not! As part of its defences your body makes lots of germ-killing chemicals. How was this discovered? Well, the story's a bit of a weepie.

A tearful story

1. In 1921, scientist Alexander Fleming was breeding germs for an experiment. He had a bad cold. A drop of snot splashed the germs and they all died!

2. Fleming realised that snot must contain a germ-killing chemical. He experimented using blood plasma, spit and tears.

3. Tears were good germ killers. To get more, Fleming ambushed visitors to his lab and squirted lemon juice in their eyes! (Don't try this – it stings!)

4. He even picked on small children. (He paid them afterwards.)

5. Further experiments proved that egg-white also killed germs. So Fleming started breaking eggs.

6. Then he discovered that fish eggs killed germs too. So he went fishing – oddly enough this was his hobby!

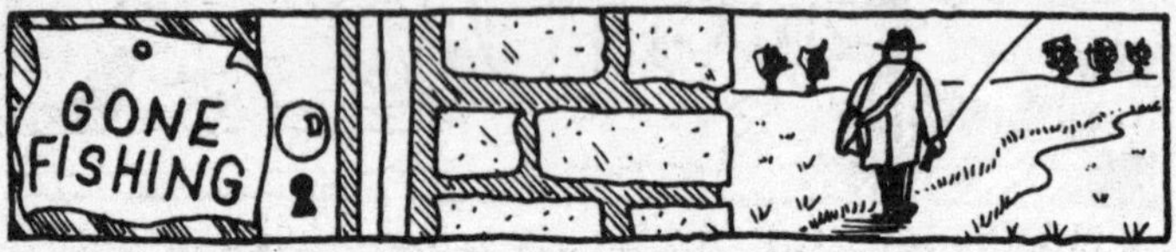

A rotten result

In 1965 scientists found that the germ-killing substance was an enzyme called lysozyme (lie-so-zime). It's found in all the things that Fleming tested. That's the good news. But sadly, lysozyme doesn't kill all known germs – just a few of them.

Luckily you've got a built-in army to defend you from germs. Every day they fight and die on your behalf. Recognise them? They're your wonderful white blood cells – all 35,000,000,000 (35,000 million) of them! Here's what they do.

Immune system fact file

Name of body part: The immune system

Where found: A network of drainage tubes called the lymph system. Also includes your white blood cells.

Useful things they do: Fight germs and keep you healthy.

Grisly details: Pus from an infected wound consists of millions of white blood cells that have been done to death by germs.

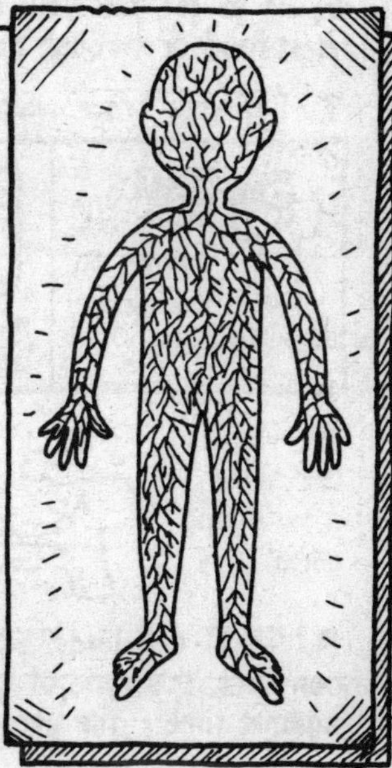

Amazing features: White blood cells "talk" to one another using chemical substances that pass on messages such as, "Bash that virus!"

1 The tubes form a drainage system for lymph – a watery fluid that dribbles from the blood vessels.

2 Nodes: These grape-sized little lumps filter out nasty germs from the tubes. They swell up and get bigger when you're sick.

3 Spleen: Helps make white blood cells in babies.

4 Thymus makes some white blood cells.

Your battling body

Here's how your body fights back. Germs are always trying to get into your body – through your nose, in your food or through cuts and scratches.

1. But your brave white blood cells are ready . . .

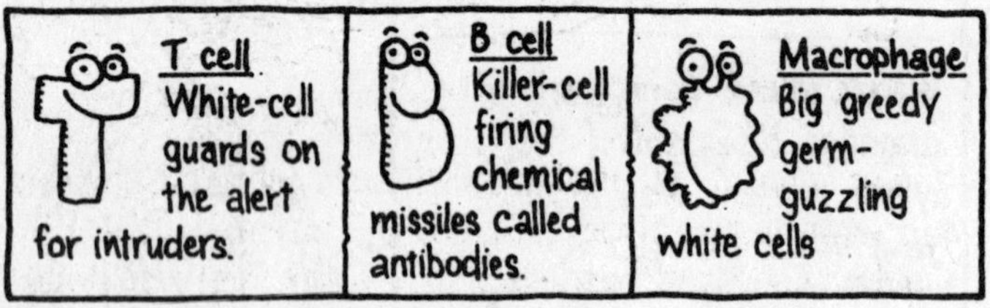

2. The T cell grabs a wriggling germ!

3. The T cell finds a B cell that makes antibodies that can stick this type of germ together. It's a desperate race against time – the germs are breeding fast!

4. The B cell fires antibodies to gum the germs together.

5. The T cell orders the B cell to make loads of copies of itself to attack any other germs loitering nearby.

6. The macrophage flows round the stuck-up germs. Reaches out long jelly-like arms to encircle them. Then it gobbles the germs! It can grab and guzzle 20 bacteria at a time and dissolve them whilst they're still alive! Congratulations, you win!

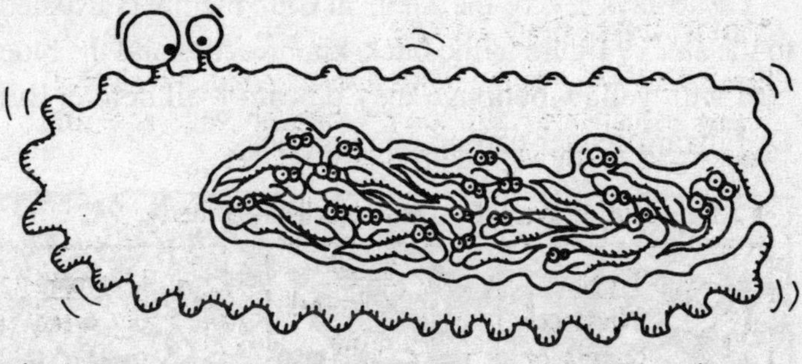

You've won if you destroy all the germs without losing too many white blood cells. It's OK to lose a few hundred thousand but lose a few billion and you're in trouble! Meanwhile bits of half-digested bacteria are left lying around on the battlefield.

How to be incredibly immune

Once you've had a certain illness, you needn't worry about getting it again – ever. Some of your white blood cells store the information about how to make the antibodies. This way, your body can store details of an incredible 18 billion types of antibody.

But sometimes your immune system needs a boost. That's why you need nasty injections. When you have a jab you are being injected with dead germs. YUCK!

These allow your body to make the antibodies needed to fight the actual full-blown disease. Yuck! This painful process is called vaccination. Here's how the modern form of vaccination was developed in 1796.

Just the jab

Some of the audience yawned rudely or snorted angrily. One muttered under his breath, "That Jenner's going on about cowpox again!"

These days few of the Medical Club members listened to the stocky figure in the buckskin breeches and the blue coat with yellow buttons. They'd heard it all before. But Dr Edward Jenner carried on regardless.

"Smallpox kills millions of people. It causes fever and covers the body with pus-filled spots. People lucky enough to survive are scarred for life. I believe that those who get the milder disease of cowpox are protected from getting smallpox."

"Why don't you experiment?!" someone shouted.

"Yes," yelled another, "On yourself!"

"But," shouted Jenner above the uproar, "many country people also believe it to be true!"

The audience exploded with laughter – they didn't think much of country folk.

Jenner sat back down – humiliated once again. He remembered going to the doctor's as an eight-year-old boy. He was terrified of the physician and the huge needle with its thread dripping with pus from a smallpox victim. This was the traditional form of vaccination using live germs and it was very dangerous. The needle scratch was supposed to cause a mild smallpox and somehow prevent the full-blown disease. But it gave young Jenner such a terrible fever that he nearly died.

There had to be a better way. Jenner was certain that people who got cowpox from milking infected cows never got smallpox. If only he could prove it. . .

One day, a young milkmaid named Sara Nelmes came into the tiny garden hut that Jenner used as his surgery. The girl was in a bad way.

She'd scratched her hand and as the doctor examined her he noticed bluish raised-up spots.

"You have the cowpox, Sara?"

"Yes, sir," the milkmaid blushed. "But at least I won't get the smallpox."

Jenner smiled. "Sara, with your permission I would like to perform a small experiment."

With a needle Dr Jenner took a drop of pus from Sara's hand and then. . . This was the moment for which he had waited for over 20 years. He decided to inject the pus into an eight-year-old boy named James Phipps. Then Jenner saw the fear in the child's eyes and remembered his own terror of the doctor with the huge needle.

So Jenner closed his eyes and gritted his teeth as he made two scratches on the boy's arm. In the next few days James would suffer the sores and discomfort of cowpox. But would this be enough to ward off the more deadly threat of smallpox?

Six weeks later Jenner held his breath as he scratched poor James again – this time with pus from a smallpox victim. Now came the real test. There would be a two week pause and then . . . what? Perhaps the boy would suffer crippling backaches, the fever and shivering and the deadly killer spots. Supposing Jenner was wrong . . . the child might even die. And then the doctor would face the death penalty for murdering his young patient!

But weeks passed and James remained healthy. The child was now immune to smallpox. Some people still jeered. They sang songs about people turning into cows after a cowpox injection.

But Dr Jenner soon hit back with a book packed with tasteful colour pictures of pus-filled cowpox blisters. More physicians backed the doctor and soon richer people began to ask for the treatment. It proved to be "just the jab" for beating smallpox. Dr Jenner grew rich and successful but he never forgot the boy who had made it possible. What did he give James as a thank-you present?

a) His very own thatched cottage with flowers round the door.

b) A needle made from solid gold.

c) One shilling (that's equivalent to 5p).

Answer: a)

Smallpox smashed

The virus that caused smallpox was living on borrowed time. Throughout Europe and North America governments began to organise vaccination programmes. By 1980 a determined world-wide campaign of vaccination led to a historic announcement from the World Health Organisation . . . smallpox had been wiped off the face of the Earth. Meanwhile, scientists had discovered vaccines for many more diseases. In 1994 all British kids were given measles jabs. Ouch!

But even if you manage to remain healthy your body never stays the same. There's always something going on even if it's a bit of a pain. Oh well – it's all part of growing up.

GROWING PAINS

You might not always like your body – but it'll grow on you. You were growing even before you were born and you spend your first 20 years getting bigger. Growing is a bit of a pain for your parents because you always need new clothes and shoes. But after you stop growing you start ageing – and that's even more of a pain!

Relatively painful

Some of the biggest growing pains are caused by stupid comments from your relatives. Every Christmas they burst into your home to inspect you from head to toe and exclaim, "Haven't you grown!" At this point the best thing to do is look rather sad and say. . .

On second thoughts – better keep quiet or you won't get any presents. Here are a few things you need to know about growing.

Tall stories

1 You don't grow at the same speed all the time. You grow quickly in your first two years. Then up to the age of ten your growth steadies before speeding up again in your teenage years.
2 As you grow the proportions of your body change. For example, a baby's head takes up about 25 per cent of its length. But in an adult the head is only 12.5 per cent of its body length.
3 It's lucky these things happen otherwise you'd look pretty odd. You wouldn't want a giant-sized head – would you?

But why do people grow? If you asked a scientist this interesting question you wouldn't just get one answer – you'd get two!
1 The fairly simple answer.
2 The excruciatingly complicated but fascinating answer involving large dollops of scientific gobbledy-gook.
So which do you want to hear first?

The fairly simple answer

The speed at which you grow is affected by diet. Eat a normal balanced amount of food and you'll grow taller than if you lived off scraps that the pigs won't eat. (No, I'm not talking about school dinners!) Health is also an important factor. Some bone diseases stop people from growing properly.

The excruciatingly complicated answer. . .

The speed at which you grow is controlled by a hormone produced in your brain. So what exactly is a hormone? I'm afraid you've got to know this before you can begin to understand the excruciatingly complicated answer. . .

Horrible hormones fact file

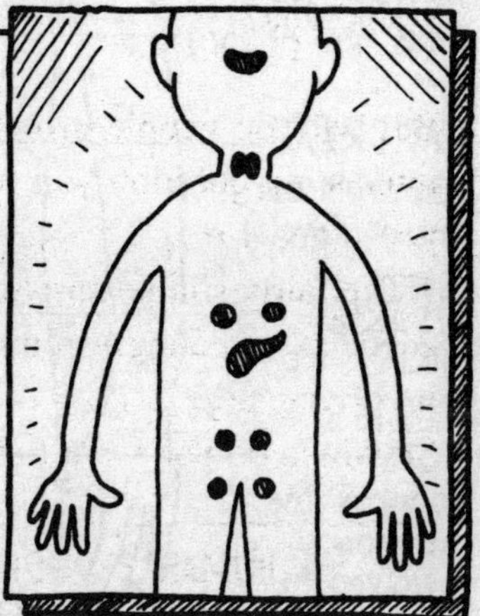

Name of body part: Hormones

Where found: Made by glands in different parts of the body

Useful things they do: Cause changes in the body. For example, some hormones give teenagers a grown-up appearance.

Grisly details: Hormones cause horrible problems (see below).

Amazing features: Cortisol (cor-tis-sol), made by the adrenal glands, is a chemical alarm clock that wakes you up!

Where to find your glands. . .

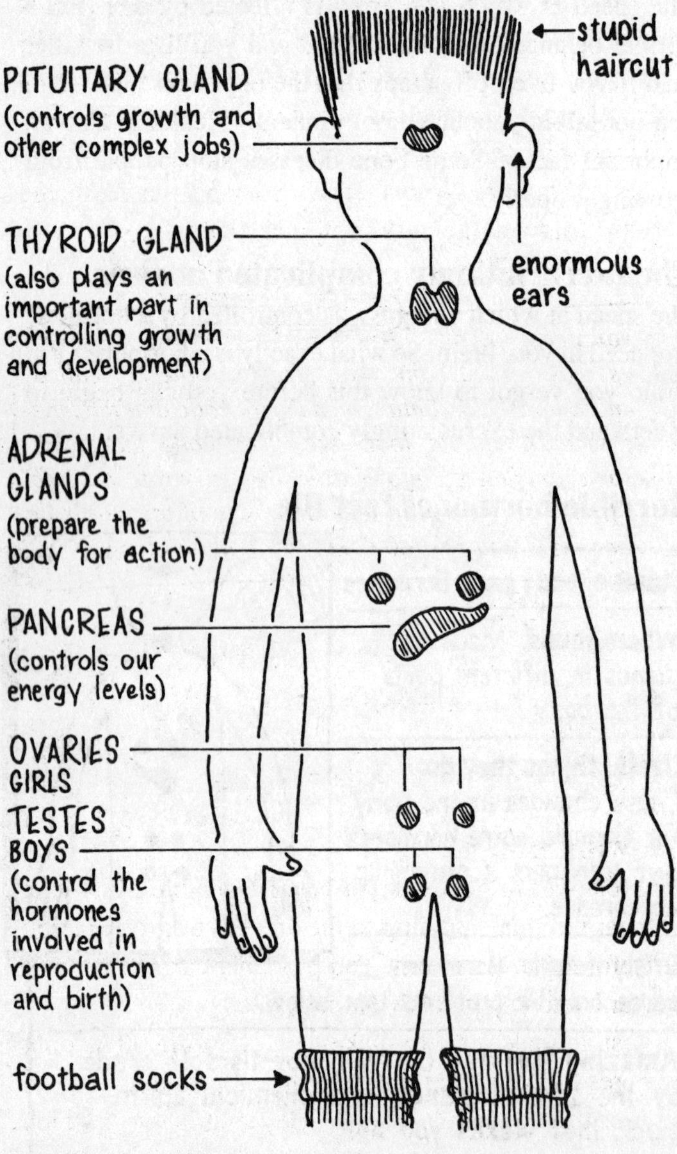

Horrible hormone problems

Here lies the answer to the question, "Why do people grow?" The pituitary also makes the hormone that tells your body to grow! Growth hormone burrows through a cell and into the nucleus to meet – the genes. The hormone tells the genes to order the cells to grow and divide so your body can grow. So what on earth are genes? (Told you this was complicated!)

Bet you never knew!

Genes are found on 46 stringy objects called chromosomes. They contain a chemical code that tells the body what it should look like. This code stores an awesome amount of information. If you wrote out the code from just one cell in letters the size of the words in this book it would be 10,000 km (6210 miles) long.

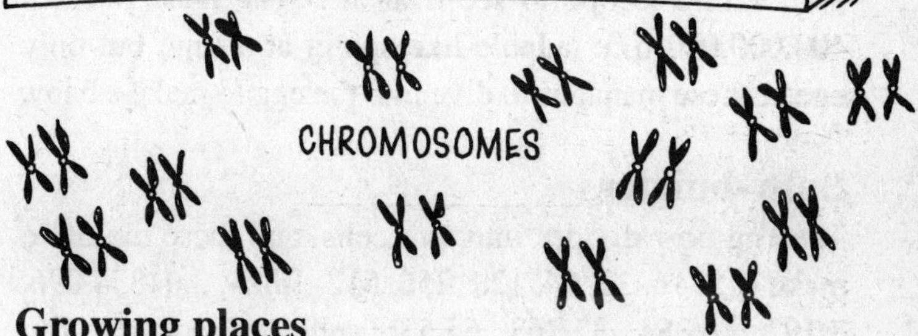

Growing places

Your relatives might think you've grown quite a bit in the last year but that's nothing to the amount of growing you did before you were born. You probably can't remember that far back – so here's what happened.

Most animals mate to make new offspring. (The only creatures that don't are tiny jelly-like things that you can only see through a microscope. They split in two – which sounds really painful.) But we humans also mate to make children. Well, just imagine your poor parents having to split in two to make your little brother!

The aim of mating is to allow the male and female parents to mix their genes up. That's why children end up looking a bit like both their parents.

The genes are carried in special cells called sperm and eggs. The male makes sperm cells in his testes and the female releases an egg cell from her ovaries. (In humans the egg cell is far smaller than a hen's egg – in fact you need a microscope to see it at all!) The male releases 400,000,000 tiny tadpole-like sperm at a time but only one of these manages to dive into the egg to make a baby.

Baby-builders

The egg now divides into two cells, and these divide to make 4, 8, 16, 32, 64, 128, 256, 512, 1,024, 2,048, 4,096, 8,192, 16,384, 32,768, 65,536 cells and so on. (You continue this list if you really want!)

So from two original cells come all the cells in the body – your muscles, bones, teeth, brain, liver, eyeballs, sweat-glands and everything else. This process of division and sorting goes on until the tiny ball of cells turns into a baby. A tiny, incredible, brand-new human being.

Incredible infancy

Now you might think that babies are pretty useless and definitely disgusting. After all, they do nothing much except sleep, dribble, throw up and other unmentionable things. But babies are incredible (just ask their mums and dads!) and babyhood is an incredible time for the body. Which of the following are too amazing to be true?

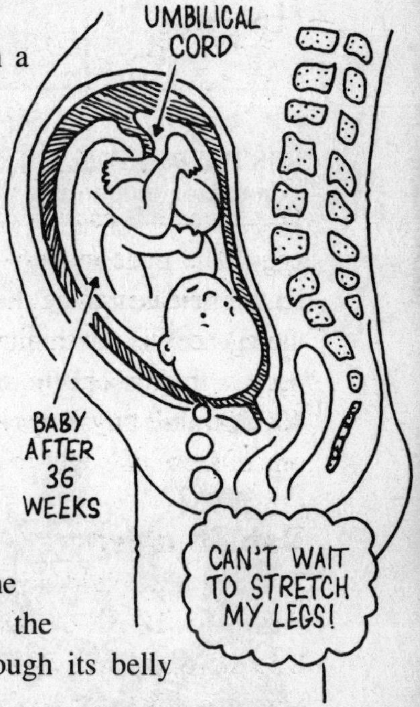

1 In the 238 days before birth a baby's weight increases 5 million times. (Lucky you don't put on weight so quickly nowadays!) TRUE / FALSE

2 During this time a baby floats around happily in a salty pool inside it's mum's womb. It turns somersaults and even scratches itself with its fingernails. TRUE / FALSE

3 The baby is fed from the mother through a tube called the umbilical cord that passes through its belly button. TRUE / FALSE

4 Babies go through a stage before they are born when they are covered in tiny hairs. TRUE / FALSE

5 Babies have a natural sense of rhythm. They kick their little hands and feet in time to music even before they are born. TRUE / FALSE

6 When they are born babies can't see in colour, only in black and white. TRUE / FALSE

7 Babies can taste food better than grown-ups because they have about 9,000 more taste-buds. TRUE / FALSE

8 Babies can remember faces. TRUE / FALSE

9 A baby can tell when someone is talking in a foreign language. TRUE / FALSE

10 Babies sleep more but dream less than adults. TRUE / FALSE

Answers: 1-4 TRUE **5-6** FALSE But unborn babies do kick in response to loud noises! **7-9** TRUE **10** FALSE Babies dream more.

In the first year after they are born, babies get 6.3 kg (1 stone) heavier. Within two years they can walk and talk. At five they're old enough to go to school. And after that it's downhill all the way.

Appalling old age

Age does funny things to people. The older a grown-up gets the less willing they are to admit how old they are. You might think that your teacher is about 98. But if you dare to ask him he might well say, "I'm in the prime of life." (Teachers are ALIVE?!) Well anyway, here are a few sure signs of ageing to look out for in your teachers.

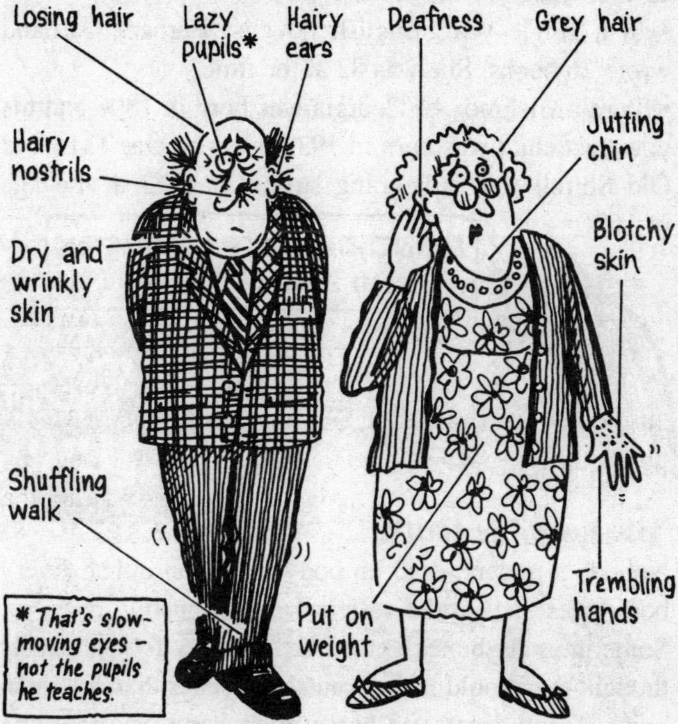

AMAZING old age

BUT don't assume that your poor old teacher is a clapped-out old has-been. Remember . . . older people (and that includes your more mature teachers) have a vast store of wisdom and learning. Many famous people have made their greatest contribution to world history in their later years.

• Genghis Khan (1162-1227) the Mongolian soldier was

conquering most of the known world when he was in his sixties.

• William Gladstone (1809-1898) was Prime Minister of Britain when he was in his eighties.

• In a single year, English novelist Barbara Cartland wrote 26 books. She was 82 at the time.

• Shirali Mislimov of Georgia was born in 1806 and his youngest child was born in 1937 when he was 131. And Old Shirali was still going strong in 1973 at the age of 168!

The horrible truth

Nobody's perfect. And no body is perfect either. Every body ages, aches and suffers from disgusting diseases. Sometimes its bones get broken, too. A few scientists thought they could make something better than a human body. A new improved home-made body or a machine that could replace the body.

But was it worth the effort? For all its faults, the body is the most fantastic, the most incredible machine in the entire universe. And it's all yours! Your body can do things that no machine could ever do. It can grow, and when it works harder its muscles grow too. It can walk thousands of kilometres and not wear out. The soles of its feet even renew themselves and thicken to make walking easier.

Your body can do 101 different things, and the most amazing thing of all is that you can do them ALL AT ONCE!

- You can ride a bicycle and digest your dinner.

- Kick a football and imagine you're playing in the Cup Final.

- You can listen to music and do your homework and still guzzle a packet of crisps!

The body suffers from disgusting diseases, it's true. But then it gets better. It actually heals and repairs itself. All you have to do is to give it proper food and exercise. Treat your body well and it'll last a lifetime.

Of course, if you went into Dr Frankenstein's lab and saw all the body bits, the bones and bottles of blood you might say, "Yuck! How horrible!"

But you've also got to admit that the body is more than just horrible. It's horribly amazing too! And that's horrible science for you!

DISGUSTING DIGESTION

Introduction

Here's a disgusting science story…

It's ten minutes to the end of a particularly boring science lesson. The hands on the clock are crawling round like dozy snails. You're struggling to stay awake. It's so tedious.

So you try to think about something – anything to stop yourself from dropping off. Lunch, perhaps? Yes, that sounds like a good idea. OK – so it's only school lunch but breakfast was centuries ago. You're so hungry. Couldn't you just murder a scrumptious steaming pudding oozing with hot jam and custard?

But then your teacher asks a tricky question.

Dead silence.

No one answers. Just then your tum lets rip with a huge, hearty rumble. It sounds deafening – just like a massive rumble of thunder. The echoes bounce off the classroom walls. Everyone stares at you. What do you do?

a) Turn scarlet and mumble "Sorry".

b) Blame the smart, goody-goody kid next to you.

c) Jump up, and close all the classroom windows saying, "There must be a storm coming, wasn't that thunder?"

A scientist, of course, would know the scientific answer. Some scientists actually spend their lives delving into digestion. Digestion is when food is taken into your body to help you stay alive and grow. It sounds about as thrilling as last night's dirty dishes.

But it doesn't have to be.

Digestion is disgusting. Amazingly disgusting! And this disgustingly amazing process is going on inside your body right now. In this book there are some foul scientific secrets and disgusting discoveries served up with a hearty helping of belly-laughs. And afterwards you'll be able to answer your teacher's question like this…

* (Bor-bor-rig-mus) Posh medical term for a rumbling tummy. The stomach walls squash the gas and liquids inside. The surrounding area wobbles too – making the sound louder.

After all, there are plenty of laws in science but not one of them says it's got to be boring. So now there's only one question. Have you got the stomach for some really disgusting discoveries?

Better read on and find out…

The young medical student turned white. His eyeballs bulged in his head and his mouth opened in a soundless scream. He wanted to yell but nothing came out. Not even a muffled gasp. He wanted to run. Run anywhere. But his legs wouldn't budge. He wanted to wake from his nightmare but this was no dream. It wasn't a scene from a horror film either. This was real life.

There really were sparrows flapping around the room. They were pecking at bits of dead body on the floor. And that really was a huge hungry rat skulking in the corner and gnawing greedily on a lump of human bone. This was a room in a hospital … and the year was 1821.

Don't panic! Hospitals aren't like this any more. But when 18-year-old medical student Hector Berlioz (1803-1869) visited a dissecting room in Paris this is what he really saw. (A dissecting room was where dead bodies were cut up so that their different parts could be studied.) This is just one example of the disgusting conditions endured by doctors and scientists in the past as they probed the secrets of digestion.

Disgusting digestion dates

The ancient Egyptians were into dissecting 5,000 years ago. In fact, every time they made a mummy they got their hands on the human guts. They always removed the intestines, or guts, and other vital organs and put them into jars because they would rot easily and spoil the preserved mummy. They kept all the body bits in jars for the mummy to use in the afterlife.

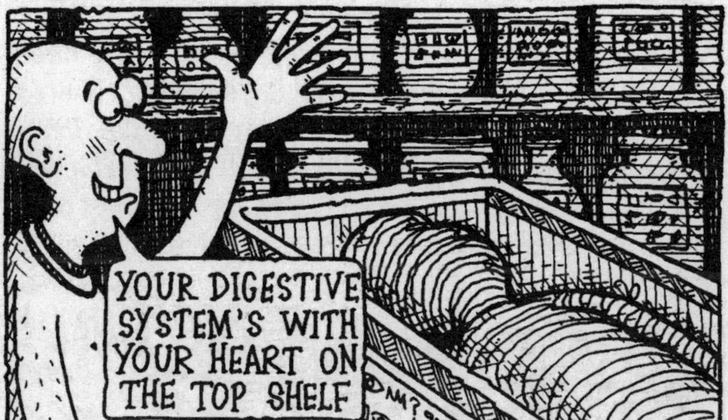

But the Egyptians weren't interested in the structure of the guts or how they worked. One of the first people to be genuinely interested in the guts was a foul-tempered Roman doctor.

Horrible Science Hall of Fame: Claudius Galen (AD129-201) Nationality: Roman

Galen said:

Hope *your* mum isn't like that. Sadly Galen inherited his mum's temper and nothing much from his dad.

Young Galen was disgustingly clever. He wrote three books before he was thirteen and another five hundred after that. Some of them had intriguing titles like *Bones for Beginners*, *On the Black Bile*, and *On the Usefulness of Parts of the Body*. One day Galen kept 12 scribes busy as he strode up and down dictating the words for 12 different books at the same time.

Galen reckoned he had the last word on medicine. He once said:

Modest, eh? The problem was Galen wasn't always right. In fact he was often WRONG. For example, he reckoned blood was made in the guts and went to the liver where it turned blue.

WRONG. Blood is made in the bone marrow and spleen. Just goes to show you can't believe everything you read in books. Galen said that humans only have 16 teeth. WRONG AGAIN – it's incredible that he never bothered to count them!

Galen made silly mistakes because he got his ideas from cutting up dead animals rather than humans. But no doctors dared to argue with him. They were scared of Galen's famously foul temper. (Once Galen had even dared to shout insults at an opponent in the sacred

Temple of Peace.) And they were even more scared he might ask his pal the Roman Emperor to dispose of them in a disgusting fashion.

For about 1,500 years doctors believed Galen's theories. They could have cut up a few bodies to check for themselves. But few did. Governments often banned dissection and where it *was* allowed doctors felt they were too grand for all the messy, gory cutting up stuff and left that to their humble assistants. Then a doctor came along who was…

A cut above the rest

Andreas Versalius (1514-1564) had a horrible habit. He stole dead bodies. And he wasn't particular either – anybody's body would do. Young, old, men or women – it didn't matter as long as the corpse wasn't too rotten. While he worked in the Belgian town of Louvain he used some disgustingly dodgy tricks to gain his revolting ends. He would:

- dig up bodies in cemeteries.

• steal the bodies of criminals left on public display.

• attend executions and sneak the body away at the end of the proceedings.

Then he would hide the bodies in his room. And late into the night by the flickering flame of a candle, he probed their grisly innards. Andreas Versalius wasn't crazy. He was a scientist and he was determined to go to any lengths to solve the mysteries of how the body worked. The appalling methods he used were the only way to get any answers. Dissection was banned, remember.

Things became easier in 1536 when Versalius became Professor of Anatomy in Padua, Italy. Here, the authorities were sympathetic to dissection. They even fixed execution dates so that the criminal's body would be nice and fresh for anatomy classes.

You'll be pleased to know doctors no longer need to steal bodies to practise dissection. Some people actually agree to allow their bodies to be dissected after death to help train medical students.

Bet you never knew!
Here's how to play Andreas Versalius's favourite game.
1 *Allow yourself to be blindfolded.*
2 *Ask your friends to hand you a selection of human bones.*
3 *Identify them by their shape and the way they feel.*
4 *You win if you get them all right.*

Rotten reading

Versalius discovered more about the inside of the human body than anyone before him. He was the first person to describe the structure of the human guts accurately. In 1543 he published his discoveries in a book *The Fabric of the Human Body*. It was packed with tasteful pictures of bits of bodies and skeletons with lovely scenery to make the revolting subject matter nicer to look at. The book was a bestseller.

But Versalius came to a disgusting end. According to one story he was cutting up a nobleman's body when it twitched. The "corpse" was still alive! Versalius decided to make himself scarce and embarked on a long sea voyage. But poor old Versalius was shipwrecked and starved to death on a lonely island. And what's more he had no body to keep him company!

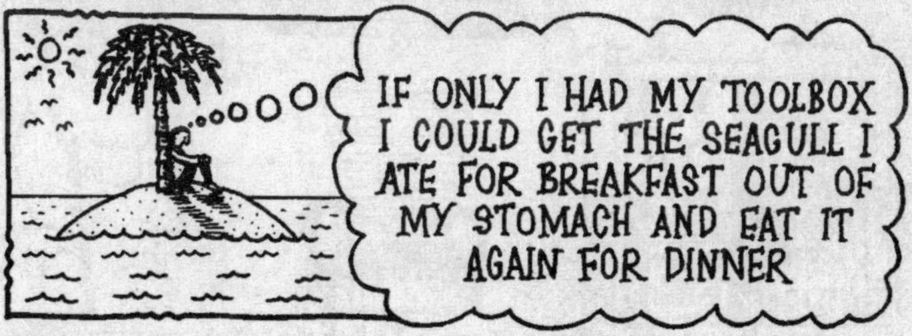

Could you have made these disgusting discoveries? Here's your chance to probe those gruesome innards and their grisly secrets. Delicate readers may find this next chapter not quite to their taste. It's a little bit sick.

Disgusting digestive bits 'n' pieces

Would you want to inspect the guts in grisly close-up detail? It's a horrible job but sometimes it's vital to check on problems. The scientist in this chapter has a real problem. He was absent-mindedly sucking his pen when he swallowed the top. It got stuck somewhere in his guts.

As luck would have it he'd just invented an incredible shrinking machine.

So all he needed was a volunteer to shrink down to 2.5 cm (1 inch) high and venture into his guts in search of the missing top. Any takers? Unfortunately, every doctor the scientist asked seemed to have an excuse. So he hired hard-bitten Private Eye, M.I. Gutzache for this unpleasant job.

First Gutzache had to change into special protective clothing so he wouldn't be digested during his hazardous mission.

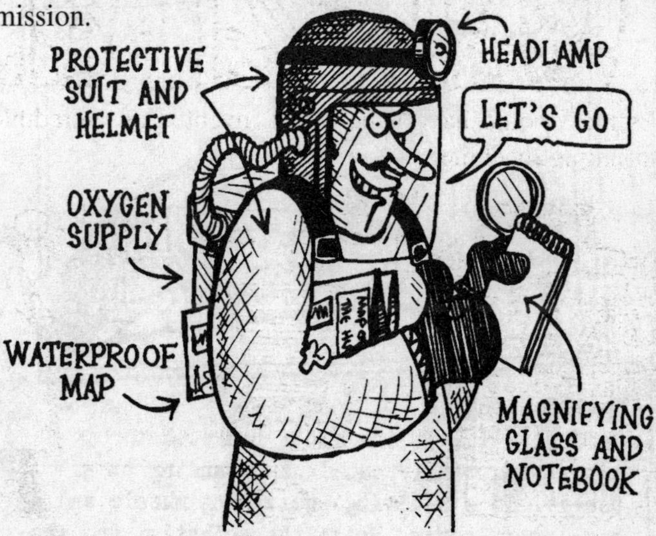

Here's Gutzache's report. Go on take a look, you know you want to – it's fascinating.

Digestive bits and pieces

It seemed a cinch. Just a quick surveillance operation. "No problem," I said. So I took the job. That was my first big mistake. I may be a small-time private eye but under the shrinking ray I started to feel even smaller. But the worst was yet to come. I was going to be swallowed by a scientist!

Tough teeth

The teeth looked tough. There were several types. Some geared for biting, and some for chewing, gnawing or nibbling. They all looked mighty mean to me. Teeth are as hard as they come - d'you know you need a diamond to cut into them?

Tasteful tongue

Suddenly, I felt the floor heave. Not surprising really, as I was standing on a tongue. It's a living, quivering muscle and a real smart mover. While the scientist guy was talking, his tongue tossed a lump of carrot into a huge puddle of spit, and another piece came flying in between his teeth. It's awesome what that muscle can do! But if I didn't act fast I figured I'd be next for a spit dunking. I cast around for an exit.

Salivary (sal-i-very) glands

But I was too late, all of a sudden I felt wet and hot. Looking down I saw I was up to my knees in saliva (that's spit to you). It looked like trouble - but trouble is my business. I knew there were six hidden glands pumping this stuff out. I was going to have to swim for it. I dived down the gullet. It seemed the safest place to be. But I was wrong.

The scientist writes …

I was trying hard not to bite Detective Gutzache. It was actually quite lucky that he fell into my saliva - it helped me to swallow him. Spit may seem disgusting stuff, but it's full of proteins called enzymes that are vital for digestion.

1. An enzyme joins on to another chemical in the food.

2. The enzyme splits up food molecules until they are small enough to be sucked through my gut walls. (There's a lot more of this going on inside my small intestine!)

Then disaster struck. Gutzache got stuck in my gullet, or oesophagus (a-sof-fer-gus), to use the technical term. What would happen to him now?

Oesophagus

Just my luck to get wedged in his throat! The scientist guy started coughing and spluttering. My body shook as he gulped. Then I felt all this water flooding over me – I was on the move! Now, I often find myself in tight spots and I can tell you this next one was seriously tight. The sides of his gullet squeezed together forcing me down. Then I hit some half-chewed food. The gullet walls squeezed the food into a ball. I knew that I could be squashed too. I wanted out. But it was too late.

The scientist adds …

My oesophagus walls squeezed together behind Mr Gutzache and pushed him down. This is called peristalsis (perry-stal-sis). It's Greek for "push around". It was lucky he didn't fall down my windpipe. That would have started me choking until I'd coughed him back into my mouth.

Stomach

I hit the stomach with a splash. It was more of a bellyflop than a dive. I found myself swimming in a lake of mush. It looked and smelled like sick. It was sick! I felt sick too. I was churned around as the stomach walls squeezed in and out. I felt like a sock in a washing machine. I figured the juice was acid because I could see it dissolving the food. I was real glad of my protective suit!

The scientist writes ...

My stomach lining makes up to 2 litres (3.5 pints) of acid juice every day to dissolve the food I eat. And there are enzymes at work too.

Small intestine

After a few hours I managed to squeeze through the exit below the stomach. I found myself in a long tube that looked like a subway. I switched on my headlamp and peered at my waterproof map. My route was clear. I should head down the duodenum (dew-o-dee-num), jejunum (gee-june-num) and ileum (ill-ee-um). Whatever they were.

The map said "small intestine" - but it seemed endless. I knew I had to keep moving. The gut walls were closing behind me and I wasn't hanging around to get squashed again. So I walked. My feet squashed on the soft rubbery ground. Just then I saw something large and blue trapped in a fold in the wall. Success! It was the missing pen top. I gingerly pulled it out and tucked it under my arm. Now all I had to do was to get out without getting digested on the way.

A squirt

Suddenly I was splattered with digestive juices. I felt like an automobile in a car-wash, except I wasn't getting any cleaner. I was covered in brownish slimy bile from the liver and pale juice from the pancreas, I didn't stop to admire the view. I made tracks for the large intestine.

The scientist writes ...

It's me again. I just wanted to explain that my bile breaks up the remains of greasy, fatty foods. It comes from my gall bladder, which is a little bag under the liver. My pancreas is about 18cm (7 inches) long and it's draped under my stomach. Besides enzymes, it makes vital chemicals that control the amount of sugar in my blood.

Appendix

In the large intestine I saw a weird sight. A little tube, about 5cm (2 in) long, leading to a dead end. In the end I figured it out. It was the appendix. It wasn't doing much – just hanging out, I guess.

The scientist writes …

Gutzache's got it right for once! My appendix spends its life doing nothing and I'm not even sure why it's there. My large intestine is definitely there for a reason though, it sucks up any spare water and minerals from my food.

The rectum

I was dead beat. So I sat down. Big mistake. I sank into something soft and brown and it didn't smell too good. I was in the rectum. It was the final stretch of the large intestine. And there was only one way out. I could see the toilet bowl. It seemed a long way down but there was nowhere else to go. I shoved the pen top out and it splashed into the water far below. *My turn next*, I thought.

The scientist writes ...

The large intestine is where waste food is stored. Most of the spare water is sucked out of the waste and through the sides of the gut. Er . . . 'scuse me a minute. Got to dash . . .

Splash-down

It was time to check out. I never liked parachute jumps. After I crawled out of the water I quit the job. The scientist wanted me to check out his liver but I'd had enough. I needed a vacation. Fighting violent crime seemed easy after this.

Disgusting expressions

Answer

Hope not. This is the medical word for a lump of poo. The main reason why doctors say "stool" is that they'd feel silly saying "poo" all day. So when you visit the doctor make sure that you don't ask for a stool to sit on. By the way the other medical word for poo is faeces (fee-sees).

Bet you never knew!

1 Some people have worms in their guts. It's true! Roundworms, pin worms and flukes can all live in the guts and feast on half-digested food. They generally get there in infected food. And once in, they lay eggs that pass out of the body with the faeces ready to infect someone else. But don't panic! Nowadays these nasty little suckers can be beaten using drugs.

2 The gut also contains microbiological bacteria or as you might know them – germs. Up to 400 types of bacteria happily swim around in the colon where they make nasty smells. And they make up 1.5 kg (3 lbs) of your total weight! But most of them are harmless and some even make useful K and B vitamins to keep us healthy (see pages 235-238 for more details).*

**Microbiological means the study of tiny life. Go on, say it. It's a brilliant word to chuck into a Friday afternoon science lesson. It means you need a microscope to see these bacteria because they're so small. You could actually find hundreds on the pointy end of a pin.*

More bits'n'pieces

In his hurry to get away, Gutzache missed out a few important digestive bits and pieces. It's time to take a closer look at...

The life-saving liver

Tiny bits of digested food molecules in the blood go to the liver to make vital substances your body needs. The liver also does hundreds of other vital jobs such as making bile (see page 180).

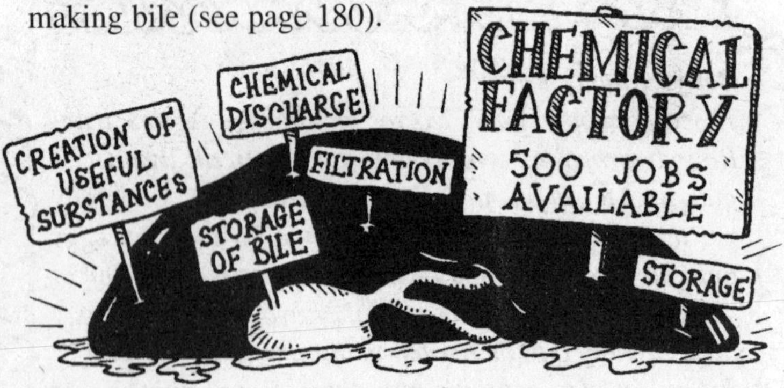

The vagus (vay-gus) nerve

The vagus nerve is like a long telephone wire that "vaguely" snakes round the guts carrying messages to and from the brain. These include orders to squeeze the gut wall and move the food ball on to its next destination.

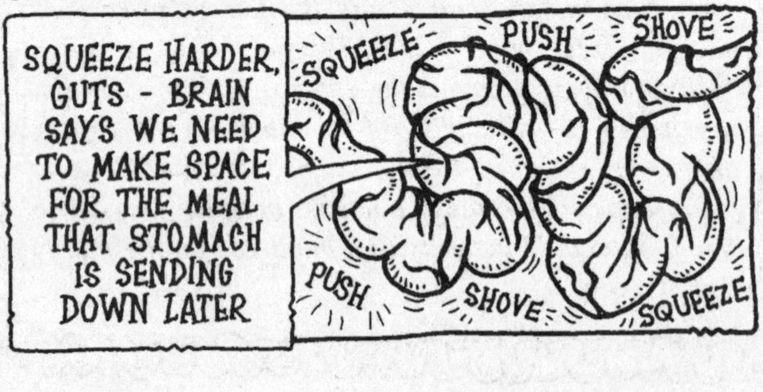

Crucial kidneys
These are the body's filters. As blood passes through them they clear out all the spare water and waste products and send them down for storage in the bladder.

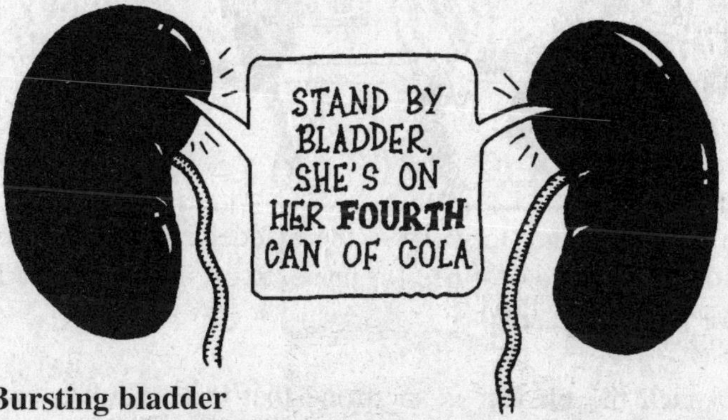

Bursting bladder
This is an incredibly wrinkled sack. It looks like a prune after a really long bath, but as it fills up, it gets bigger and it looks more like a balloon. The speed this happens depends on how much a person has had to drink. Most people need to pee about four to six times a day.

How can you tell when someone's bladder is full? Easy. They start twitching, writhing and dancing around looking for the nearest loo. If you were feeling heartless you could…

a) Join in the dancing.

b) Tell them not to worry – the bladder can store up to 400 ml (14 fl oz) of pee (or urine, to use the posh word for it) fairly easily.

In fact, the bladder is so strong that in an adult it can swell to 10 cm across without going pop.

Disgustingly odd bits'n'pieces quiz

Now you've checked out the main digestive bits, you've just got time to check out the obscure nooks and crannies. Doctors were probably having a laugh when they dreamt up some of the weird names for certain body bits. Can you guess which bits are inside you and which are made up?

1 Deaver's Windows
2 Islets of Langerhans
3 Crypt of Lieberkühn
4 The Pustule of Volvo
5 Flint's Arcade
6 Ferrein's Pyramid
7 Fibres of Mummery
8 Verheyen's Stars

Answers

1 TRUE. These are spaces in the flesh that hold the guts securely in position. The spaces are named after their discoverer, American scientist John Blair Deaver. **2** TRUE. These are areas in the pancreas which make a hormone called insulin which controls the speed your body turns its food into energy. They're named after eagle-eyed German doctor Paul Langerhans who spotted them in 1869. **3** TRUE. And what's more they aren't crypts where dead bodies are buried. They're tiny pits in the small intestine that produce digestive juices. But you'd be a dead body without them because they're vital to digest your food. **4** FALSE. The Volvo is a Swedish car. **5** TRUE. These are arch-shaped blood vessels in the kidneys and nothing to do with amusement arcades. They're named after their discoverer, American professor Austin Flint. **6** TRUE. An area of the kidney above Flint's arcade. These pyramid-shaped bits were named after a French professor of surgery called Antoine Ferrein, who wrote about them in 1746. They're nothing to do with the pyramids in Egypt and you won't find a mummy skulking inside one. **7** TRUE. These are stringy bits inside the teeth. They're nothing to do with mummies or pyramids either. **8** TRUE. These are star-shaped veins on the kidney named after Philipe Verheyen who described them in 1699. Verheyen was planning to be a priest but he had an accident and doctors had to chop his leg off. He was so fascinated by this horrible ordeal that he gave up the priesthood. He decided to study medicine instead and became a professor.

Congratulations! You've finished the chapter. Feeling peckish? Desperate enough to eat a school dinner? Better scoff some now before you read about the vile food in the next chapter. It really takes the cake ... or is it the biscuit?

Foul food facts

This chapter is about food. It's about what we eat and how much we eat. But don't expect a mouth-watering feast. This is Horrible Science, remember, so you'll be reading about really foul foods. Got a brown paper bag handy? Good – you might need it!

Enormous eaters

In your lifetime you'll guzzle about 30 tonnes of food – that's the weight of six elephants or 20 rhinos. In one year the average greedy grown-up can munch their way through 78 kg (34 lbs) of potatoes, 26 kg (11.8 lbs) of sugar, 500 apples, 150 loaves of bread and 200 eggs, and still have room for pudding.

If you only ate boring pieces of bread and butter all the time you'd still get through about 250,000 slices in a lifetime. But some people eat a lot more than that.

All-time glutton Edward "Bozo" Miller of Oakland, California used to guzzle 11 times more food than anyone else. In 1963 he scoffed 28 chickens in a single stomach-splitting feast and became a legend in his own lunchtime. Now you might think that's a lot, but compared with some animals it's just a tiny snack.

• An elephant can knock back up to half a tonne of leaves and bark every day.

• Every day a blue whale swallows four tonnes of tiny sea creatures called plankton – that's more food than a human eats in a year. Mind you, the whale is 2,000 times heavier than a human.

• Even tiny creatures can munch more for their size than humans. For example, the 2 gram (0.07 oz) Etruscan shrew scoffs up to three times its own weight every day. That's like a human eating one entire sheep, 50 chickens, 60 family-sized loaves and 150 apples every day. You'd never cram all that into your lunch box, would you? So why do the shrews stuff their little faces? Well, they have to. Shrews need the energy all this food gives them to keep active and warm in cold weather.

Could you be a scientist?

If you like food, you don't have to become a chef. You could become a scientist instead. Yes, scientists have performed some mouth-watering experiments. Can you predict the results?

1 In the 1970s a group of American scientists went to a party and watched people eating. (Don't do this at parties – it's rude.) The scientists found that overweight people ate more than thinner people. The scientists quickly grabbed the food and took it into another room. What happened next?

a) The overweight people went into the next room to get the food.

b) The overweight people couldn't be bothered to move. The thinner people went next door and helped themselves.

c) A fight broke out and the scientists were chucked out for spoiling the party.

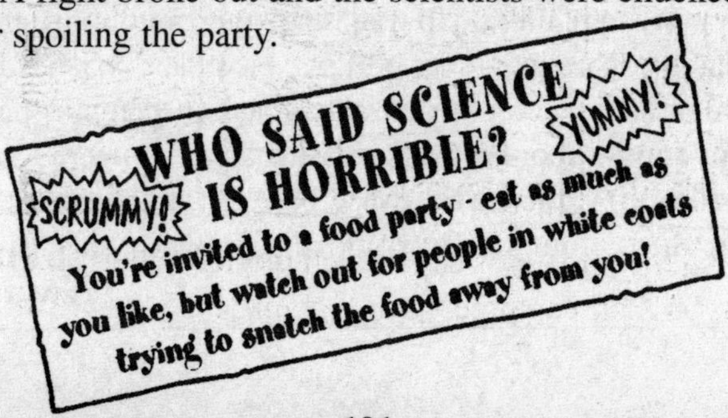

2 In the 1970s scientists at Virginia University, in America asked a group of people to sample a selection of yummy ice-creams after first slurping down a rich, sweet milk-shake. (And this was a science experiment?!) The aim was to see which group ate the most ice-cream. What did they find?

a) People who were trying to lose weight ate more ice-cream.

b) People who were trying to lose weight ate less ice-cream.

c) Everyone scoffed as much as they could because the food was free and then threw up everywhere.

Answers

1 b) The overweight people only ate more if the food was available. If food wasn't available, the thinner people ate more because they were more willing to go and find it. **2 a)** The people trying to lose weight were upset. The scientists had told them that the milk-shake was fattening and that they'd broken their diet. So they pigged out on ice-cream because they felt they might as well enjoy themselves.

Enormous appetites

The amount you can eat depends on how big your stomach is. After all, you've got to put all that food somewhere. This is also controlled by a pea-sized lump on the underside of the brain called the hypothalamus (hi-po-thala-mus). This signals to your brain when it's time to eat and when to stop. If you don't want to stop, then chances are that you're eating something you really enjoy. And if you don't want to start eating, then you're probably sitting in front of your school dinner…

Foul food favourites

Food is vital. It does more than simply fill you up. It supplies the chemicals that your body needs to stay healthy and grow. But we all have foods we love. And we all have foods we love to hate. Here's a school dinner menu. Which dishes might tempt you?

It's really strange, but some teachers and even a few otherwise quite normal people think school dinners are the height of good taste! Because that's all a favourite food is – just a matter of taste. Like most people you probably chose your favourite foods when you were about two years old. But all over the world people enjoy different foods. Including some that might seem horrible to you. We managed to talk fearless Private Eye M.I. Gutzache into sampling a few of these foreign delicacies.

Foul food report

It seemed like a good idea. No more swimming about in stomachs, no more parachute jumps. Just a lunch date. My kind of assignment, I thought. A private eye like me needs a strong stomach, so I reckoned I could face up to anything. I was wrong!

1. Tasted good - I like the savoury taste of onions and herbs and meat. I was just enjoying my second helping when someone mentioned that the meat was sheep's heart and lungs wrapped up in its stomach. I suddenly needed some fresh air.

2. This was really good. Nice crunchy batter. Then they told me it was chopped pigs intestines with corn meal fried in lard. I swallowed hard and went on to the next dish.

3. I could see what this dish was. I shut my eyes and took a bite. It tasted like watery chicken. I'd prefer chicken any day.

4. Tasted a bit fishy. No, I don't mean fishy suspicious - just fishy and kind of salty. But when I learned the fish had been squashed to paste and left to rot for a few days, I decided they could keep their rotten fish.

5. I took one look at the eyeballs and they took one look at me. We were eyeball to eyeball. I started to sweat. I knew what I had to do, it was staring me right in the face. "OK, that's it," I snapped. "I quit!" This job was sick.

Poor old Gutzache, he couldn't cope with the eyeball because he wasn't used to eating that part of an animal. But if he eats tongue, breast and neck, what difference does an eyeball make? It's all a question of what you're used to. If Gutzache had grown up in the Middle East he'd have been eating eyeballs since he was two – and loving them!

Bet you never knew!

***1** There's a type of chilli called a red "savina habenero" that's so hot that just 1 gram (0.035 oz) of the powder can flavour half a million times its weight in a sauce. Eat the chilli on its own and you'll turn into a fire-breathing dragon with steam pouring from your ears. Or, at least, that's how you'll feel.*

***2** Until the 1970s in Papua New Guinea it was traditional for people to eat their dead relatives. The brains were especially prized. This was considered respectful to the dead and a good way of boosting your own brainpower.*

And here's something else you shouldn't try.

Poison pills

Some people will eat just about anything. But would you believe that some people used to eat poison? In 1733 dangerously dodgy doctor Ned Ward sold antimony pills as a cure for everything including upset tummies. But antimony is a poison once used by the ancient Egyptians to bump off flies. So not surprisingly the pills caused violent stomach pains. One joker wrote a poem about Ned Ward:

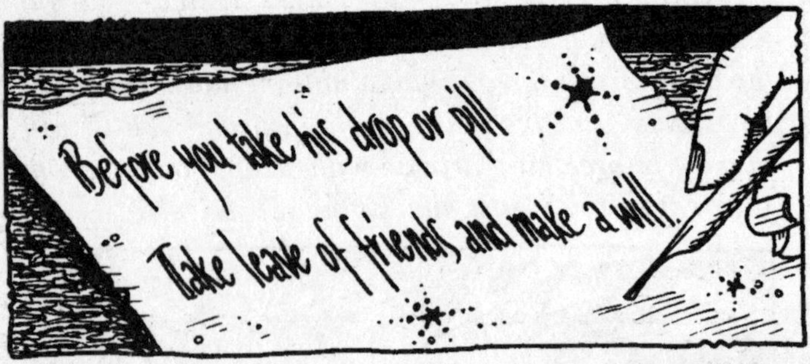

But most people believed the adverts and thought the pain was part of the cure. The doctor made his fortune. He even gave poor sick people free samples of the wonderful pills. How kind! But oddly enough Ward never tried his own pills. This may explain why he lived to a ripe old age.

But antimony is just one of a host of disgusting poisons that turn up in food. Watch out, the next chapter could give you a nasty reaction…

Fatal food poisoning

Food can be fatal. Well, not the food itself but what's lurking inside it. There may be all sorts of hidden poisons and germs lying in wait for your unsuspecting innards. So in order to protect yourself, you need to know all the disgusting details.

Disgusting poisons fact file

NAME: Poisons

THE BASIC FACTS: A poison is a chemical that gets into your body and makes you sick. Poisons include acids that dissolve the guts. Other poisons get to the brain in the bloodstream and knock the victim out.

THE HORRIBLE DETAILS: 1 Some of the deadliest poisons are called toxins. They're made by germs that get into food. Some can kill.

2 The best way for your body to get rid of a poison is to throw it back up again. That's why people spend the whole night throwing up after eating a dodgy dinner that's alive with germs.

Teacher's tea-break teaser

Try this teaser during a teacher's tea break. It'll be as welcome as a snail in a salad bar. Tap lightly on the staffroom door. When the door creaks open your teacher will be holding the regulation mug of sludgy mud-coloured coffee. Smile sweetly and say:

Answer

Coffee can be poisonous if you drink too much too fast. It contains a chemical called caffeine (also found in tea and cola drinks) that makes the heart beat faster. Normally it's quite harmless but scientists reckon that if someone drank 100 cups in four hours the caffeine would be strong enough to put their heart and blood vessels under fatal pressure.

Some good and some bad news

Here's the good news: it's not easy to get poisoned. As long as you're sensible about what you put in your mouth, you're not going to get poisoned by man-made chemicals. If it isn't a drink don't drink it, and if it isn't food don't eat it. And food poisoning caused by germs is fairly rare, too.

Now the bad news: crowds of germs hang around in the hope of causing some really foul food poisoning. At best these awful invaders cause an upset tummy. At worst they can kill – as you'll discover in the next chapter.

So what does food poisoning do to you? We've managed to get hold of a doctor's notes on a case of food poisoning. See if you can decipher the doctor's dodgy handwriting.

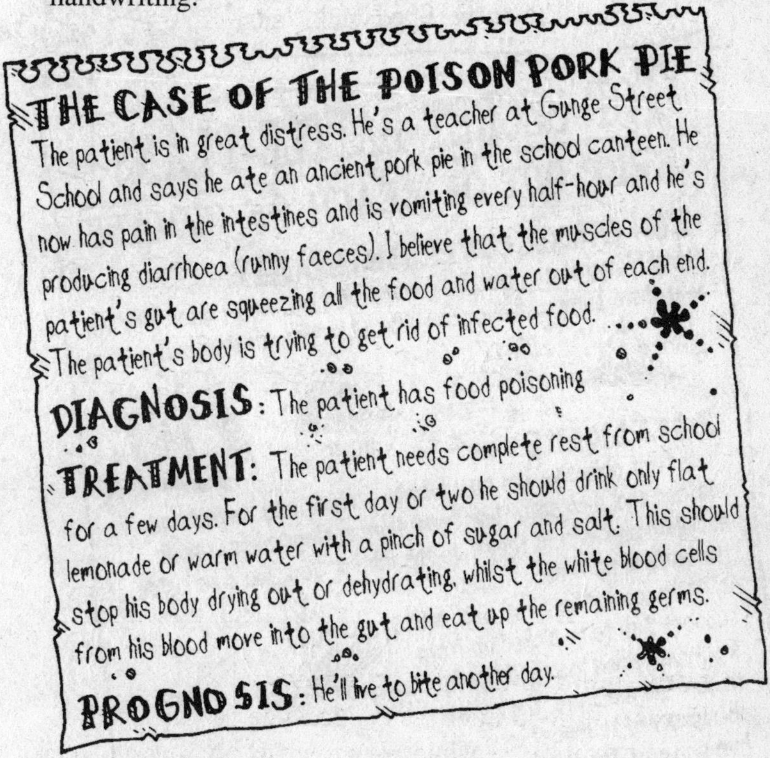

Yes, germs are always ready to attack us. As you'll find out on page 206, our favourite private eye M.I. Gutzache is hot on the trail of the germs. But the germs are hatching their own dastardly plans...

Germ top secret war plans

3 GET STUCK IN

Start eating. Squirt out enzymes that turn the food into slime and suck it into your body. Be sure to make plenty of waste chemicals to make the food rotten and stinking.

4 GET NEW RECRUITS

Another simple task: pull yourself in half. Again and again. Soon you'll have hundreds, then thousands and millions of reinforcements. This will provide overwhelming numbers for the big attack on the guts.

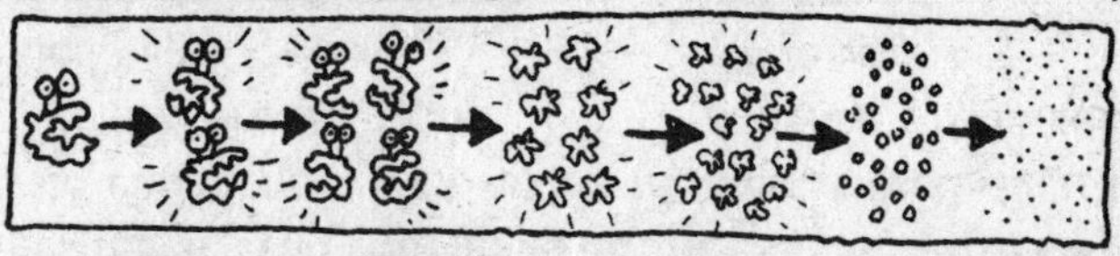

5 A FINAL WARNING

Humans will try to fight back with every weapon at their disposal. Be on your guard for antibiotics – medicines made from chemicals that us germs produce to defend ourselves against rival germs. And watch out. If a human uses enough antibiotics your entire army could be wiped out.

Dare you discover for yourself ... how things rot?

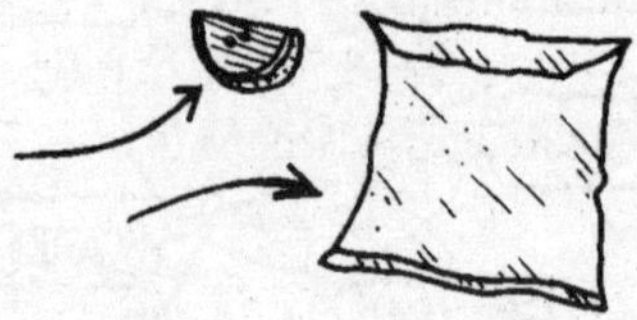

What you need
a piece of orange
a large polythene bag

What you do
Seal the orange in the bag and leave it in a warm place for six days.
What do you notice?

a) The orange stays the same.
b) The orange goes mushy and smelly.
c) The orange grows bigger.

Answer
b) Germs have been feeding on the orange and slowly digesting it. The foul pong in the bag is caused by waste chemicals given off as the germs feed. Don't touch the orange again. Throw it away inside the sealed bag.

How NOT to handle food

Here are some sure-fire ways to give germs a helping hand into your food...

- Sneezing into food.

• Coughing into food. This shoots germs from your mouth and nose into the air. Use a handkerchief. Do not wrap your food in the handkerchief or use it as a bandage afterwards. Germs can also get into your body through unwashed wounds.

• Handling food without washing your hands. (There are usually a few germs hanging around on your hands.)
• Picking your nose or biting nails. This is a marvellous way to pick up a few million germs. It's especially anti-social if you try to do both at the same time.

• Picking bits of food from your teeth with your fingers and then eating it. Not recommended.

Disgusting detective work

Following the sad case of the food-poisoned teacher (see page 201), we decided to investigate the school kitchen that was suspected of foul play and even fouler pork pies. It needed someone with experience, with dedication and above all … with guts. There was only one man for a case like this…

Another dirty job by M.I. Gutzache

FOUL FOOD REPORT by M.I. Gutzache

At last, some real detective work! Something undercover. I'd heard that school kitchens were clean places that were inspected regularly by public health officers. But this one was different. It proved a real dirty business. Stomach churning, in fact, but I got the pictures in the end.

Can you spot the germ danger signs in each picture?

Answers

1 Hair can carry germs even when it's clean, so it's a bad idea to comb it in a kitchen because germ-laden dandruff and old skin could fall into the soup. **2** Hair not tied back or covered. An ideal way to leave greasy germ-laden hairs in the jelly. **3** Blowing on food to cool it. A wonderful way for germs to get from the mouth onto the food. You might as well dribble into it. **4** Dirty hands, fingernails and clothes, and not wearing overalls. If they touch food they'll pass on loads of germs. **5** Flies should be kept out of kitchen. On pain of death – to the flies that is! **6** Fridge door left open so the food isn't being kept cold. The cold should stop the germs from breeding so fast. **7** All kinds of food mixed up in the fridge so germs can slop and spill from raw meat to cooked meat where they will breed happily. **8** Litter bins overflowing and full of rotten food are a luxury hotel for germs to breed. **9** Cockroaches love slinking about in damp, dark places. And they're happy to pass on their germs when they investigate any food that's been left out. **10** Get that cat off the table! You might like Tiddles but you won't like her germs. Do you really want germ-encrusted cat fluff in your butter?

Fresh food quiz

If cooks manage to get rid of bacteria they can keep food fresh for longer. Which of the following methods will work?

1 Boiling food and sealing it in an air-tight container.

2 Squashing the food and germs into a plastic box.

3 Mixing the food with lots of sugar or salt.

4 Smoking the food over a really smoky fire.
5 Sucking all the air out of the food so the bacteria can't breathe.
6 Freezing the food with the bacteria in it.
7 Drying the food out so the bacteria can't drink.
8 Spinning the food around really fast. The germs get so dizzy that they die.

Answers
1 Yes. Any thorough heating, as in cooking, will kill bacteria. Keeping food in an air-tight container such as the cans you buy in a supermarket will stop bacteria from getting back in. **2 No.** The bacteria will still live and breed, and destroy the food. **3 Yes.** The sugar draws water from the food and the bacteria can't live without water. That's why jam doesn't go rotten. **4 Yes.** The smoke covers the food with chemicals such as nitrites that kill the bacteria. This is what keeps smoked fish such as kippers fresh. **5 Yes.** This is what happens when food is vacuum packed. The food will keep in this form for months. **6 Yes.** The cold kills the bacteria. That's why food stays fresh in the freezer. **7 Yes.** The bacteria can survive as tiny seeds called spores, but drying out stops them from being active. **8 No.** Bacteria don't get dizzy.

We've painted a pretty grim picture of the germ world and maybe we're being a bit unfair. After all, they're just doing what comes naturally – for a germ that is. And we can't get rid of germs altogether. There are different germs in different countries and some will always manage to get into our bodies. Then our bodies have to fight against the disgusting, deadly digestive diseases that are lurking in the next chapter. BEWARE!

Deadly digestive diseases

If there's something even more disgusting than digestion then it's the dreadful digestive diseases that germs can cause. There's a long, horrible list of them and many are not just disgusting, they're deadly, too. We asked our Private Eye M.I. Gutzache to compile a dossier on the worst villains. Gunge Street School was in trouble. More teachers and some children too were going down with dangerous diseases. The kitchens needed inspection, there were various germs under suspicion. Gutzache was ready for the job.

A DEADLY GERM DOSSIER

by M.I. Gutzache

They're a real mean bunch of no-good low-lifes. Even I was shocked at the things these guys get up to. I shuddered to think they were hiding out in the very school kitchen I'd visited. These germs hit the young and the old hardest. That's bad news for young kids and tired old teachers. These germs must be stopped before they close down the school.

NAME: Salmonella
KNOWN HAUNTS: A real shady character – hides out in raw meat and eggs. Its favourite bolt-holes are chicken guts. I saw a chicken in the fridge at Gunge Street. It didn't look too healthy.
ALIASES: Over 1,000 varieties – just take your pick.
KNOWN CRIMES: Causes repeated vomiting and diarrhoea. Responsible for hundreds of thousands of attacks all over the world. A killer.

NAME: Listeria
KNOWN HAUNTS: Soil, dung, dirty water, cheese, chicken or salads. I've got my doubts about the cheese at Gunge Street. It smelt kind of prehistoric. The germ's known to be at home at –5°C (24°F). So putting the cheese in the fridge won't do

much good. This character is tough - it can even live at 42°C (106°F). If a human got that hot they'd need a doctor fast.
KNOWN CRIMES: Causes violent sickness. These germs could spoil your whole day.

NAME: Staphylococcus
KNOWN HAUNTS: Nostrils, on skin especially in cuts and boils. The Gunge Street cooks must have been crawling with these germs. The germs hang out on food that should be kept in the fridge but that's been left out too long. Like the awful smelling Gunge Street mince that was left out mouldering for three whole days.
MODE OF OPERATION: Gets on to food from unbandaged cuts on hands.
KNOWN CRIMES: Causes diarrhoea, vomiting and painful cramps in the guts. These germs could spoil your whole week.

NAME: Clostridium botulinum
CAUSES: Botulism
KNOWN HAUNTS: Soil, fish, meat and vegetables.
MODE OF OPERATION: Thankfully no one's seen this germ at Gunge Street.
KNOWN CRIMES: Botulism causes double vision, weakness, difficulty talking and . . . DEATH.
WEAPONS: The toxin produced by this germ is deadly. Just 10mg (0.154 grains) could poison every human on Earth.

Conclusion

These guys are bad news. They must be rounded up. But it's going to be a tough job. They're a big mob and they've got so many hideouts. There's just one weapon that'll get them beat – and that's cleanliness!

USEFUL WEAPONS

But some germs are much more deadly and hopefully we'll never come across these criminal characters in Gunge Street kitchens ...

NAME: Vibrio cholerae
CAUSES: Cholera
KNOWN HAUNTS: Water mixed with faeces from another cholera sufferer.
MODE OF OPERATION: Gets into the body through eating shellfish that live in this dirty water. (Must be careful next time I eat oysters.) More usually spread by drinking the dirty water itself. Drinking water sounded like a real dumb move. So I checked out the local water company and they said they had the problem sussed. They put chlorine in the water to blow the germs away.
KNOWN CRIMES: Causes violent vomiting, deadly diarrhoea and painful cramps. The victim's body dries out and turns blue. You could easily wake up to find yourself DEAD.

CHOLERA VICTIM

NAME: **Salmonella typhi**
KNOWN HAUNTS: The faeces of someone who has had the disease and survived. Typhoid is a relative of the notorious salmonella crime family – only these guys are even more vicious.
MODE OF OPERATION: Gets around on dust or flies or dirty fingers.
KNOWN CRIMES: Causes a rash and a nasty cough. Turns the victim's faeces into a green and runny soup. If untreated it kills 20 per cent of its victims. Hey, that's nasty!

NAME: **Shigella dysenteriae**
KNOWN HAUNTS: The guts and faeces, dirty water and food.
KNOWN ALIASES: Can be caused by amoeba – the scientist guy says that's a microscopic blob-like animal. I'll take his word for it. I just don't want to find this blob anywhere near my hot dog.
KNOWN CRIMES: Spreads from the guts to the liver and causes a deadly fever. It can even make holes in the gut.

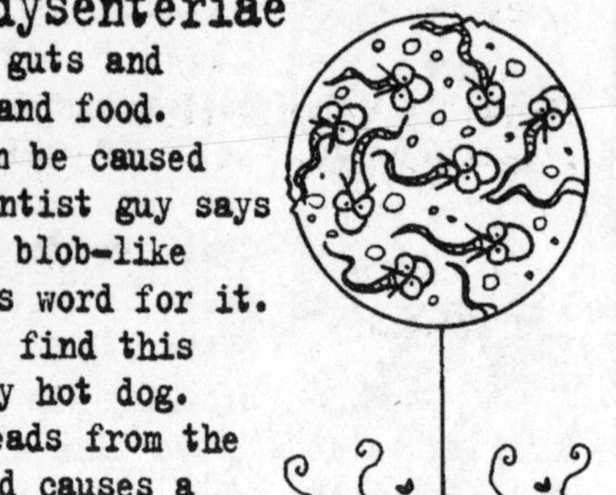

Conclusion

I'm feeling sick. During my mission to the school kitchen I came over kind of hungry. Figured a piece of fruit wouldn't do any harm – now I've got pains in my gut and I'm feeling feverish. It's dysentry . . . I'm sure of it. ARGHH my guts! QUICK – where's the bathroom?

Bet you never knew!
Dysentery can be deadly for doctors even if they don't catch the disease. In the year AD*580 Queen Austrichildia, wife of the King Guntram of the Franks had the disease really badly. She was tended by two doctors. Half-crazed with fever, she thought they weren't trying to save her. So she made her grief-stricken husband promise that if she died the doctors would be executed at her grave. She died – and the unlucky doctors got the chop.*

Over 1,000 years later one man was determined to stamp out the curse of dysentery and all the other deadly digestive diseases.

Horrible Science Hall of Fame:
Louis Pasteur (1822-1895) Nationality: French

Louis Pasteur had embarrassing table manners. He would fiddle with his bread. He'd tear a slice into crumbs and inspect them for dust and wool and bits of cockroaches. If he found anything suspicious he would examine it at the table using a portable microscope. (Don't start getting ideas now!)

Next Pasteur would study the glasses. He'd wipe away tiny specks of dirt that no one else could see. And if that wasn't bad enough he'd launch into a loud and detailed account of his latest gruesome experiments with mice or bits of mashed up body and germs. This was because Louis Pasteur was obsessed with germs. He was so desperate to keep germs off his hands that he wouldn't shake hands with anyone. But oddly enough Mrs Pasteur didn't complain about her husband's habits. She was his most devoted helper.

Louis Pasteur was the deadliest enemy the germ world ever had. He hunted germs like a determined cop hunts a master criminal. With a total and ruthless dedication he worked weekends and evenings – refusing to give up ever. But then Pasteur had every reason to hate germs. Two of his children had died of typhoid.

At school no one thought young Louis was especially clever. His teachers said he was "passable" at Physics and "mediocre" at Chemistry. But Louis stuck at his science studies and eventually became a Professor of Chemistry. These are just a few of his achievements:

• He proved that germs make wine and beer go sour. This work involved going to vineyards and sampling wines (all in the interests of science, of course). Pasteur discovered that if you heat liquids to 72° C (161° F) for a few seconds you can kill germs without spoiling the taste. He had invented pasteurisation – which is used today to stop your milk going off too quickly.

• He went on holiday leaving a mix of chicken cholera germs and broth. (Chickens suffer a different type of cholera to humans.) When he got back he found that many of the germs had died. He gave the mixture of weakened germs to some chickens and found they stayed healthy. The chickens' bodies had produced chemical defences against the dead germs that they could use to fight living germs. We call the dead germs a vaccine and it's what you get when you're vaccinated against a disease.

• Pasteur went on to develop vaccines against the killer diseases anthrax and rabies. The rabies vaccine was particularly welcome because rabies *always* kills its victims. Trouble is, the rabies vaccine had to be delivered by painful injections, but at least the victim gets to live.

Could you be a scientist?

In 1860 Pasteur climbed a mountain carrying sealed flasks containing yeast extract broth and sugar. At 1,500 metres (5,000 feet) he opened the flasks and filled them with cold mountain air then re-sealed them. Pasteur believed that the broth would only go off if germs from the air could get to it. He had already filled other flasks with air from the top of one hill, then another higher hill, and a cellar. What were the results?

a) All the flasks showed the same amount of germs. This proved that germs are found at all heights.
b) The most germs were found up the mountain and on the higher hill. This is because the wind blows germs up in the air.
c) The most germs were on the lower hill. The least germs were found up the mountain and in the cellar.

Answer
c) Pasteur proved that germs spread on specks of dust. The cellar was well sealed so the dust couldn't get in easily and the mountain air had even less dust so there were fewer germs. The germs couldn't get into the sealed flasks and their contents stayed fresh. In fact, one of the flasks from 1860 is now a museum exhibit and the broth is still fresh ... anyone want to try it?

Typhoid marches on...

Despite Pasteur's hard work he couldn't trace the deadly germ that had killed his children. The typhoid germ was eventually tracked down by Karl Joseph Eberth (1835-1926) in 1880. But the disease continued to claim lives. Edith Claypole (1870-1915), a talented American scientist, died of the disease in 1915. She was in the middle of a study of ... typhoid fever. And in 1909 doctors faced the killer disease again. Here are the facts in a story that tells how they might have happened.

Typhoid Mary

New York, 1909

Mary Mallon was a killer and her lethal weapon was ice-cream. Delicious, home-made ice-cream. But could it really kill people? Guns or bombs, maybe – but ice-cream?

And Mary didn't look dangerous. She was a shy woman of about 40 years of age with grey hair tied neatly in a bun. She wore small round spectacles and her plump figure seemed an excellent advertisement for her wholesome cooking. No wonder Dr George Soper felt confused as he stood in the kitchen in Park Avenue.

Surely Mary wouldn't harm a fly?

Then the doctor noticed Mary's hands. Big red raw hands that were used to hard kitchen work – hands that hadn't been washed in a week. They weren't just dirty – they were filthy. Every hollow and vein and knuckle was smeared with grime, and there was thick, black dirt under her fingernails.

"Well, sir, why did you want to see me?" she asked in her soft Irish voice. "I haven't got all day. The people here are taken badly. The daughter is dead and the servants are sick. I've lots to do."

The doctor pulled himself together. He had difficult and unpleasant things to say. "Mary Mallon, I have reason to believe you are spreading an infectious and fatal disease."

Mary didn't even blink. It was as if the doctor had said something about the weather.

"I don't know what you're talking about, sir," she said quietly.

"Let me explain," said the doctor. "Last year you worked as a cook at Oyster Bay, Long Island. Six people in that house fell sick with typhoid fever."

"So they got sick. People do – what's that to me?" asked Mary sounding a bit more annoyed.

"I talked to the family and I checked what they ate. The family all said they enjoyed eating ice-cream. Your ice-cream that you always make by hand."

Mary's mouth drooped crossly at the corners and she slowly pulled open a drawer under the table.

"You've had eight jobs in seven years," continued the doctor grimly. "And in seven of those eight houses there have been cases of typhoid fever."

Mary's filthy fingers groped for the meat cleaver.

"Mary," said the doctor coldly, "I think the typhoid was spread on your dirty hands."

"ARRRGGGGH!" With a banshee wail Mary threw herself on the doctor. She screamed in fury, "I'll learn ye. You meddling doctor – I'll chop ye up for sausages. I'll have ye for breakfast. I'LL KILL YE!"

Dr Soper leapt sideways just in time. The heavy cleaver hacked into the table top. He tore round the kitchen chased by Mary brandishing her weapon.

Dr Soper escaped and gasped out his story to New

York's Chief of Police. The police moved in swiftly. They raided Mary's house and found her hiding in an outside toilet. It took seven policemen to carry her shrieking and wailing to a waiting ambulance.

A few months later at the Riverside Hospital for Communicable Diseases in New York, Dr Soper sat in his office a little uneasily. The time had come for a talk with Mary. Or "Typhoid Mary" as the newspapers were now calling her.

"Typhoid is a terrible disease," began the doctor. "You get fever, spots, stomach pains, a cough and bowel movements that look like pea soup. But you'll remember all that, won't you Mary?"

"Why should I remember anything?" asked Mary grumpily. She glared up at Dr Soper's two hefty assistants who stood either side of her. Ready for the first sign of trouble.

Dr Soper sighed, "Our tests prove that you've had the disease. Although you got better, the germs are still in your gall bladder. They pass out of your body every time you visit the toilet. Some germs get on your hands and if you don't wash them they also get onto food."

"I don't understand," moaned Mary, "I'm a cook. I do

me job but no one tells me nothing."

Then Dr Soper offered his reluctant patient a choice. She could give up cooking or she could stay locked up in the island hospital. For ever.

"You can't keep me here," protested Mary. "Why are you doing this to me?"

Dr Soper grimly shook his head. "Oh, but we can keep you here, Mary. We have the legal power. But you do have another choice. Allow us to cut out your gall-bladder. It's a risky operation, but you'll be free of germs after we've done it. And then we'll let you go."

"I'll kill ye!" spat Mary struggling with the two assistants. "I'll never let ye near me gall-bladder – whatever that is."

But three years later Mary had a change of heart. Not about the operation, though. She agreed to give up cooking and report to Dr Soper every three months. But after she left the hospital she promptly disappeared.

In 1915 an epidemic of typhoid fever hit New York's Sloane Hospital for Women. Two members of staff died. One morning the kitchen maid was having a laugh with a friend. "That old cook, Mrs Brown," she sniggered, "she's so grumpy and guess what? She looks just like that woman in the papers a few years ago. What's-her-name – Typhoid Mary!"

Listening at the door, the cook, who was really Mary Mallon, clenched her dirty fists in rage.

Once again Mary disappeared but this time the police were on her trail. She was arrested soon afterwards. Mary Mallon had knowingly spread typhoid and people had died. How do you think she was punished?

a) Mary Mallon was executed for murder. The judge said: "Mary, you are too dangerous to live."

b) Mary was drugged by Dr Soper and while she was unconscious he removed her gall bladder. When she was completely free of typhoid germs the doctors let her go.

c) She was locked up on the island for the rest of her life.

Answer

c) Mary spent the rest of her life in prison. She was the first known carrier of typhoid fever and although she was never charged with a crime she was judged a menace to public health. In 1923 the doctors built her a cottage in the hospital grounds and gave her a job working in the hospital lab that studied germs – such as typhoid.

Today Mary Mallon is world famous as "Typhoid Mary." All she ever wanted to do was to make ice-cream. But her name is linked for ever to a disease she never truly understood.

The fight goes on

Louis Pasteur's work showed scientists how to discover germs and how to develop new drugs and vaccines to combat them. Today doctors cure typhoid using drugs. Meanwhile, the world-wide battle against other diseases continues. For example, in the 1970s 4,000,000 children a year were dying of cholera. In 1974 World Health Organization scientists invented a drink made from clean water, minerals and sugar which can be given to cholera victims to stop them drying out. This simple drink, named ORT (oral re-hydration therapy), has saved the lives of thousands of children.

So that's the answer. If we can keep germs at bay we can all live happily ever after. Er, no. Here comes the really bad news. Eating clean food can make you ill! Some people even die from their diets! Will you be able to stomach the next chapter? Better read on and find out…

A horribly healthy diet

There's a lot more to food than meets the eye. There are loads of vital ingredients that you must have in your daily diet. To find out more we persuaded Private Eye M.I. Gutzache to sneak back into the school kitchens to collect samples. At first he said he couldn't face going back to that revolting place. But after a bit of bribery and gentle persuasion with a roll of banknotes he dragged himself off his sick bed.

Gutzache goes into ... school dinners

It was time for the protective suit. And I insisted on a gas mask for this dirty job. Some of the samples smelled kind of ancient. They were days old, and I figured they could be emetic. (Hey, I'm starting to talk like a scientist! An emetic is something that makes you sick as a dog.)

Sample 1 - A school potato

This rather sad potato was about to be boiled in a school dinner. But it was still a healthy specimen. This is what I found hiding inside it:

Slug*
81 per cent water
0.4 per cent protein
16 per cent carbohydrates (in the form of a chemical called starch)
0.1 per cent fat
0.8 per cent fibre
0.7 per cent vitamins
1 per cent minerals

* The slug also contains these ingredients but in different amounts. At least this time it didn't get cooked with the potato.

Sample 2 - A glass of water

It wasn't much to look at, but my investigation revealed that you need about two litres (3.5 pints) of this clear runny stuff every day. Half of this comes from water in your food (like the watery potato), and half from what you actually drink. You've got to top up your water supply 'cos your body is two-thirds water and bits such as your brain are 80 per cent water. So you know what'll happen if you don't drink enough of it - pea-brain!

Sample 3 - Jam pudding

This pudding is oozing with sticky sugar. It looked good enough to eat, but the news was bad.

The scientist guy says sugar gives you the energy your body needs but nothing else. He says I eat more sugar than my body needs. Seems there's enough sugar rolling around inside me to fill a jam jar. I was chewing a candy bar at the time. I put it down and decided I'd had enough sugar for one day. Only a scientist could spoil my appetite.

Bet you never knew!

Sugar hangs out in loads of savoury foods, too – just a small tin of baked beans contains two to three teaspoonfuls of sugar. And you'll find it in cereals, tinned meat, soup, tinned vegetables, peanut butter and even coleslaw. Sweet foods have even more sugar – a chocolate bar has ten teaspoonfuls. Most of us probably get through 30 teaspoonfuls of sugar a day. Wow!

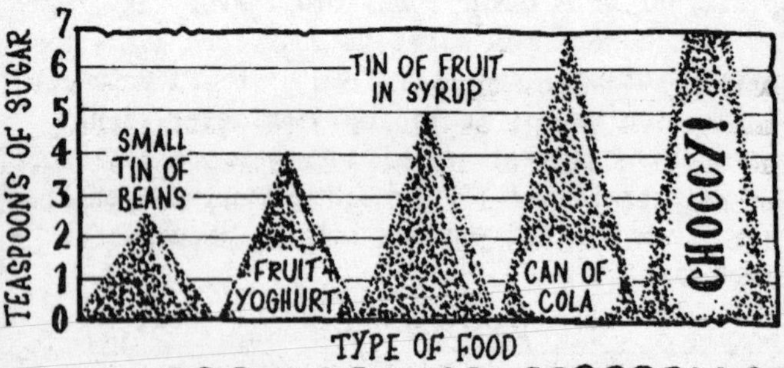

Sample 4 - Mashed swede

Hidden inside this strange and tasteless lump of orange vegetable I came across a strange and tasteless food chemical. It's called starch, a type of carbohydrate the same as I found in that potato. It's made out of sugar chemicals joined in a chain. The scientists say that inside your muscles enzymes can rip apart the sugar chemicals and free the energy to help your body move. Sounds good - why did it have to taste so bad?

Sample 5 - School dinner chips

The chips were cold and greasy and oozing with fat. They hang around in your stomach like a sack of cement. The fats stay down longer than most foods and at least they make you feel nice and full. But it seems spare fat turns into body fat slopping lazily around your stomach and backside. And get this - there's usually enough fat in your body at any one time to make seven bars of soap!

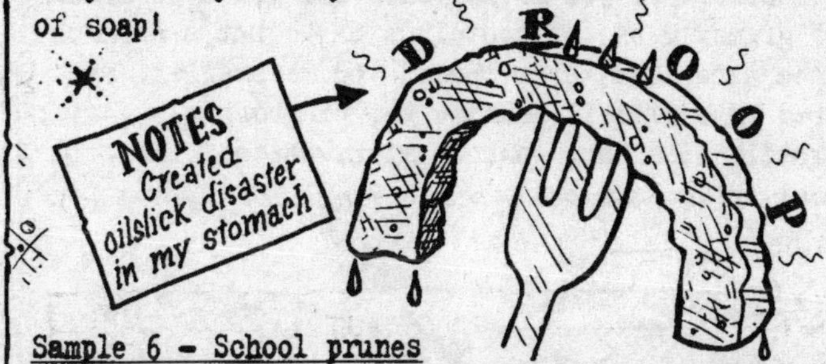

Sample 6 - School prunes

Hmm, prunes. Can't say I liked the taste, they had a weird kind of leathery texture. But my investigation showed that's 'cos they're loaded with fibre. That's the stuff that makes brown bread chewy and fruit and veg stringy. Seems your body can't digest fibre but it keeps the rest of your food moving in the gut. The gut walls can grip the fibre more easily than ordinary food. In the end this gets moving, too ... to the bathroom.

Sample 7 - Smelly cheese

Some of the kids I interviewed had strange ideas about where the cheese came from. Well, I wasn't here to find out about its past - I was looking for the inside story and I found it. Cheese is

25 per cent protein - your body uses this substance to build muscles. Although your body is 20 per cent protein you don't need tonnes of the stuff. If you're 12 years old you need about 55 grams (2 oz) of protein a day. That's as much as a grown man, even though you're smaller. You need more protein because you're growing. Protein also hangs out in milk, cheese, fish, meat, beans and nuts.

Sample 8 - Suspect salt

All this suspect food had got to me. A cold bead of sweat trickled down my face. I tried to lick it off. Ugh - salt! Try it yourself - that's what sweat contains. We use salt for killing germs and, as I found, it comes in handy for disguising the vile taste of school dinners. There are 14,000 different uses for salt - but I've got a report to finish, so I'm not going to list them all here.

Salt is vital for many of the chemical reactions that go on in your body. Sweating is one way your body gets rid of any spare salt. But salt isn't the only mineral you've just gotta have.

Mysterious minerals

The school dinner samples were loaded with mysterious minerals. They're vital in tiny amounts for building your body and making useful chemicals.

You might be amazed to learn that your school dinner contains all these strange and foul-smelling chemicals. Oh – you aren't? Well, your teacher might be...

Test your teacher

Try testing your teacher or even your school cook (if you dare) on this fascinating topic.

1 Sulphur is a foul-tasting chemical but it makes up 0.25 per cent of your body. How much sulphur is that?
a) Enough to kill all the fleas on a dog.
b) Enough to kill all the fleas on an elephant.
c) Enough to kill all the fleas on a rat.
2 Iron is a vital mineral that your body uses to give blood it's brilliant red colour. What happens when you don't eat enough?
a) Your blood turns yellow.
b) You come out in spots and a fever.
c) You become pale and tired and don't feel like eating.

3 Your body is 0.004 per cent iron (lucky it doesn't rust!). How much iron is that?

a) Enough to make the head of a pin.

b) Enough to make a 5 cm (2 inch) nail.

c) Enough to make an iron lump the size of your arm bone.

4 Calcium is a vital raw material for bones. A 12-year-old child needs 700 mg (0.02 oz) of calcium a day. What's that equal to?

a) Four plates of spinach.

b) 40 plates of spinach. (Yuk!)

c) No spinach because this vegetable doesn't contain calcium.

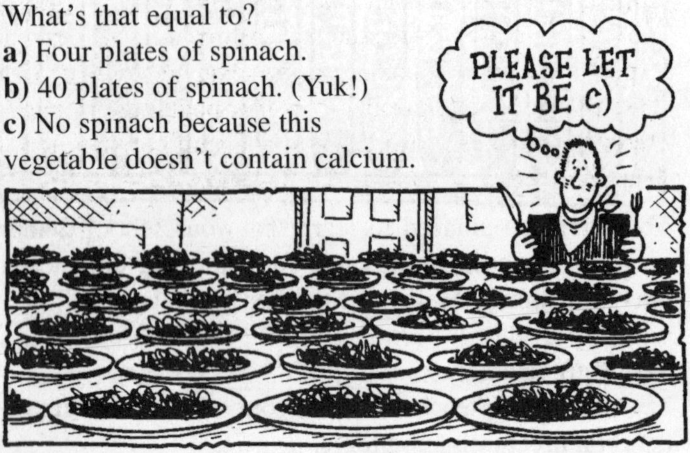

5 What's the best source of iodine?

a) Rainwater

b) Snails

c) Seaweed

Answers

1 a) That is if your dog has fleas, of course! Warning: don't eat too much sulphur or it won't just be the fleas that get bumped off. **2 c)** The red bit in blood is a chemical that takes vital oxygen around your body. Lack of iron causes anaemia (a-nee-me-a). If you don't eat anything the anaemia gets worse. **3 b)** But that's no excuse to start sucking rusty old nails. No – it's much easier to get your iron from liver, wholemeal bread, dried fruit or treacle. **4 a)** You'll find the same amount of calcium in three glasses of milk, 16 large slices of bread or 85 g (3 oz) of cheese. Take your pick. **5 c)** Iodine is the most amazing mineral of the lot. Read on to find out why...

Getting it in the neck

You only need 0.004 grams (0.00015 oz) of iodine every day. But without it life is a pain in the neck. Here's why.

Iodine comes from the sea – that's why seaweed has so much of it. The iodine gets blown inshore as sea spray and collects on plants.

You eat them. A special part of your neck called the thyroid gland uses the iodine to make a chemical called thyroxine (thi-rox-een). Thyroxine makes your body grow and use up food faster.

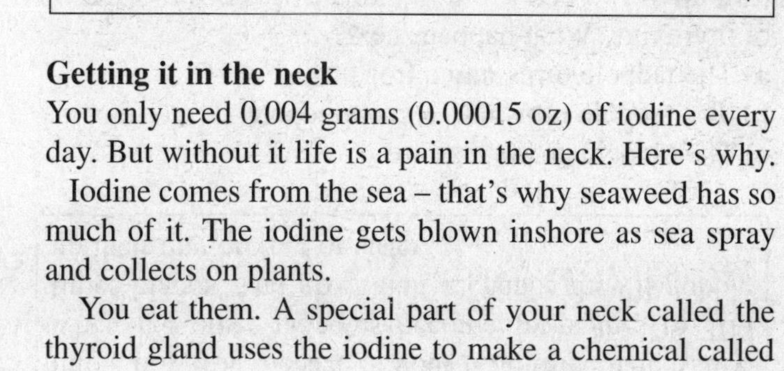

Without enough iodine the thyroid gland swells up as it tries to filter every last drop of the mineral from your blood. It forms a hideous lump called a goitre (goy-ter).

In the 1800s part of the mid-west USA furthest from the sea was known as the "goitre belt". There was less iodine there so, of course, more people developed goitres.

You'll find lots of iodine in seafood, fish and, of course, seaweed (if you can face eating it).

Could you be a scientist?

This disgusting experiment is common in university science courses. The aim is to show how thyroxine works. Take one harmless little bull-frog tadpole. It can take up to two years to turn into a frog. Feed it one drop of thyroxine. What happens next?

a) The tadpole turns into a frog.

b) The tadpole turns into a giant tadpole.

c) The tadpole grows a goitre.

Answer

a) Within a few hours the thyroxine turns the tadpole into a tiny frog the size of your little fingernail. Sadly, when the other tadpoles become frogs they're 100 times bigger. And given half a chance they'll gobble up their tiny brother or sister.

Vital vitamins

Vitamins aren't an optional extra. They're vital chemicals that keep you healthy. They're so important that you can buy lots of different pills and drinks that aim to provide extra vitamins. The adverts are everywhere:

Vit A

Drink Vita-Slurp
A brand new range of vitamin drinks.
A slurp-a-day keeps the doctor away!

Carrot-cocktail-Slurp

Do you suffer from spots? Having trouble shaking off the dandruff? Can't see in the dark? You could be missing out on vitamin A. Vit A Carrot-Cocktail-Slurp is the obvious answer.

Just one slurp and you'll be spotting black cats in coal cellars! Yes that lovely vitamin A makes a chemical called visual purple at the back of the eye, so helping your eyes to see better in poor light.

THE SMALL PRINT
You CAN get too much of a good thing. Drink too much Vit A Vita-Slurp and your hair will fall out and you could die. Yes DIE. Too much vitamin A can poison you which is why people can die if they eat a vitamin A-rich polar-bear liver.

Ingredients: extract of liver, milk, butter, eggs, fish and carrots.*

*That's why people say that carrots help you see in the dark.

Vit B

Get-up-and-go-Slurp

Drink Vita-Slurp
A brand new range of vitamin drinks.
A slurp-a-day keeps the doctor away!

Tired and run-down? You need Vit B Get-up-and-go-Slurp! Why not try all ten mouth-watering varieties?

Just one slurp and you'll be back on your feet. Yes, these vital vitamins help your body turn food into energy. Healthy nerves and blood guaranteed.

THE SMALL PRINT
Lack of vitamin B5 makes a rat's fur go grey. But humans go grey anyway. And not even Vita-Slurp can stop it.

Ingredients: extracts of wholemeal bread, yeast extract, milk, nuts and fresh vegetables.

Vit D Sunny-Slurp

Drink Vita-Slurp
A brand new range of vitamin drinks.
A slurp-a-day keeps the doctor away!

- Do your fingernails break at awkward moments?
- Are you getting enough vitamin D a day?
- One slurp of Vit D Sunny-Slurp and you'll be D-LIGHTED!

Your tough fingernails will be the envy of your friends and you'll be proud of your strong bones and gleaming healthy teeth. Ingredients: Extracts of oil from a cod's liver, milk and cheese.*

THE SMALL PRINT
Don't let the delicious taste of this Slurp make you drink too much. Overdose on Vit D and you'll be sick and constipated (unable to produce poo).

*The body also makes vitamin D from the sunlight that falls on the skin.

Vit E
Suppleskin-Slurp

Drink Vita-Slurp
A brand new range of vitamin drinks.
A slurp-a-day keeps the doctor away!

Do you have tired sagging skin? Are there strange brown marks, or liver spots, on your hands? You need a shot of Vit E Suppleskin-Slurp. In no time you'll be glowing with good health and all those nasty cuts and bruises will be healing up fine. And you'll have a healthy blood system, too! Ingredients: extracts of wholemeal bread, butter and brown rice.

THE SMALL PRINT
Some people have baths in Vit E Suppleskin-Slurp in a bid to stay young-looking. But this is going too far – it doesn't work – sorry!

Vit K
Kwik-clot Slurp

Drink Vita-Slurp
A brand new range of vitamin drinks.
A slurp-a-day keeps the doctor away!

Are you having trouble with clots? (No, not stupid people – we mean *blood* clots.) When you cut yourself, do you just keep bleeding? Essential for those more serious wounds, Vit K Kwik-clot Slurp will help your blood to clot-a-lot, so it stays where it belongs – that's inside your body, and not all over the carpet!
Ingredients: extracts of green vegetables and liver, and germs from the human gut!

OK – got the message? Missing out on vitamins makes you sick. But it took doctors many years to discover which foods were the best sources of which vitamins. Here's the story of one man's search for the truth about the most horrible sickness of all – scurvy.

The terror of the sea

Stinking bad breath, swollen purple gums, easy bruising, wounds not healing, bleeding eyeballs, tiredness and death. Yep. Scurvy was no picnic. A few hundred years ago you could walk round any port and spot the sickly seafarers a mile off. They were the ones with no teeth.

But why did sailors suffer from scurvy more than other people? For sailors in the 18th and early 19th centuries it wasn't just the sea that was rough, life on board ship was pretty rough, too. Conditions were really grim and scurvy used to be the terror of the sea. Sailors feared catching scurvy more than shipwrecks, pirates or shark attacks. But for years no one knew what caused this terrible disease.

But some captains thought they knew…

And, of course, the captains had their favourite cures…

Ship's doctor James Lind (1716-1794) felt sure these cures were useless. But he had to prove it. He reckoned that the disgusting food on board ship was part of the problem. In the days before fridges and freezers it was impossible to keep food fresh at sea. So a typical meal looked like this.

*A dried biscuit so hard that a London museum has a 200 year example. You had to tap your hard tack before you ate it to get the maggots out.

**It was so salty that it made you thirsty enough to drink the disgusting water.

But which of these foul foods caused scurvy? Or maybe as the food was so horrible, the seafarers were missing out on something in their diet. Perhaps they were getting the disease because of something they *weren't* eating. Here's how James Lind might have written up his research:

Here's how James Lind might have written up his research:

HMS Salisbury, somewhere in the English Channel, 1747.

It's so frustrating. Here I am with 12 sailors sick with scurvy. I'm sure they're missing something in their diet - but what? I can't watch them die - I'm the doctor, I've got to try something. I'll have to experiment. I've always wanted to be a scientist. I'll divide the sailors into pairs and get each pair to try a cure suggested by other doctors. One of them has to work! Here goes!!

Sailors Walker Planke and Spike de Gunn will get a few drops of sulphuric acid a day. (Note: Mustn't make it too strong or it'll dissolve their guts.)

I'll give Davy Jones-Locker and Andy Cutlass two spoonfuls of vinegar a day.

I'll give Wilby Sicke and Len Ho a cup of seawater a day.

Jim Ladd and Roger Jolly will eat garlic and horseradish bound together with smelly plant glue.

Chivers Metimbers and Downey Hatch will get a daily quart of cider. Our two stowaway female crew members Eve Too and Raisa Anchor will each get two oranges and a lemon a day.

Fourteen days later

Eve and Raisa are cured! I'm brilliant! (Shame about the others, though.) The girls leapt out of their hammocks on the sixth day and raced each other round the ship. They said they hated all that nasty sour fruit but felt much better anyway. They've offered to help me nurse the other ten who are still sick.

1 Poor Walker and Spike are in a bad way. I feel a bit sorry for them. They've still got scurvy and now they've got raging gut ache, too. Must be all that acid.

2 Davy and Andy are in a sour mood. That'll be the vinegar. And they've still got scurvy.

3 Poor Wilby and Len keep throwing up. Must be all that seawater. They've still got the scurvy.

4 Everyone steers clear of Jim and Roger. They reek of garlic and they can't stop farting. Ah, now that'll be all the horseradish. No improvement in the scurvy.

5 Chivers and Downey have still got scurvy, but at least they're happy. They keep singing "Roll out the barrel!" and shouting "Cheers!" to all the others. The rest of the crew have all volunteered to try this treatment.

Conclusion
I've cracked it - with a bit of help from these brave long-suffering seafarers! I'm really certain that scurvy can be cured by eating fresh fruit. Yes - that's the answer. I'm sure you get the disease if you miss out on some chemical in these foods.
IT'S FANTASTIC - I can't wait to tell everyone!

James Lind sent his report to Admiral Lord Anson (1697-1762) who was in charge of the Royal Navy. He thought Anson would support him. After all when Anson sailed round the world in 1740-1744 most of his crew had died of scurvy. So what happened next?

a) Lord Anson was impressed. Lind was given a £20,000 reward and in future all seafarers were ordered to eat a lemon a day. No one got scurvy ever again.

b) The Navy ignored Lind's findings and it took another 40 years before they took action.

c) The Navy decided that the acid treatment was better. Lind was sacked from his job as a nuisance and a trouble-maker.

Answer

b) Disgusting but true. The Navy decided that lemons were too expensive. They actually felt it was cheaper to hire new sailors to replace the ones who died. Things only changed after the sailors mutinied and demanded lemons to beat scurvy. Although some sailors didn't like the fruit they changed their minds when lemons and limes were added to their rum ration. But it wasn't until the 1930s that scientists found the mystery chemical that prevented scurvy was ascorbic acid – better known as vitamin C.

A disgusting diet

So, eat lots of different foods and you'll get everything your body needs to stay healthy. Brilliant! But what happens if you are vegetarian and don't eat meat or fish? Or if you're vegan and don't eat meat, fish or foods made by animals such as milk and eggs? Either way it's fine as long as you get the vitamins and minerals you need.

But eat just a few things and you won't get all the vital goodies. The most disgusting diet of all is not to eat anything. Surprise! Food is good for you, hunger is bad for you. Scientists have found that children who miss breakfast find it hard to learn new things at school. Don't try this excuse. And just look what happens to a really starving body…

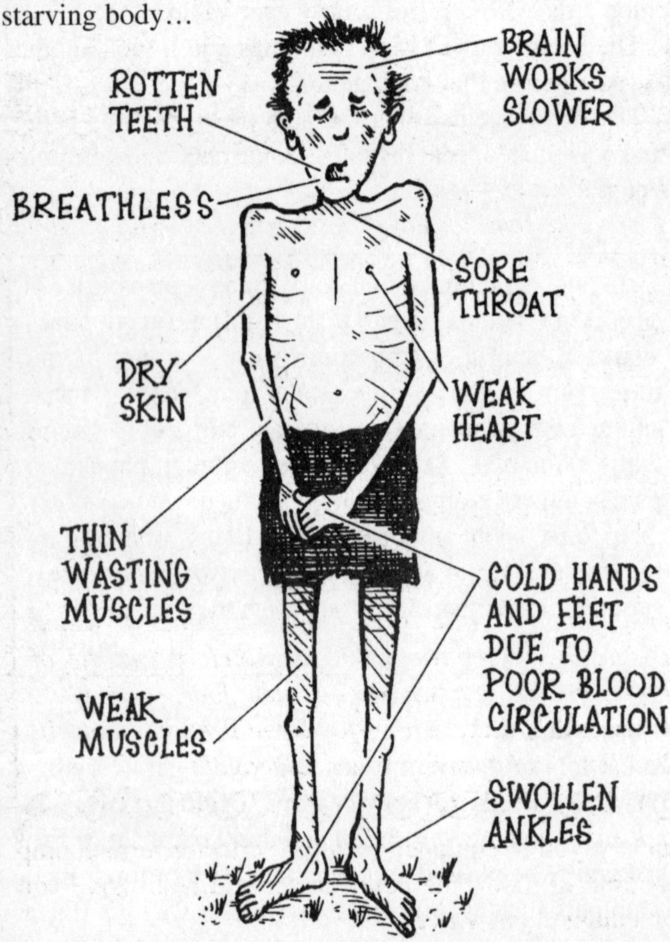

Miserable, isn't it? In the bad old days hunger was a cheap way of punishing naughty children.

Bet you never knew!

1 *Nowadays millions of people are overweight and are trying to lose weight by eating less. But scientists say there's no reason to change your body shape unless it harms your health. Meanwhile, 750 million of the world's people can't find enough food. They'd like to put on weight, not lose it.*

2 Got a food allergy? This means you get a bad reaction from a particular food that is normally quite harmless – you get sick or develop a skin rash whenever you eat it. But which type of food is making you sick? To find out you'll need to live off boiled meat, tinned fruit, potatoes and mineral water. Disgusting! After two weeks, and before you die of boredom, you can sample one new food each week. When you eat the wrong food you'll know about it. You'll get that nasty sickness back again.

Luckily, you're equipped with the perfect gear to chomp any kind of food. The next chapter will really give you something to chew over.

The mighty mouth

Shovel food in your gob and something disgusting happens. Your food, even the stringiest steak and crunchiest carrots, turn into a shredded gooey pulp before vanishing for ever down the black hole of your throat. So what's going on? Get your teeth into these amazing facts.

Dare you discover for yourself ... what's in your mouth?

Stand in front of mirror. Open wide. Go on – take a look – it won't bite you. What do you see? An amazing chewing machine – that's what.

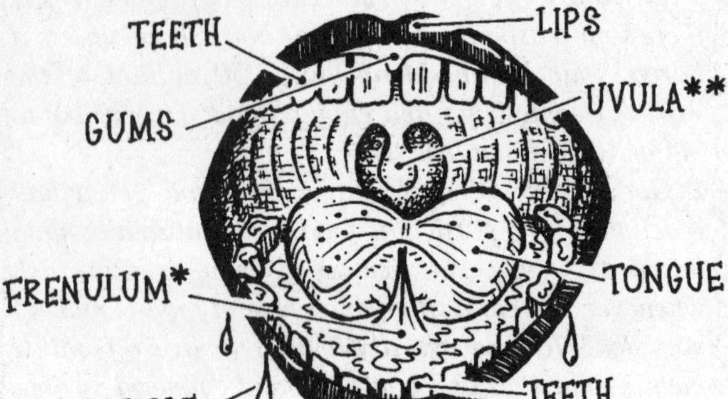

*This supplies your tongue with blood. Can you see the blood vessels? Pretty, aren't they? Well, pretty disgusting really.

**This little dangling bit hangs around in the throat and no one knows quite what it's for. It seems to help you swallow and its name means "little grape" in Latin – can you see why?

The talented tongue

The tongue is a lump of muscle. You can take a good look at it in the mirror, it's one part of your digestive system you can actually see, but don't go showing it to headteachers, parents, etc. Your talented tongue is amazingly agile. It moves around while you eat, talk or even eat and talk at the same time.

Disgusting taste fact file

NAME: Taste

THE BASIC FACTS: Your tongue is covered in tiny bumps called papillae (pap-pill-ay). Can you see them? On their sides are even tinier clumps called taste buds. Your brilliant buds pick up tastes and send the info. along nerves straight to your brain.

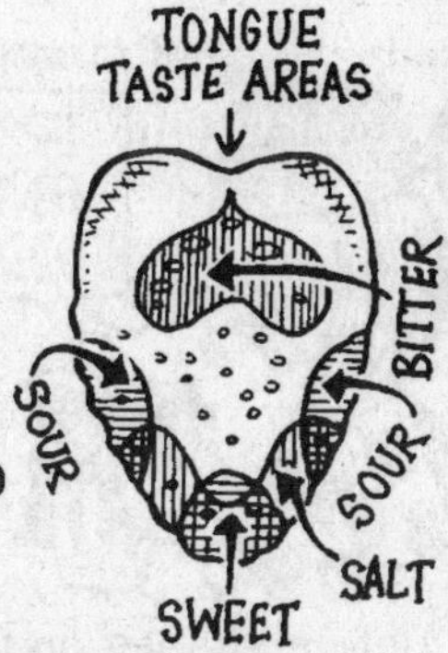

THE HORRIBLE DETAILS: There's a chemical called monosodium glutamate (mon-o-so-di-um gloo-ta-mate) that boosts your sense of taste. It's found in some Chinese recipes. But it makes some people feel sick and dizzy.

Some tasteless facts

1 According to the Chinese there are only three main tastes. Hot and fiery = spicy curry; onion/garlic = when you don't want to make any new friends; delicious = the fresh vegetables you have with your main course.

2 Western scientists disagree. They say that you can taste four tastes – sweet, sour, salty and bitter.

3 But your tongue can recognize hundreds of flavours made up of a mixture of tastes. Take crisps, for example. There are over 70 flavours including chocolate, strawberry, and hedgehog*. (It's true – manufacturers really did make crisps in these foul flavours.)

* Before you get on the phone to the World Wide Fund for Nature, they don't use any dead hedgehogs – this is an entirely man-made flavour.

4 Some people have sensitive taste buds. Cheese experts can sample a really smelly cheese and tell exactly where the cheese was made, whether the milk that made it was heated, and even what time the cow was milked. But if they're wrong they can get a bit cheesed off.

5 A doctor always looks at your tongue to check your state of health. For example, a thick white scum on your tongue might be caused by a disgusting infection called thrush (nothing to do with tweety-birds that eat worms).

6 In ancient China doctors peered at tongues too. They

believed that the appearance of the tongue reflected the health of the rest of the body. Here are a few things they looked for…

a) Whitish tongue = lack of energy.

b) Bright red tongue = body is too hot.

c) Purple/blue tongue or purple spots = blood not moving fast enough.

d) Fur-like growth* on the tongue = death will follow within a week.

*This could really be a sign the body is unwell. The "fur" may be a type of fungus which flourishes when the body's defences, the white blood cells, are weakened by other diseases.

Here are two experiments that are in the best possible taste.

Dare YOU discover for yourself 1… Test your taste

What you need

2 small cubes of uncooked potato

2 small cubes of apple

All you do is

1 Close your eyes and hold your nose. Ask someone to hand you one of the foods.

2 Put the food in your mouth and try to guess what you're eating. Now try the other food.

3 Stop holding your nose and repeat step 2. What do you notice?

a) It's easier to make out tastes when you hold your nose.

b) It's harder to make out tastes when you hold your nose.

c) Foods taste sweeter when you hold your nose.

Dare YOU discover for yourself 2...
Can you change your sense of taste?

What you need

Your favourite wine gums or fruit flavoured sweets. (Tell your parents you need them for science homework – if they believe that, you might as well go for extra pocket money while you're at it.)

2 extra extra strong mints or an ice-cube. Put it in a glass of water for a few seconds first.

HORRIBLE HEALTH WARNING!

Don't put an ice-cube straight from the freezer into your mouth. The freezing cold ice-cube might actually freeze the outside of your tongue and make it sore.

All you do is

1 Pop the extra strong mints OR the ice-cube in your mouth. Keep it there until it melts.

2 Pop the wine gum in your mouth. What do you notice?

a) You can't taste it easily.

b) It tastes twice as fruity.

c) When you take it out of your mouth it's gone black.

Answers

1 b) Your sense of smell is stronger than your sense of taste. When you think you're tasting your favourite food – you're really sniffing it. And that's why food tastes like cardboard when you have a real stonker of a cold. **2 a)** The ice numbs the tongue so it can't taste so well. The strong taste of the mint blocks out new taste signals from your tongue to your brain for a while. So the news about the taste of the sweet doesn't get through. And after that there's nothing for it. You'll have to brush all traces of the sweet off your teeth.

Disgusting teeth fact file

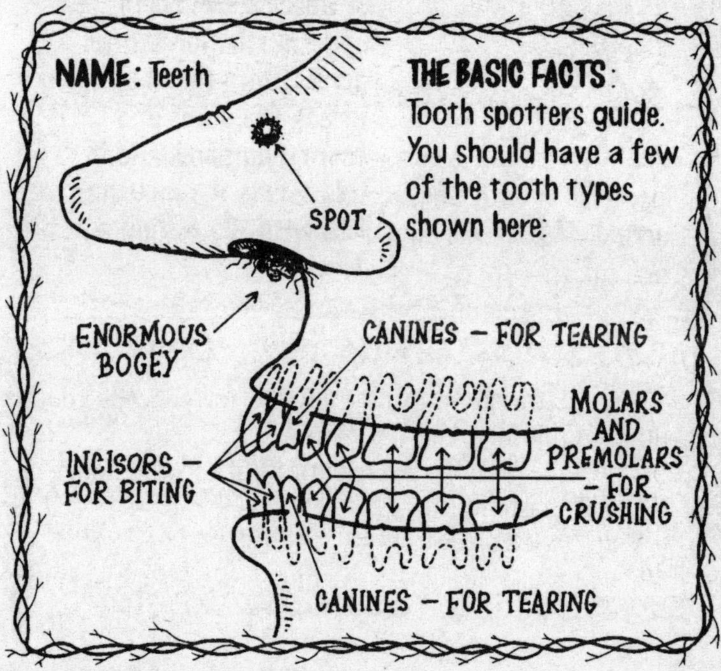

MORE BASIC FACTS: A tooth contains three main parts:

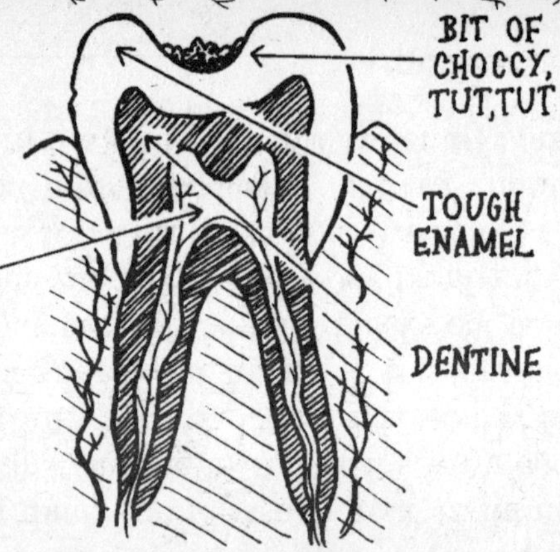

THE HORRIBLE DETAILS: If a tooth gets really rotten a pus-filled hole or abscess can form underneath. Sometimes germs from the abscess attack the gums and form a gumboil. And if this bursts the mouth fills with vile-tasting pus. Yeuch!

Bet you never knew!

Your teeth have a crushing power of 227 kg (500 lbs) – that's the weight of three men! You have two sets of teeth. Your new set grows and pushes out your first set of teeth (called milk teeth or baby teeth) as you grow older.

But that's nothing…

• Elephants have only four teeth but they are replaced six times. When the last set of teeth falls out the elephant starves.

• Crocodiles grow new teeth whenever they need them. This could be handy for humans, too. You could grow extra teeth to handle all those rubbery school dinners.

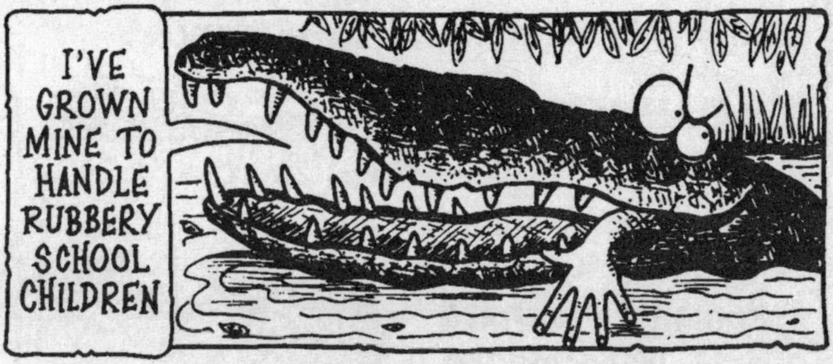

• Sharks have 12 rows of teeth and if they lose a few, more will grow in their place.

Dreadful dentures

Humans only get two sets of teeth and when these fall out we're stuck. That's why millions of people have to wear false teeth or dentures. Nowadays these are made from a tough plastic but before then people had to make do with some really disgusting dentures. Here are a few examples...

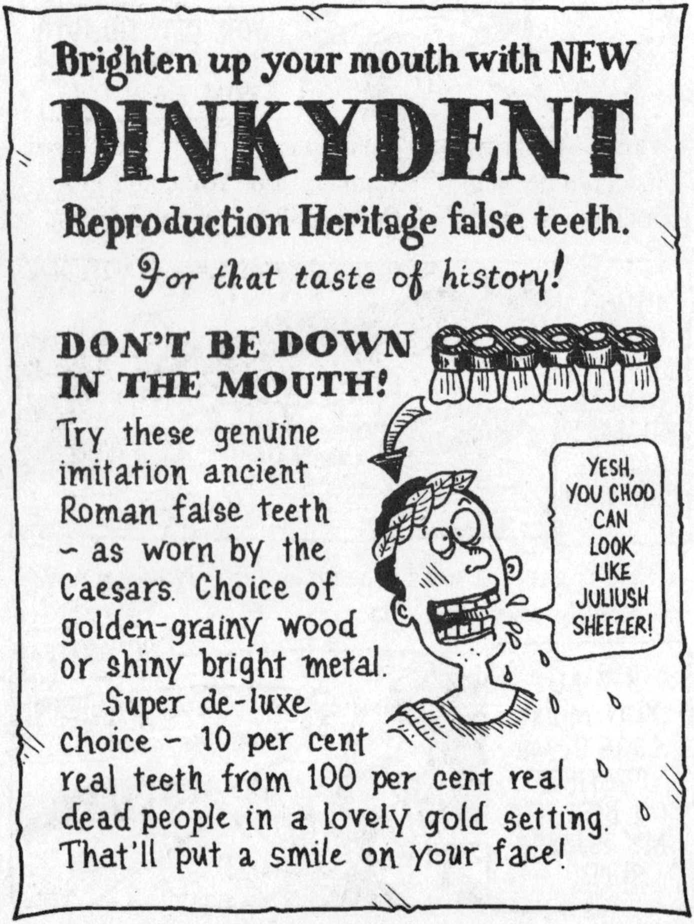

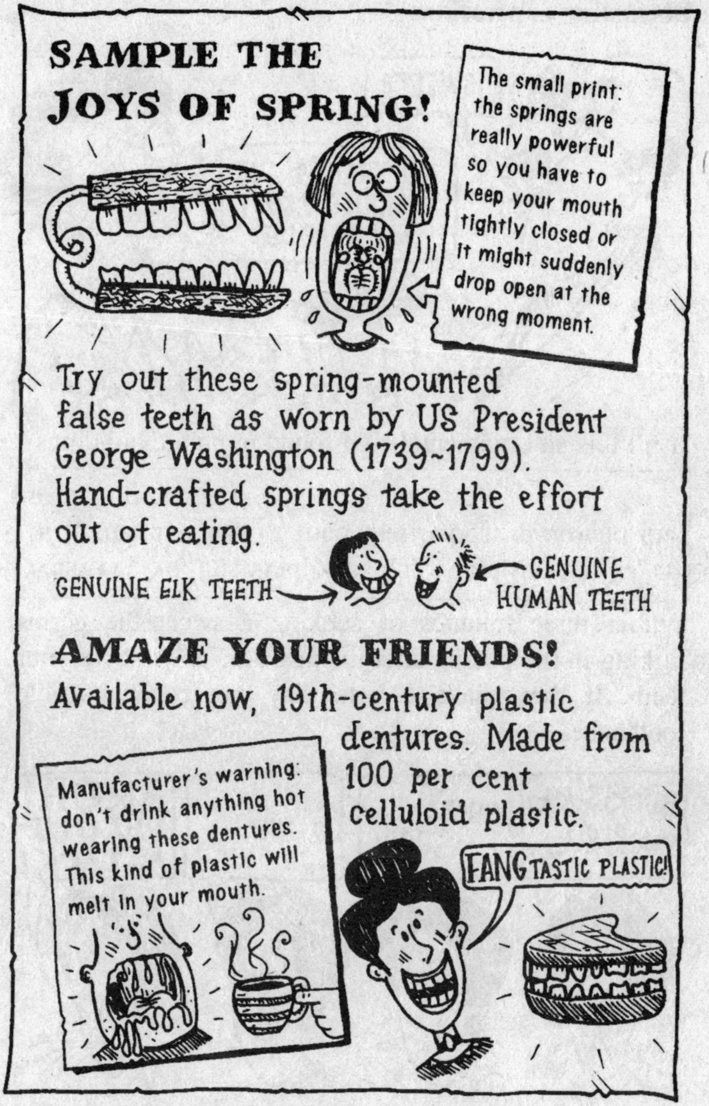

Of course, you'd probably rather not have false teeth. So it's a good idea to take care of the ones you've got.

Disgusting expressions

Isn't this an ornamental sign found in public buildings?

Answer: No, this kind of plaque is a disgusting layer of germs and bits of food that builds up around the teeth.

Within three minutes of sucking a sweet the germs lurking in the plaque start making acid to dissolve your teeth. If they make a hole they can cause horrible toothache.

Here are some disgusting ideas to help for making a clean sweep of the problem.

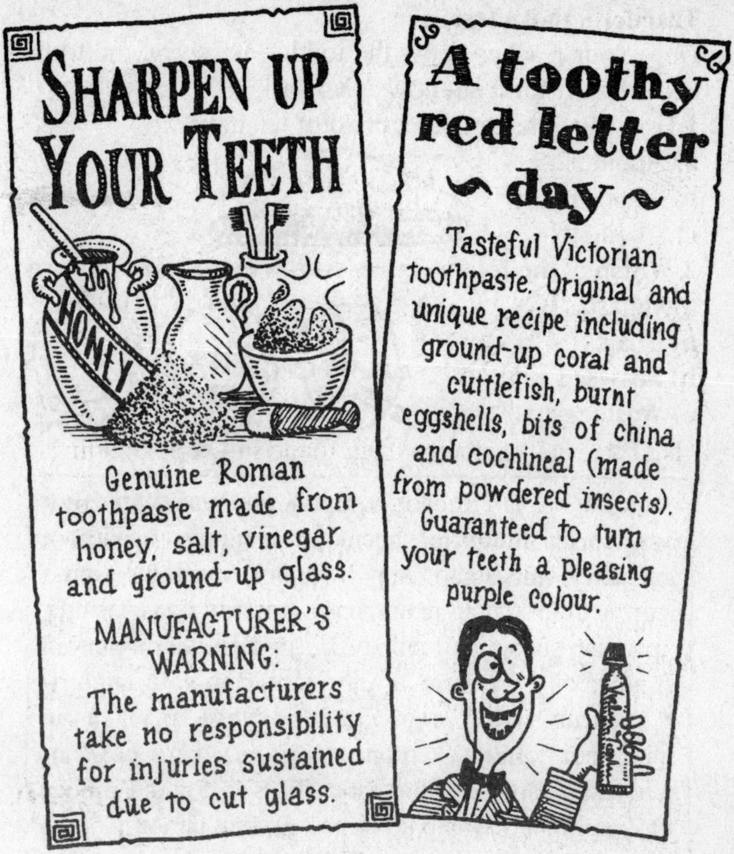

And here are some more sensible ideas.

- Flossing teeth cleans out germs lurking between teeth and near gums – some of their favourite hiding places.
- Chewing a sugar-free chewing gum makes you produce spit. Spit contains chemicals that help combat the acid made by tooth germs, and so helps to keep your teeth clean.

But don't do either of these in science lessons. Instead, you could try this…

Teacher's tooth test

Does your teacher know the tooth – er, sorry, the truth about teeth? Find out now as you ask...

1 How many teeth does a child of ten have?

a) About 52

b) About 12

c) About 26

2 Which of the following isn't a raw material of modern toothpastes?

a) Chalk

b) Seaweed

c) Washing-up liquid

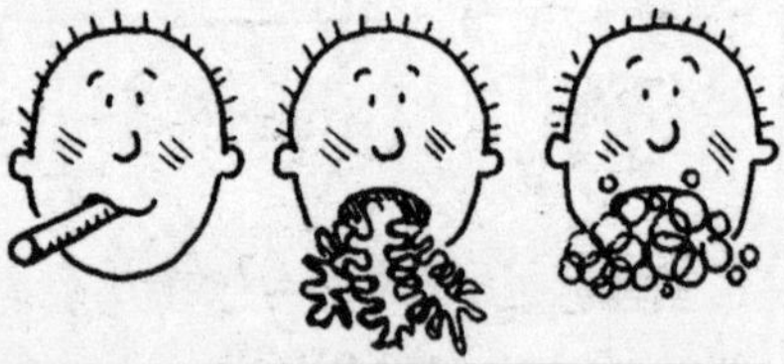

Answers

1 a) With a bit of luck your teacher will fall for this one. Although they're not all on display, a child of ten should have grown-up teeth hidden under their first set. And when you take a bite the vibration makes all these teeth twang slightly like guitar strings. **2** Another trick question. They're *all* used. The chalk is ground up to make a fine powder that cleans the teeth. The seaweed provides a chemical called alginate that binds the paste together. The detergent gives the toothpaste bubbles and makes cleaning easier. Too much detergent and you'd be foaming at the mouth.

Super-slurping spit

Picture your favourite food. A giant pizza with your favourite topping and hot bubbling cheese. Sizzling juicy burgers or crispy fried chicken and a giant pile of fries. Can't you smell that lovely just-cooked aroma? Are you drooling yet? You should be. Just thinking about food makes your mouth water – and the smell and sight of food helps even more. Your spit is ready and waiting to come out whenever you need it.

Spit is made by six salivary glands – two under your tongue, two under your jaw and two under your ears. When you get mumps the salivary glands under your ear get infected by a virus and swell up so your face looks fat. But cheer up face-ache – help is at hand…

After that embarrassing experience you probably wouldn't care about having a swollen face. Every day your sensational salivary glands squirt out 1-1.5 litres (1.8-2.6 pints) of spit. All of this you swallow. Some people spit it out instead – disgusting! Don't do it. It's a waste of good spit – look what it can do for you.

Have you ever eaten really dry food, like bread, when your mouth is also dry and there's nothing to drink? Disgusting, isn't it? By making your food wet, spit makes it easier to swallow. And spit helps you taste food. You can only taste food by detecting chemicals floating around in water. When food is dry its chemicals can't flow amongst the taste-buds so it seems tasteless.

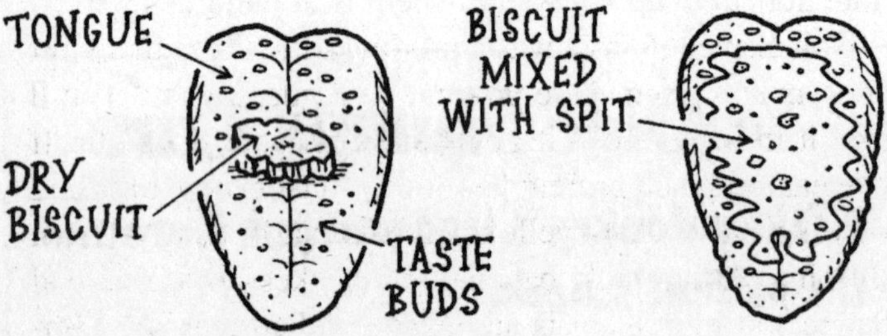

Spit has some disgusting ingredients, such as mucus – basically the same stuff that streams from your nose when you have a cold. This makes it quite slimy and stringy so you can suck it back into your mouth. There's no need to demonstrate this interesting scientific accomplishment just now.

Then there are the germs. Your spit is swarming with them. In fact, there may be 100,000,000 (one hundred million) bacteria in your mouth at any one time. Many germs end up getting eaten when you swallow spit. Hmm, tasty! But strangely enough, spit contains chemicals that kill some germs, and dentists have found that spit helps to keep your mouth clean and free from infection.

Spit also contains a waste product called urea that your body makes from spare protein. And guess what? You'll find it in urine too – it gives urine its yellow colour. If you eat too much protein your body makes more urea and your spit also turns yellow. Either that or you've been slurping extra thick banana milkshakes. But the real magic spit ingredient is an enzyme called amylase (am-me-laze) that rips carbohydrates apart into the sugars that make them up. (You can find out more about enzymes on page 285.)

Disgusting eating habits

Mealtimes used to be tough for kids.

Bet you never knew!

1 While you're swallowing, you can always think how lucky you are compared to birds. They can't do peristalsis (that is squeezing the sides of the gullet to force food down). Spot the difference.

That's what the bird has to do to ensure the worm slips down its gullet and not out of its beak.

2 Some people have difficulty swallowing. The sides of their oesophagus squeeze together so that food sticks halfway down. This condition can sometimes be triggered by gulping a cold drink too fast. The best thing to do is to sip a nice warm drink to relax your muscles. Ahh – that's better.

One of the worst things to do when you're eating is to eat too quickly. Like these people…

Fast food facts

- Do you like pickled onions? If you find them disgusting you'll be horrified to hear that Pat Donahue crunched 91 in 68 seconds in Victoria, Canada in 1978.

• Peter Dowdeswell ate 144 prunes in 31.27 seconds in Rochester, New York, in 1986. Prunes are full of fibre and are well known for making you want to go to the toilet. So you can guess what the next world record was…

• In the same year Peter also ate 91.44 metres (100 yards) of spaghetti in 12 seconds in Halesowen, Britain. And then … well you can guess what happened next.

Disgusting digestion expressions

Is this dangerous?

Answer
No. Eructation is just the posh scientific word for letting air from your stomach escape from your mouth. You probably call it burping.

Bigger, better burps

Huge hearty great burps are just your body's way of getting rid of some of the air you swallowed with your food. The faster you eat and the more you talk as you eat the more you burp. It's easier to burp when you're standing up. So imagine a posh party where people are eating and talking, and drinking fizzy drinks (with lots of gas) and standing up, too. They all want to burp but they're far too polite.

By the way, if you ever go to lunch in Arabia it's OK to burp loudly after the meal. It's considered a sign of good manners. This is sensible because you've got to let the air out somehow.

CONGRATULATIONS! You've managed to eat your supper without hiccups, heartburn, burping or food dribbling out of your nostrils. NOW for the tricky bit. Can you keep it down?

The Staggering Stomach

You're in control. You decide what you eat, don't you? Think again. There's a part of your body that seems to have a mind of its own. It's a muscular bag just under the left part of your chest. It makes you feel sick, it makes you feel queasy and it rumbles. And it does a whole load of other tricks, too … it's staggering!

Disgusting stomach fact file

NAME: Stomach

THE BASIC FACTS: The stomach is a storage tank for your food. Its job is to mix and squash food to make it easier to digest. The stomach also makes enzymes that digest protein and milk. And it does all this while you get on with your life.

THE HORRIBLE DETAILS: The stomach is staggeringly horrible. For example, there's a type of germ that lives quite happily in the stomach eating up your half-digested food.

Staggering stomach statistics

The human stomach can hold up to 4 litres (7 pints) of food.

Mind you, that's nothing.

- It takes your speedy stomach just 60 minutes to digest a cup of tea and a jam sandwich.

• Milk, eggs and meat take a bit longer. Eat a boiled egg with a ham sandwich washed down with a milk-shake and it'll take 3-4 hours to clear the stomach.
• But if you really want your stomach to work harder try a huge three-course dinner with soup and meat, and fruit for afters. That'll take your tired-out tum 6-7 hours to process.

• A wolf's stomach can hold 4.5 litres (8 pints) of food. Does that mean they have to "wolf" their meals?
• Cow stomachs can hold 182 litres (40 gallons) of food – that's enough to fill a bath if the cow sicked it up again. (Cows have an advantage – they actually have four stomachs not one.) One stomach is used for storing the grass before they sick it up and re-chew it – lovely! This is known as "chewing the cud" – or rumination (roo-min-ay-shun) as the scientists call it. The other stomachs are useful for storing the re-chewed grass whilst it rots. (Rotten grass is easier to digest.) Yum-yum!

• The mangrove monkey eats leaves all day. It needs an extra big tum to hold all those leaves and its stomach weighs as much as the rest of its body. If you had a stomach this big you really would be staggering.

Staggering stomach quiz

How well do you know your own stomach?

1 The word stomach comes from the Greek word for "throat". TRUE/FALSE

2 Butterflies in your stomach aren't anything to do with the stomach. TRUE/FALSE

3 It's possible to live without a stomach. TRUE/FALSE

4 It's possible to eat and eat until your stomach bursts. TRUE/FALSE

5 When you eat ice-cream the cold freezes your stomach. TRUE/FALSE

6 Your stomach stops moving when you're asleep. TRUE/FALSE

7 Your stomach produces an acid strong enough to dissolve a lump of bone. TRUE/FALSE

Answers

1 TRUE It makes you wonder how much those Greeks really knew about the body. **2** TRUE They're caused by a throbbing blood vessel over the heart. When you're nervous you're more sensitive to this throbbing. It's nothing to do with real butterflies. **3** TRUE Some people do. You just need to eat regular small meals instead of three big meals. **4** FALSE Don't worry this is impossible. If your stomach gets really full the opening at its base simply widens to let more food into your guts. But that's not an excuse to go and pig out. **5** TRUE That's "freeze" in the sense of stopping it moving, not turning it to ice. The cold stops your stomach churning for up to half an hour. **6** FALSE The stomach carries on churning slowly even while you're dreaming. In fact, if you dream you're eating, your stomach thinks the dream is real and makes extra digestive juices. **7** TRUE The stomach wall contains 35 million pits that make 0.5 per cent hydrochloric (hi-dro-cloor-rick) acid. This is strong enough to dissolve a lump of food in a few hours. A boa constrictor's stomach juices can even turn a whole pig into goo. Yuck! A more concentrated form of the acid is used in industry to dissolve out zinc from scrap iron (don't try this at home).

The vital goings on in the stomach were first probed by a scientist with a taste for staggeringly sick experiments.

Horrible Science Hall of Fame: Lazzaro Spallanzani (1729-1799) Nationality: Italian

Brainy Laz wanted to be a lawyer until his even brainier cousin Laura Bassi (1711-1778) talked him into becoming a scientist. As luck would have it, Laura happened to be the world's first woman professor of physics and introduced Laz to her scientist pals. So Laz became interested in many areas of science including such scintillating topics as where thunder clouds and sponges come from. (That's the sea creatures, not the cake you eat for tea or the thing you use in the bath.)

Laz had a hands-on approach to science. When locals claimed that Lake Ventasso in Italy had a giant whirlpool, the brave scientist built a raft and sailed across the lake – so proving the whirlpool didn't exist. In 1788 he decided to study volcanoes so he climbed a series of Italian craters. At Mount Etna in Sicily he had to be rescued after getting knocked out by poisonous gases. Undaunted he climbed Mount Vulcano but gave up when his walking stick caught fire and his feet got burnt.

Finally, by watching Mount Stromboli he discovered that gas explosions are the reason rocks fly out of volcanoes.

It took more than a few disgusting sights to stop Laz in his tracks. In 1765 he became interested in how some animals can re-grow parts of their bodies. So he cut up thousands of unfortunate worms, slugs and salamanders.

(He discovered that younger animals are best at re-growing.) He took the same fearless approach to his work on digestion. Would you want to make yourself sick? Laz did – in the interests of science – umpteen times.

Then he studied vile vomit. Amongst other disgusting discoveries he found that stomach acid could dissolve soft bone and gristle but this took longer than ordinary meat.

Disgusting digestion expressions

One doctor says to another:

Should you take cover?

Answer: YES. It's the posh word for being sick.

This can be triggered by:

a) Fear – e.g. a science test.

b) A horrible sight or smell – e.g. a revolting science experiment.

c) Disgusting food or poison or germs – e.g. a school dinner.

Oddly enough, doctors also use the term to describe leaking of the blood from a dodgy valve in the heart.

A sickening story

You're dizzy, you turn pale, you sweat and your mouth is full of spit. You're about to chuck up. Run for the bathroom! The muscles in your lower body and stomach all squeeze together until your half-digested food erupts from your gullet. Vomiting, as it's called, is controlled by a part of your brain known as the vomiting centre. It's well-known that throwing up can be triggered by fear. Scientists don't quite know how this happens. They think that your nerves produce chemicals that make your stomach heave when you're scared of something.

What your vomit looks like depends on how long it's been in your stomach. If it's only been there for a few seconds it won't look too different from when you ate it. Especially if it happens to be carrot stew. But if it's been down for a couple of hours it will be a thick soupy mess. Scientists call this disgusting substance chyme (pronounced chime). How chyming, er, sorry, charming.

Could you be a scientist?

Have you ever bent over and thought you were about to be sick? Don't try to do it now – take my word for it, it happens. The half-digested food slips out of your stomach. The acid mixture can burn the oesophagus so badly that some sufferers think they're having a heart attack. This is called heartburn. Some scientists looked at the effects of exercise on heartburn. They measured the amount of acid stomach juice there was in the oesophagus one hour after…

a) Running

b) Weightlifting

c) Cycling

Which do you think caused the most heartburn?

Answer

a) Perhaps the jogging up and down made the stomach contents slop upwards? Cycling was the least likely to cause heartburn. You can get heartburn if you go to bed straight after a big meal. If you lie down with a full stomach its contents can leak into the oesophagus. So you've got an excuse to stay up late? No such luck. You'll just have to eat earlier. No more midnight feasts and raiding the larder is definitely out.

Unbearable ulcers

Life can be tough for the stomach, too. One of the nastiest things that can happen to a stomach is when it starts digesting itself! This is what's known as an ulcer. Ulcers can be unbearably painful and need to be treated with substances such as chalk (yes, chalk) that neutralize the acid.

Your stomach has three lines of defence.

1 A thick layer of jelly-like mucus (the same stuff as slimy, runny snot, remember). This stops the acid leaking out and causing an ulcer.

2 A wall of 800 million cells wedged together to block

any acid that does escape. The cells are being replaced and every three days you get a brand new shiny pink stomach lining!

3 If the stomach gets too acidic the cells make a chemical called bicarbonate of soda. This is actually the same chemical you find in alka-seltzer and other medicines that settle an upset tum. The chemical neutralizes the acid so it isn't so strong.

Normally, though, ulcers only happen to stressed-out grown-ups.

Scientists reckon that ulcers are caused by bacteria that stop the stomach lining from making so much lovely protective mucus. This allows the stomach's acid to make a hole in the lining – and that's the ulcer. Sounds painful.

Talking about the guts, which we were a moment ago, it's time to leave the stomach and check out the intestines. And the going is going to get seriously disgusting from now on.

Disgusting gut feelings

Welcome to the intestines – the most horrible bit of your digestive system. The place where it's all happening. It's where fats, carbohydrates and proteins get broken down to smaller chemicals and sucked into the blood. And it's home to all sorts of disgusting goings-on.

Remember Gutzache's epic journey through the guts? Here's the map he used. It'll help you find your way around this chapter, too.

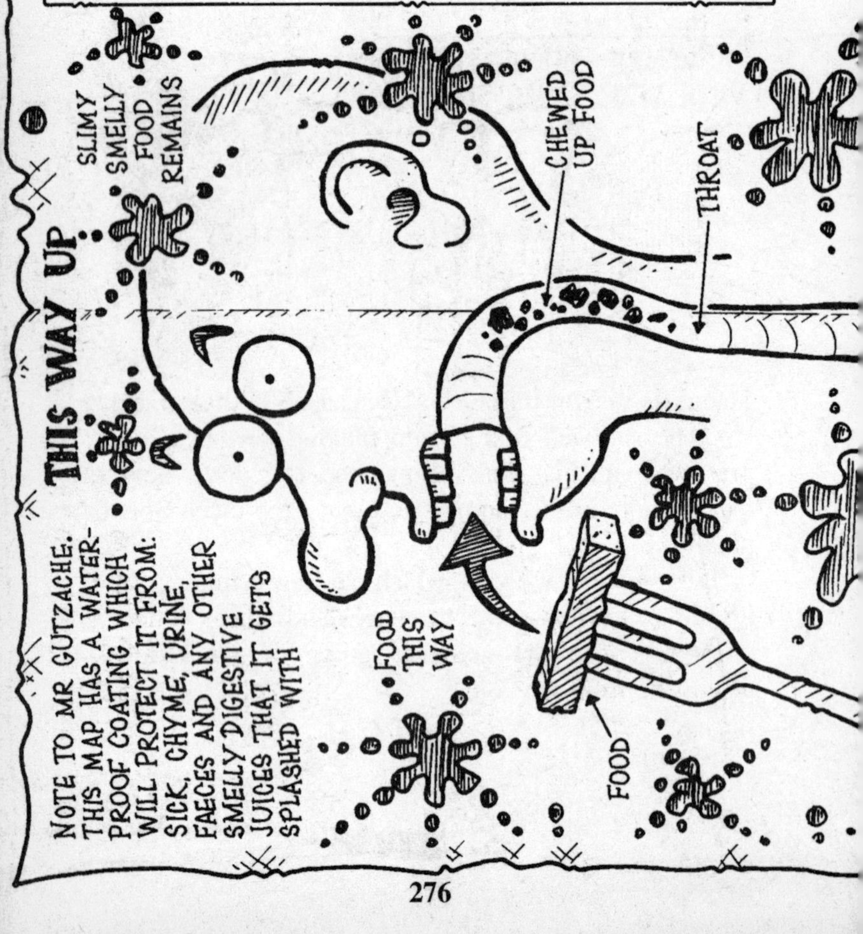

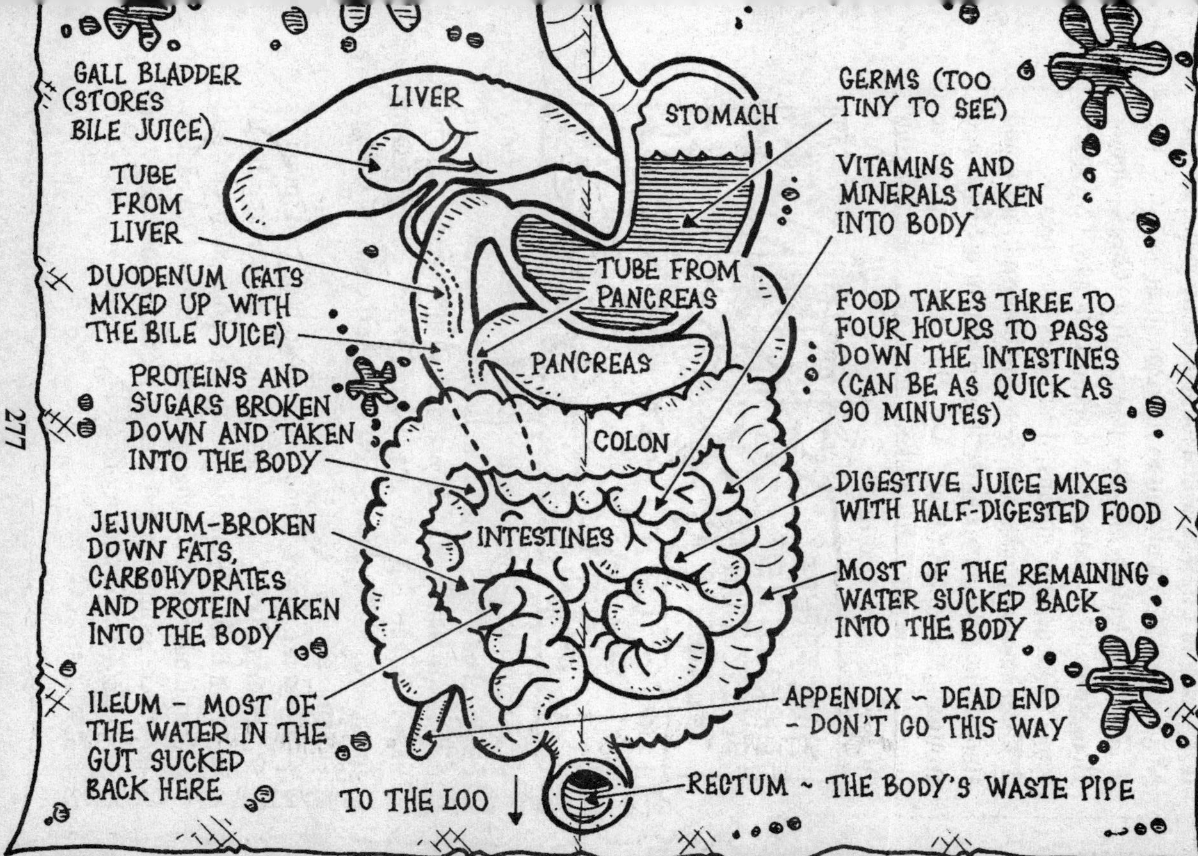
GALL BLADDER (STORES BILE JUICE)
LIVER
STOMACH
GERMS (TOO TINY TO SEE)
TUBE FROM LIVER
VITAMINS AND MINERALS TAKEN INTO BODY
DUODENUM (FATS MIXED UP WITH THE BILE JUICE)
TUBE FROM PANCREAS
PANCREAS
FOOD TAKES THREE TO FOUR HOURS TO PASS DOWN THE INTESTINES (CAN BE AS QUICK AS 90 MINUTES)
PROTEINS AND SUGARS BROKEN DOWN AND TAKEN INTO THE BODY
COLON
DIGESTIVE JUICE MIXES WITH HALF-DIGESTED FOOD
INTESTINES
JEJUNUM-BROKEN DOWN FATS, CARBOHYDRATES AND PROTEIN TAKEN INTO THE BODY
MOST OF THE REMAINING WATER SUCKED BACK INTO THE BODY
ILEUM - MOST OF THE WATER IN THE GUT SUCKED BACK HERE
APPENDIX ~ DEAD END - DON'T GO THIS WAY
TO THE LOO
RECTUM ~ THE BODY'S WASTE PIPE

Gruesome guts facts

1 The human intestines are nine metres (27 feet) long and if they weren't tightly coiled and curled up you'd have to be 11 metres (36 feet) tall to fit them all in.

2 The duodenum got its name after Greek doctor Herophilus (4th century BC) claimed it was 12 fingers long. ("Duodenum" means "12 fingers" in Greek.)

3 The ancient Greeks and Romans believed you could foretell the future by sacrificing a sheep to the gods and peering at its intestines. On the whole, the more unhealthy the intestines looked, the more unhealthy your future was supposed to be.

4 The inside of the small intestine looks like a furry carpet. The "fur" is thousands of tiny sticking out bits called villi that suck in digested food and transfer it to the blood. Ironed flat this area would cover 20-40 square metres (215-430 square feet) – about the size of a large classroom.

5 Gruesome stones made from waste food and minerals sometimes form in the guts. These bezoar (be-zo-ar) stones are also found in sheep and goat stomachs and were thought to have magical powers. In the 17th century they were ground up and used as medicines but they were as useless as a square football.

6 In fifth-century India doctors were not afraid to perform operations to remove blockages in the guts. They cut open the patient and afterwards joined the sides of the cut using … ants. Yes, ants. They got a giant black ant to bite the sides of the wound then cut the ant's head off. This left the jaws in position just like a little stitch. Luckily your guts can't feel pain apart from a bit of cramp. So at least the operation didn't hurt the human patient, even if the ants were a bit cut up about it.

Dare you discover … what bile juice does to fats?

What you need

washing-up liquid
a bowl of warm water
cooking oil

All you do is

1 Pour a little cooking oil into the water. The oil will float on the water. This is like the fat in your intestines.

2 Add a drop of the washing-up liquid representing the bile juice. Give the mixture a rapid stir.

What happens next?

a) The oil sinks to the bottom of the bowl and forms a kind of sludge.

b) The oil, washing-up liquid and water mix together in lots of little bubbles.

c) The oil, washing-up liquid and water form huge bubbles that don't burst easily.

Answer
b) The washing-up liquid (bile juice) breaks up the cooking oil (fats) so that it mixes easily with the water (liquid in your intestines). In this form it's far easier for the gut walls to take it into your bloodstream.

Gruesome greetings

You might wonder how all this activity is controlled by your body. Why doesn't the food in one part of the intestine simply stop moving so that the rest of your supper piles up behind it?

In fact, special chemicals in the blood called hormones carry messages from one part of the body to another to control this vital job. Just imagine if you could hear these messages – what would they say?

One hormone is called secretin (see-creet-in) and here's its message…

Another hormone is called cholecystokinin (kole-sis-toe-ki-nin) – we'll let it speak for itself.

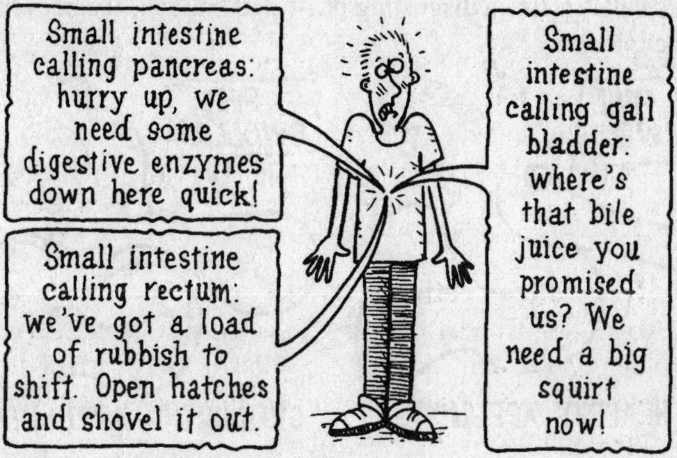

Meanwhile, the guts also keep in touch using nerves like a kind of telephone line. Let's listen in to a few more conversations

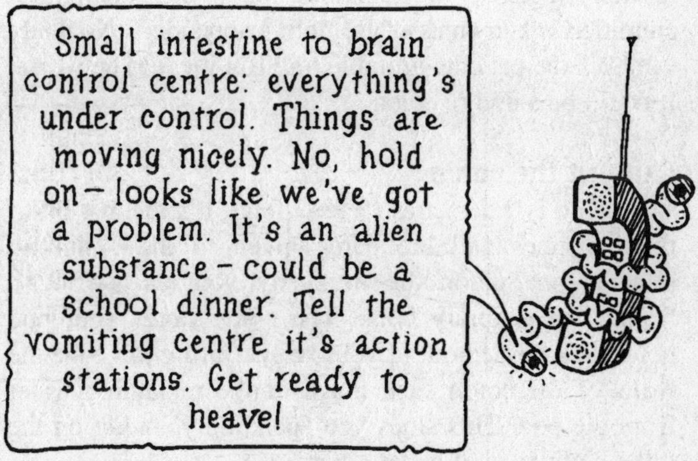

The grumbling appendix

Sometimes when the appendix gets infected by germs it swells up like a disgusting pus-filled balloon. It can even explode.

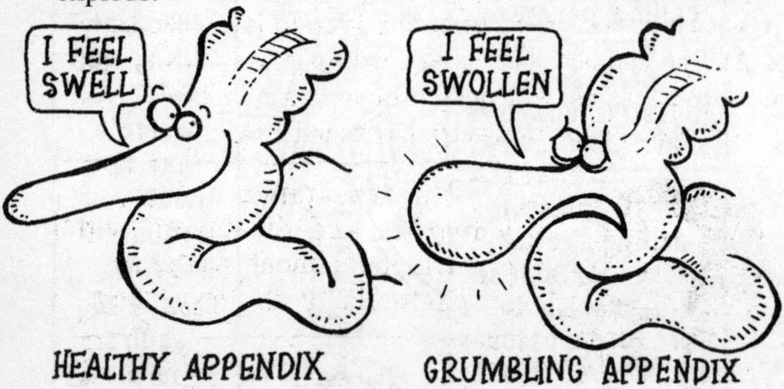

This appalling ailment is called appendicitis and in serious cases the appendix has to be removed. But if the infection isn't too bad the body's white cells guzzle most of the germs and the appendix gets better. If the germs multiply again you get more pain. This delightful condition is known as a "grumbling appendix". No doubt it makes the patients grumble too. But it could be worse. It could be a dodgy colon.

Cut out the colon

The colon is 1.5 metres (5 feet) long. It's the last bit of the intestines and the name given to the : sign in punctuation. So don't be surprised if your teacher finds a "colon" in a library book. The colon stores your poo before it's pushed out of your body. During this time the walls of the colon suck much of the remaining water from the poo. This stops you spending your life on the toilet getting rid of watery diarrhoea.

Top surgeon Sir William Arbuthnot Lane (1856-1943) was keen on ballroom dancing and designing new types of surgical instruments. But he wasn't too keen on colons. He thought they were useless and caused disease when germs escaped from the colon to infect the body. And he claimed the victim smelt of graveyards. Willie also said people with dodgy colons had cold, bluish ears, cold noses, clammy sweaty hands and …

Well, Willie was in the know when it came to colons. His claim to fame was to discover the sudden twists and turns in the colon now known as Lane's kinks.

Worried about the appearance of his patients, Willie invented an operation in which the offending colon was removed. This was fine, so long as the victim, sorry patient, didn't mind the consequences. These involved spending the rest of their life with a hole in their guts through which their poo passed into a bag. Yuk! Fortunately, other doctors criticised Lane for performing the operation unnecessarily. And so Lane's treatment of the colon came to a : er, sorry, a full stop.

Meanwhile, back in the intestines things are really hotting up. Boiling and bubbling as mysterious chemicals get to work. Enter the energetic enzymes. Is your gut getting fizz-ical? Better find out now…

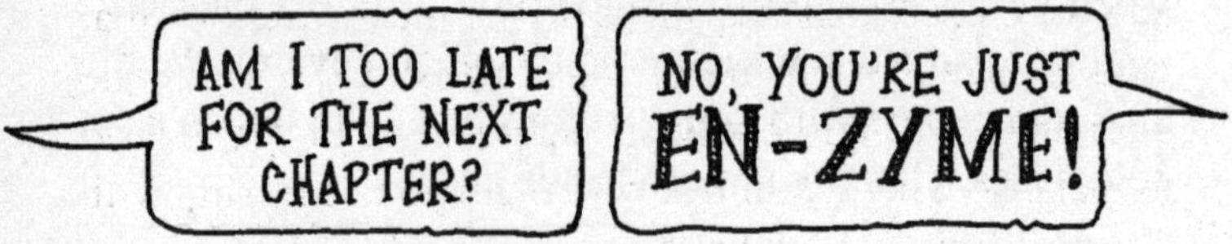

Energetic enzymes

Look inside your body and you'll see a gruesome assembly of bones, muscles and blood. But look closer and you'll see a fizzing mass of chemical reactions that would make most chemists green with envy. It's all done with enzymes. Without them digestion would be a dead loss and so would you. But with them you're fizzing with physical fitness. So what do enzymes do all day?

Disgusting enzymes fact file

NAME: Enzymes

THE BASIC FACTS: **1** An enzyme is a protein that changes other chemicals. In digestion, enzymes break other chemicals to pieces.

2 Every cell in your body contains over 3,000 different enzymes.

THE HORRIBLE DETAILS: If you didn't have enzymes the only other way to digest your food would be to heat your body. This also breaks the food chemicals up. Unfortunately, your body would need to be 300°C (572°F) to do this. So you'd need to cook yourself to enjoy your food.

Dare you discover ... how enzymes work?

What you need

a hard-boiled egg. (Ask an adult to help you boil the egg for ten minutes.) Cool the egg and peel off the shell.

biological washing powder

a jar

a spoon

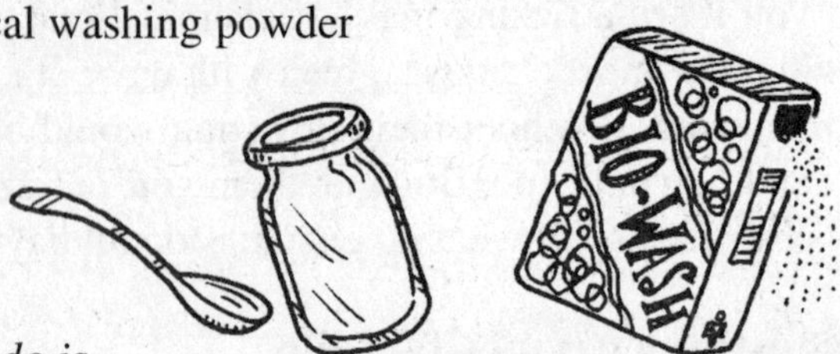

All you do is

1 Add eight tablespoonfuls of warm water to the jar.

2 Mix in one tablespoonful of washing powder. Stir until the powder disappears.

3 Add a piece of the boiled egg white (not the yellow yolk).

4 Wrap the jar in a towel and leave in a warm place such as an airing cupboard for two days.

5 Take a look at the piece of egg white. What do you notice?

a) The egg is a horrible brown colour.

b) The egg has turned into a white liquid.

c) The egg has got smaller.

Answer

c) The washing powder contains enzymes that break down the protein in the egg into smaller chemicals that dissolve in the water. This is exactly what happens in your guts.

Bet you never knew!

Enzymes make heat as they rip chemicals to pieces inside your guts. That's why Arctic sledge drivers give their dogs butter to eat in very cold weather. Butter is digested by enzymes and this makes enough heat to warm the dogs. And if enzymes make heat, let's visit a few hot spots.

Disgusting pancreas fact file

NAME: Pancreas

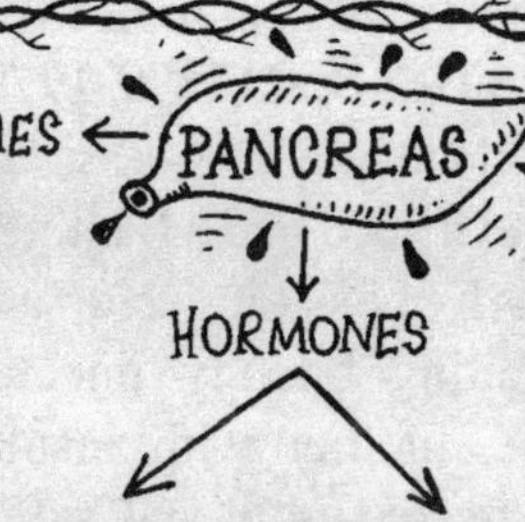

THE BASIC FACTS: The pancreas is like a chemical factory pumping out enzymes to digest carbohydrates, fat and protein. It makes 1.5 litres (2.6 pints) of digestive juice a day.

THE HORRIBLE DETAILS: The pancreas also makes two hormones – insulin and glycogen that control the sugar that gets to your muscles to provide energy. Lack of insulin causes a horrible disease called diabetes.

A worthy winner?

Scientists toil away for years until at last they make a great discovery. But who should get the glory for discoveries? Take insulin, for example. When scientists found out about insulin they were able to give extra insulin to people with diabetes. Thousands of lives were saved. In Sweden a committee met to award the 1923 Nobel Prize for Medicine… But who should get credit? These were the main contenders:

Frederick Banting (1891-1941)
A First World War hero. Like many scientists of his time, Banting was convinced there was something in the pancreas that prevented diabetes. He discovered insulin in 1922.

Charles Best (1899-1978)
Brilliant laboratory assistant who helped make Banting's work possible. He and Banting bravely injected one another with insulin to make sure it was safe.

James Collip (1892-1965)
A talented chemist. Showed Banting and Best how to make a pure kind of insulin suitable for injecting into humans.

John Macleod (1876-1935)
In charge of the lab in Canada where Banting and Best worked. Didn't think much of Banting as a scientist. Was on holiday when insulin was discovered.

Two scientists were awarded the coveted Nobel Prize in 1923 – but which two?

Answer
Macleod and Banting. Although Macleod had been on holiday at the time, he was honoured because he was in charge of the lab. Which just goes to prove that science can be disgustingly unfair. Fortunately, Macleod decided to share his prize money with Collip and Banting generously shared his prize with Best.

Disgusting liver fact file

NAME: Liver

THE BASIC FACTS: It's brown and weighs about 1.5kg (4.4lbs). It has hundreds of jobs including making bile which helps to digest fats. After food has been digested, the liver stores food chemicals and vitamins.

Liver fact file continued . . .

THE HORRIBLE DETAILS: Bile is disgusting stuff, it's thick, brownish and bitter tasting. After the bile has digested fats, the salts in the bile are taken back into the blood and end up back in the liver. Then they're used to make more bile . . . this sickening cycle can continue up to 18 times.

One man played a vital role in probing the liver's secrets…

Horrible Science Hall of Fame: Claude Bernard (1813-1878) Nationality: French

Bernard was the son of a humble grape picker but when he died he was the first French scientist to enjoy a full state funeral. Well, maybe "enjoy" isn't the right word since he was dead at the time. Young Claude Bernard didn't want to be a scientist. He wanted to be a playwright. Fortunately (for science), his plays were so bad that Claude took up medicine instead.

He discovered that carbohydrates are broken down into sugars during digestion and fats are broken down by bile juice. Then he found that the liver can make sugar. He fed a dog on a sugar-free diet and then opened up its liver to find that sugar had mysteriously appeared there.

Mrs Bernard was just one of many who believed that Claude's experiments were cruel to dogs. No dog owner would allow Claude near their pets and the scientist soon found that his programme of research was in trouble owing to a shortage of subjects.

So he took to kidnapping dogs for his research. One day one of Bernard's stolen dogs escaped from the lab and ran home to its owner. Unfortunately, the owner happened to be the Chief of Police and he came round to ask the scientist some awkward questions…

What do you think happened next?

a) Claude Bernard was sentenced to three years' hard labour for cruelty to dogs. Mrs Bernard was the chief prosecution witness.

b) The scientist was let off after paying a hefty fine and making a big donation to the local stray dogs home.

c) Bernard made a grovelling apology and was let off with a caution.

Answer

c) And you'll be pleased to know the dog lived happily ever after with his owner.

Disgusting liver diseases

The ancient peoples of Babylonia (modern Iraq) had a disgusting method of finding out what liver disease a person was suffering from. Let's take a look at this ancient tablet. *

* That's a clay tablet, not the sort of tablet you'd take for an upset tum or sore throat.

Stones similar to those in the guts can also appear in the liver. They often form in the gall bladder where they do no harm unless they get big enough to stop bile from reaching the guts. If there is a blockage, the bile leaks into the blood and ends up in the skin and eyeballs. Bile contains colours made from waste chemicals from the liver and these turn the skin and eyeballs a tasteful yellow. This disgusting condition is known as jaundice.

Nowadays, it's easy for surgeons to crush the stones or in the worst cases simply whip out the gall bladder in one easy operation. Meanwhile, your body is busy using up all your hard-digested food.

Juicy joules

Your blood carries the juicy digested food chemicals to all parts of your body. In your muscles the chemicals are ripped apart to produce the energy that keeps you going. We measure this energy in kilojoules (ke-lo-jools) or kJ for short.

Bet you never knew!
A boy aged 9-11 needs 9,500 kJ of food per day to keep going and between the ages of 12 and 14 this goes up to 11,000 kJ. A girl of 9-11 needs only 8,500 kJ per day and at 12-14 she needs 9,000 kJ. So why do girls need less food? Some girls are smaller or less active than boys. Or maybe they're just not so greedy.

Compare that with…

- A canary needs just 46 kJ a day to avoid hopping off its perch for good.
- An elephant uses up a jumbo 385,000 kJ a day.
- A rocket needs 100,000,000 (one hundred million) kJ to get into space.

Confusing isn't it? Maybe this quiz will help you digest the facts.

Energy quiz

Can you find the food with the right amount of energy to keep you going through each challenge?

CHALLENGE	FOOD
1 Shovelling snow for an hour. 	a) A glass of milk. 418 kJ 
2 Cycling for ten minutes. 	b) 4 apples. 840 kJ 
3 Scrubbing the floor for twenty minutes. 	c) A bar of chocolate. 1255 kJ 
4 Swimming round the pool for four minutes without touching the sides. 	d) A slice of of buttered toast. 314 kJ 
5 Dancing for ten minutes. 	e) 300 grams (10.6 oz) of sausages. 3000 kJ 

WARNING If you eat too little food you'll feel horribly hungry and weak and light-headed. You might even faint. Eat too much and you'll put on extra fat.

Answers

1 e) The fat in the sausages is full of energy and you'll need it for all that shovelling in the cold.

2 d) You also use this amount of energy keeping your body ticking over for 75 minutes when you're asleep.

3 b) Although you'd want more than just apples as a reward for scrubbing the floor.

4 c) Now you're talking. You use the same energy tidying your room for an hour or sitting a three-hour Science exam. Wouldn't you rather tidy your room?

5 a) You'd have to watch TV for 75 minutes to use up this amount of energy.

A hot problem

Producing all that energy also generates heat. That's why you feel really hot and sweaty after a run. Every day we produce the same heat as burning 500g (1 lb) of coal. Twelve people sitting in a room give off as much heat as a small electric fire. Luckily, the blood takes the heat outwards to the skin where it escapes into the air through the pores in your skin. Phew – that's a relief!

Sometimes the heat takes water away from your body in the form of sweat and this also cools you down. But if you've got too much water in your body there's another way to get rid of it. Any idea what that might be?

Going round the bend

You can't get away from the toilet. Ultimately it will command your presence with all the power of a giant magnet. Once your breakfast has worked its way through your system, your body will insist on it. It doesn't matter how busy you are – even if it's the middle of a vital science test. You've gotta do what you've gotta do.

But why? The story starts with a couple of rather crucial organs – the kidneys.

Crucial kidneys fact file

NAME: Kidneys

THE BASIC FACTS: You've got two – one on either side of your body – although you only need one to stay alive. Each one is about 11 x 6cm (4 x 2 inches) and its job is to filter spare water and waste chemicals from your blood.

THE HORRIBLE DETAILS: The waste stuff is urine – that's pee to you.

SUPPER'S READY. IT'S YOUR FAVOURITE – STEAK AND KIDNEY PIE

KIDNEYS? ACTUALLY I'M NOT VERY HUNGRY, DAD

Fantastic filters

Every day about 2,000 litres (440 gallons) of blood flows through your kidneys. Now, as you may have noticed, you don't have that much blood. So we're talking about the same blood going through the kidneys lots of times.

Here's what happens…

Just imagine your kidneys as a pair of fantastic coffee filters. (They do filter coffee along with everything else.)

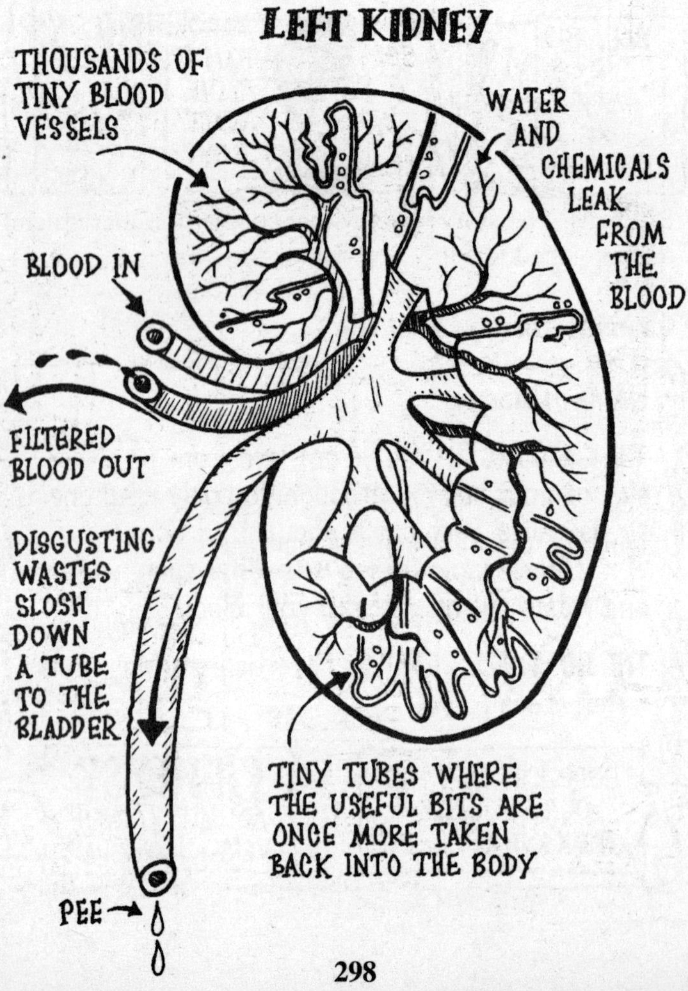

Bet you never knew!

People with defective kidneys can be wired up to an artificial kidney. This is known as dialysis (di-al-lis-sis). The first artificial kidney was made by US scientists in Baltimore in 1914. The blood passes out of the body and along a tube where the wastes are filtered out just like in a real kidney.

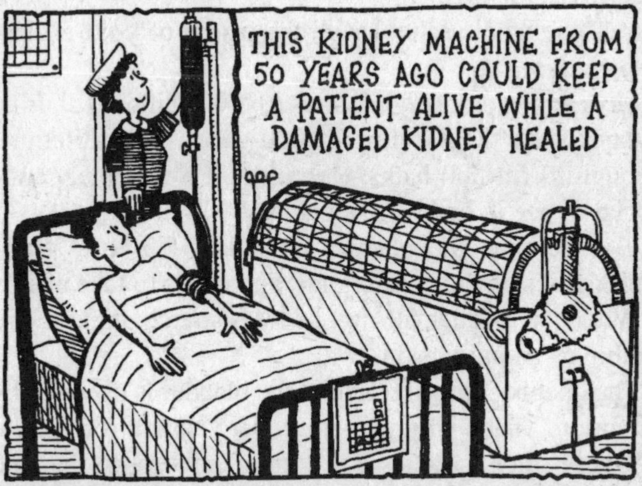

Disgusting digestion expressions

Shouldn't she be in hospital?

Answer
No. This is just the posh scientific word for weeing. Coffee contains a chemical that stops the kidneys taking back so much water from a person's urine. So they end up making more urine.

Useless urine facts

Shock the whole school with the extent of your useless knowledge.

1 Most adults produce 1-2 litres (0.2-0.4 gallons) of urine a day. That's 40,000 litres (8,000 gallons) in a lifetime, enough to fill 500 baths. (Warning: it's extremely anti-social to pee in one bath, let alone 500.)

2 By the time the bladder has about 0.3 litres (0.07 gallons) it's already feeling full and needs to take a leak.

3 When the bladder fills up, its sides stretch until they're as thin as an onion skin.

4 The opening at the bottom of the bladder is operated by the brain. That's why you don't wet yourself (or at least not very often). Babies don't know how to do this and that's why they wear nappies. When you go to sleep, messages from your brain keep the opening locked to prevent little disasters in the night.

5 When you go to the toilet you usually hold your breath. (It's true – see what happens next time you pee.) This allows the diaphragm, a muscle above your liver, to push down on your guts. This in turn squashes the bladder and forces the urine to squirt down its exit tube.

6 Urine is about 96 per cent water. The rest is a mix of urea (remember, that's a waste chemical made by your body), and a bit of waste protein and salt. It's a bit smelly but it's usually germ-free...

7 That's why urine was once used to wash wounds on the battlefield. No need to try this next time you get a cut.

8 Most of the time urine is yellow – that's the urea. But sometimes it can be a different colour – such as red, that's when you've eaten too much beetroot. And disgusting facts such as this were once incredibly useful to a breed of...

Useless urine doctors

Sometimes your doctor will ask for a sample of your urine. This can help to detect certain diseases. But for hundreds of years doctors thought that you could identify every kind of disease by looking at the patient's urine. Some doctors even tasted it, too. Erk!

In the Middle Ages Spanish urine doctor, Arnold of Villanova, said:

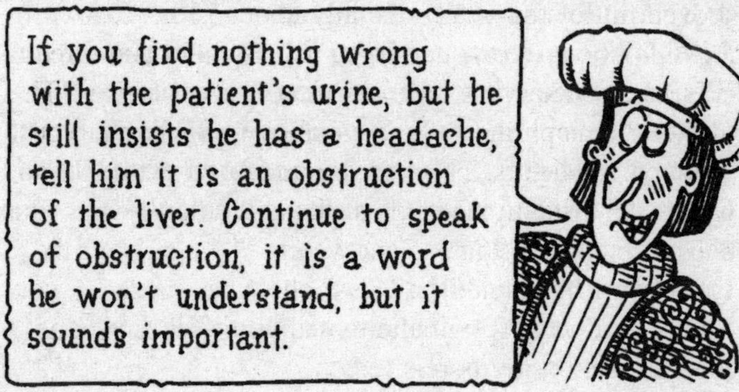

Surely doctors aren't like that nowadays. They wouldn't use long words just to confuse their patients … would they?

Disgusting expressions

How should she answer? Clue: it's nothing to do with Christmas paper chains, they're *decorations*.

Answer Defaecation is the posh medical term for making poo. For most people this is once a day or once every two days. But people who eat lots of fibre can defaecate *five times* per day. Bet they get through a fortune in loo rolls.

Foul faeces

You remember all that waste food piling up in the colon? Well, it's got to go some time. So every day some of it is shoved out of the anus – usually about 150g (22 oz) for a child. About three-quarters of this is water and the rest is waste food such as fibre and dead germs. Lovely!

Note: anus = the hole in your bum where the waste products come out. Not to be confused with Uranus which is a distant planet. Clearly you wouldn't want your anus to be that distant.

Could you be a scientist?

You are a doctor. Two patients see you. One says …
Doctor, doctor, my poo is red.

1 What do you say?
a) It's blood. You'll be dead in a week.
b) You've got a liver disease that's turned your bile red.
c) Stop eating so many tomatoes.
The other patient says...
Doctor, doctor, my poo is blue!
2 What do you say?
a) You have a rare colon disease.
b) That's impossible – you must be an alien.
c) Stop eating those blackberries.

Answers 1 c) 2 c)

Crunched-up constipation

When you're very worried you'd think your body would help you feel better. But it doesn't. Instead the vagus nerve for some reason doesn't send the signals from the brain that make you go to the toilet. As a result the poo piles up in the colon where its moisture is sucked back into the blood. The poo becomes dry and crammed together – that's constipation. So it's painful to get rid of – and that really is a worry. And here's another worry – sometimes stress can speed up peristalsis resulting in diarrhoea and extra farts.

If this happens to you, maybe you'd like to try Sir William Arbuthnot Lane's patent constipation remedy...

The paraffin acts like oil in a rusty bike chain. It gets the poo moving again. No, on second thoughts better not – you wouldn't want your guts to turn into a paraffin lamp would you now? And there are enough dangerous gases down there already.

Disgusting digestion expressions

Does this need surgery?

Answer:
No, just a clothes peg over the nose. Flatulence is the scientific name for farting. It's nothing to do with being flat – although you might feel a bit flattened after being given this diagnosis.

Ten things you always wanted to know about farting but were afraid to ask

1 Kings and Queens fart. Presidents fart and so do Emperors. Children fart and even teachers are said to do it once in a while. The only difference is how much, how often and how loudly they let it out.

2 The first known account of farting was by ancient Greek playwright Aristophanes (about 448-380 BC) who makes a character in one of his plays say,

"My wind exploded like a thunderclap."

Sounds nasty.

3 Farting is simply your body's way of getting rid of air that you've swallowed by eating too fast, talking while eating, or swallowing bubbly spit. Of course, you can burp some air up. The more you burp, the less you fart. Better not try explaining this important principle at family meal-times.

Or this one…

4 This air gets mixed up with poo in the gut. If there's a lot of air in poo it'll float.

5 Amazingly, a group of fearless scientists analysed the chemical ingredients of a fart. (Did they wear gas masks?) They bravely discovered that a fart is a mixture of five different gases – mainly nitrogen (59 per cent) which is a boring gas that floats about in the air without people taking too much notice of it. Except when someone farts!

6 Well, the smell comes from the chemicals indole and skatole. These are given off when germs get to work on bits of protein from your food.

7 Sometimes a gas called hydrogen sulphide forms in farts. This happens when chemicals from different foods get together in the guts. You'll know all about it because the fart smells like rotten eggs. It's bad news – and not only in the social sense. Hydrogen sulphide is poisonous and it can explode if too much of it mixes with oxygen in the air.

Crisps are full of little air bubbles. Chewing gum makes you swallow air. Like the air in crisps this may re-emerge as farts. Fizzy drinks are full of bubbles.

8 Beans, brussel sprouts, cauliflowers and bran contain a type of carbohydrate that the germs in your gut can change into gas.

Scientists reckon that meat contains many of the chemicals that cause some of the smelliest farts.

9 US astronauts are banned from eating certain foods, especially beans, before a space-flight. Well, how would you fancy being cooped up in a cramped spacecraft on a ten-day space mission with someone who had a bit of a bottom problem?

10 Mind you, flying can make you fart. As a plane flies higher the air pressure around the passengers drops. This makes the air in the guts expand and the result is . . . well, I think you can guess.

When it comes to getting rid of smells there is one invention that has proved more than a flush in the pan.

Flushed with success

1 The first loo that could be flushed with water was in the palace of Knossos, Crete. This 3,500-year-old loo even had a bung you could stick down the pan to block nasty whiffs from the sewers.

2 In the Middle Ages most people had toilets that were nothing more than seats over smelly holes in the ground.

3 In 1590, Englishman Sir John Harrington invented a loo that could be flushed with water.

4 But the loo really came into its own after 1778 when inventor Joseph Bramah devised the ball valve which automatically filled the cistern and the "U" bend.

5 Gradually toilets became more and more popular with anyone rich enough to afford them.

But there was a problem.

Something in the air

The problem had been festering for some time, growing ever more gross, ever nastier with each passing year. And with each year the truth became ever more unpalatable, ever more horrible. London, one of the greatest cities in the world, stank. It didn't just pong, whiff or smell – it STANK. By the 1850s it reeked of rotting sewage and filth and every kind of loathsome rubbish. And it stank because London's sewerage system had broken down.

The London Times

4th August 1857

A BIG JOB?

Today we bring you an exclusive interview with genuine London "tosher" - Bert Smellie.

Bert's unenviable job is to crawl into the sewers in search of valuables accidentally flushed down toilets.

On a good day Bert finds coins, bits of rag and bones. "The work's all right," he says, "it's good money but it's dangerous too!"

"What sort of dangers?" I ask him.

"Them sewers is diabolical," says Bert. "Falling to bits - they can fall on you without warning and you'd be

Bert Smellie

buried alive. Others have deep pools that'll suck you down in rotten slime. And the smell is bad enough to make you heave.

"And then there's the rats. Yeah. Giant rats big as cats some of them. At night they come out of the sewers into houses. They've been known to attack babies. Even some of my mates have been attacked by rats. All we ever found was their skeletons. Horrible . . . and to think, it could have been me."

"Come off it Bert," I laugh. "Pull the other one!"

Then Bert holds up

one of his hands. It's covered in white scars. Rat bites.

Blimey!

The Editor writes . . .

We at the *London Times* say something must be done about this disgrace. London must have new sewers. The politicians must get their act together and pay for it . . . this issue STINKS and we believe there's a real whiff of corruption here.

Eventually the sewers couldn't take it any more. And so began the Great Stink. It was the most horrible smell anyone could remember. In the hot summer of 1858 the smell of the sewage-clogged River Thames was so foul that people were physically sick. Eventually people kicked up such a stink about it that the politicians were forced to act. The problem was so urgent that the Government agreed to fork out for a brand new sewerage system. At once!

Super sewers

In all, 209 km (130 miles) of new sewers were constructed. They mainly ran downhill to take the waste away from London. And the system is still operating today. Nowadays complex sewage systems are commonplace in large cities. But in the 19th century some of them were considered so amazing that they became tourist attractions. Can you imagine it?

For a holiday with a difference . . .

The Municipal Sewage Experience

GREAT VALUE - IT WON'T BE A DRAIN ON YOUR POCKET!

A unique thrilling close-up view of how our fascinating sewage system deals with waste water from washing and toilets, and rainwater from gutters.

GASP WITH AMAZEMENT

as the watery mass of sewage is filtered to remove large objects and then left to settle.

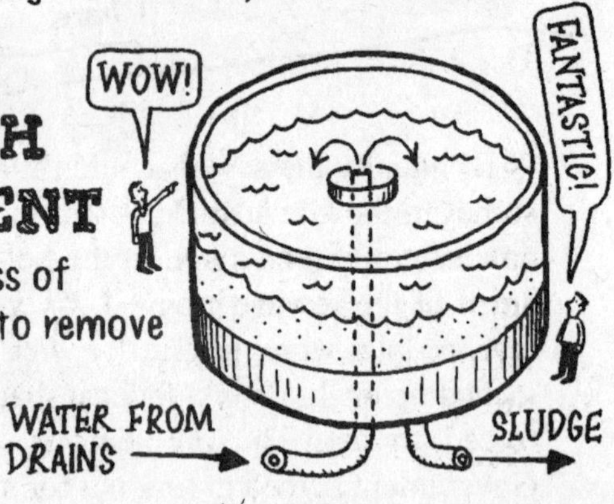

BE TOTALLY GOBSMACKED

as watery waste is left in tanks where much of it is eaten by hungry germs. Or we can use the poison chlorine to bump them off!

HOLD YOUR BREATH

as the sludgy solid sewage is left for a few weeks for germs to feast on.

YES, NOTHING IS WASTED

This pongy process gives off smelly gas that can be used to power the sewage works. And it can even be used to light gaslights in the streets.Even the smelly sludge is dried and used as fertilizer.

So sewage makes excellent plant food! Ideally suited for growing crops. Crops to make into a school lunch.

A school lunch. But that's where this book started, isn't it?

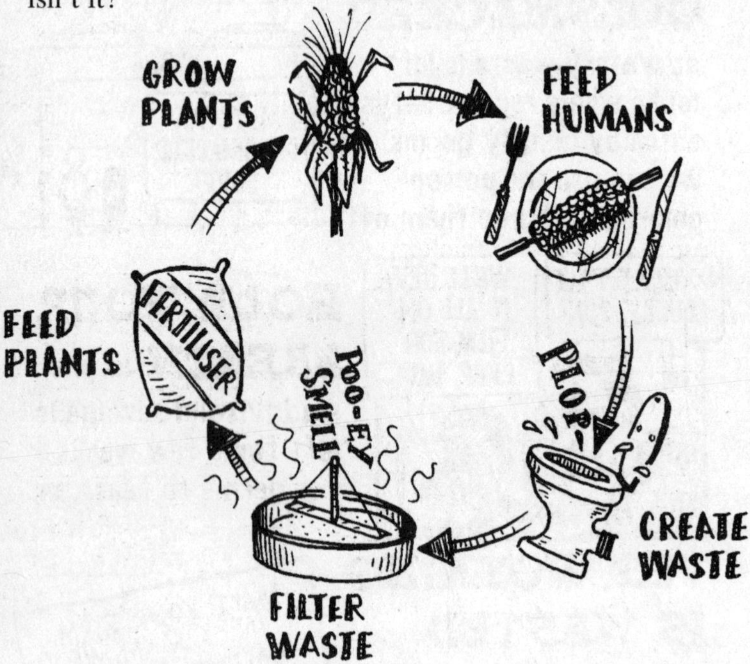

Something to chew over (food for thought)

Food's brilliant. We think about it, we talk about it, we even dream about it. And when it's on our plates we play with it before we eat it. But what goes inside our bodies is even more fascinating.

If your digestive system was a machine it would be the most amazing and incredible machine ever invented. Every day it systematically sorts through whatever you choose to feed it with. It sorts out the bits your body can use and chucks out the bits it can't.

All the time you're busy watching TV, sitting in a science lesson or chatting with your friends, your guts are quietly (leaving aside the odd gurgle) getting on with this vital task. They hardly ever protest – OK, so they make you throw up from time to time, but only if they've got a good reason.

So how long has it taken you to read the first bit of this chapter? About one minute? Right, prepare to be amazed… In just one minute:

- Your stomach has churned three times.
- 500,000 new cells have been made for lining your stomach.
- The food in your guts has moved 2.5cm (1 inch).

• And your kidneys might have filtered out 1.4ml (0.05 fl oz) of urine that even now could be trickling into your bladder.
• Meanwhile all the glands and organs in your digestive system are happily pumping and squirting away: salivary glands, stomach, liver pancreas. All of them producing their vital juices and enzymes.

And so it carries on 24 hours a day. Even when you're asleep. Even when you're in a Science lesson and not thinking about food at all. You've got to admit, it's fascinatingly disgusting.

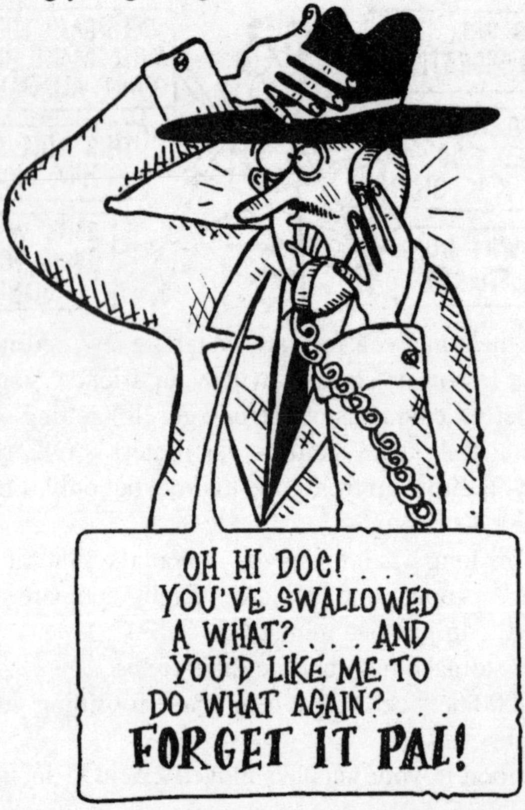

BULGING BRAINS

INTRODUCTION

To hear some scientists talk you'd think they knew everything about science...

But don't be fooled – scientists *don't* know everything. After all, if they did there would be no need for any new experiments. Scientists could sit around all day with their feet up. But, in fact, there are lots of mysteries left to solve. Lots of things we don't know or don't understand.

For example, there's one object that's so mysterious it makes the brainiest scientists scratch their heads. It's wet and squishy and looks revolting – and oddly enough, it's found between their ears. What is it? No, it's not their disgusting, snotty nose. It's the bit *inside* their heads – their bulging brain. Scientists aren't even sure how it works...

But if scientists are puzzled by their own little grey cells what chance do the rest of us have? No wonder learning about your brain can make your head ache.

Well, if science scrambles your brains, help is at hand. This book is bulging with brain facts. For example, bet you never knew that in 1998 US scientists found the part of the brain that makes you laugh. They gave an electric shock to this area of a girl's brain and she started giggling uncontrollably.

And that's not all. Did you know that in one brain experiment children were forced to sniff their little brother's stinky old T-shirts? (Page 364 will give you all the smelly details.) Now that really is cruelty!

So by the time you've finished reading this book your knowledge will be so vast you could easily become the brains of your class. And who knows? Your teacher might even mistake you for a scientific mega-genius. But to enjoy the full benefits you've got to ask your brain to help you read this book.

Your eyeballs scan the letters, your brain makes sense of the words, and your memory reminds you what they mean. But hold on – looks like you've already started ... oh well, don't let me stop you. Now ask your brain to send a message down thousands of nerves to tell your finger muscles to gently lift the next page.

BULGING BRAIN BASICS

Dr Funkenstain felt a rush of excitement as she gazed into the glass tank. For five years she had been planning this experiment. Now she had done it and she was looking at the result. The tank was bathed in an eerie light. And floating ghostlike in the tank's centre was a strange and horrible looking object. It was pink like a sausage and wrinkled like an old walnut. And it gave out the faintest whiff of blue cheese.

Could it be an unknown creature from the depths of the ocean? Or perhaps an alien from another world? Dr Funkenstain knew better. She was gazing at a real human brain. A very special human brain because...

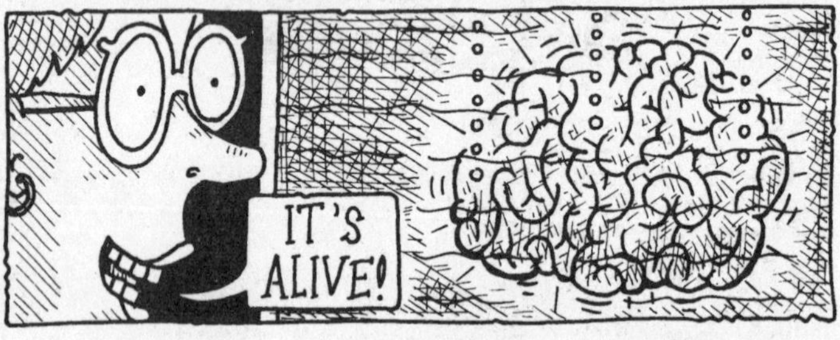

Dr Funkenstain whispered excitedly. Peering closer she could see the tiny wormlike blood vessels crisscrossing the brain's surface. Dr Funkenstain had done it. She was the first scientist in history to keep a brain alive outside the body.

DON'T PANIC! It's only a story. Scientists can't keep human brains in tanks – yet. But this technique might be possible in the future. Perhaps you'd like to become the first brain surgeon to keep a brain in a tank? If so beware: it's a bad idea to rush into brain surgery without getting to know a bit about your subject. Important facts like...

What's your brain for?

The brain is the part of your body that tells you what's going on around you. You can use your brain to order your body around and even to order everybody else around. But there's much more to your brain. Much, much more.

Inside your brain are your precious memories, your dreams, your hopes for the future and the knowledge of everything you love and care about. In your brain you can sense lovely smells and tastes and colours. Your brain helps you feel great and happy about life and that's the good side. But your brain also creates horrible fears and worries that can make you miserable.

Your brain makes the thoughts and feelings that make your personality. Your brain turns your body from a living object into *you* the person. Without a brain you'd be as dead as a dodo's tombstone, so it's good to know that you've got your very own bulging brain right now between your ears ... hopefully.

Inside the bulging brain

Still want to be a brain surgeon? Excellent. Now you've found out a bit about what the bulging brain does, you're ready to check out how it works...

Bulging fact file

NAME: The brain

BASIC FACTS: The brain is made up of three main parts:

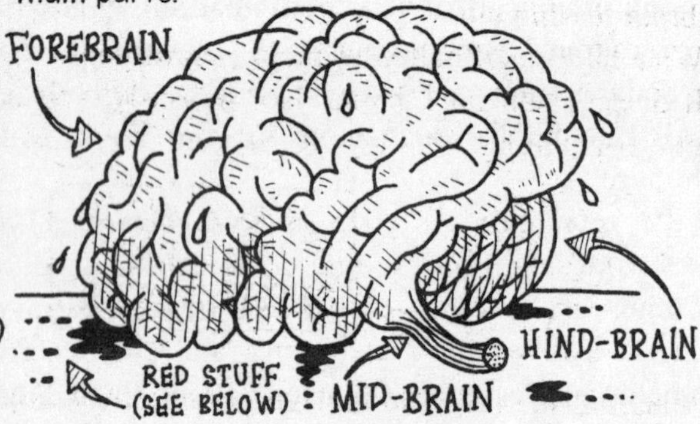

Each area is made up of smaller bits with different jobs. (For more details see page 344-348.)

DISGUSTING DETAILS: The brain needs energy from the sugar and oxygen carried in the blood. So it sucks in about 750 ml (one pint) of the red stuff every minute. All this hot blood gives out lots of heat – that's why your brain is the hottest part of your body.

Bet you never knew!

Your brain weighs less than 1.3 kg – that's a little less than the weight of a large bag of sugar or the weight of all the germs swarming in your guts. In fact, the brain is only one-fiftieth the weight of a grown-up man and it's far lighter than your guts, your blood, your skin or your bones.

Have you got a bulging brain?

So just how clever is your brain? Well, if you're going to be a brain surgeon you'll need to know all the answers to this brain-teasing quiz:

1 What happens if half your brain is damaged?

a) It doesn't half hurt, ha-ha. No, seriously, you can't remember anything.

b) You die. No one could survive such a terrible injury.

c) You can live normally although you have to re-learn vital skills such as talking.

2 What happens if someone cuts your brain in two?

a) Your brain becomes twice as clever.

b) Your brain functions normally but you may find yourself doing your science homework twice.

c) Each side of your brain behaves like a separate person.

3 Imagine you were born without 97 per cent of your cortex (cor-tex) – that's the wrinkly part of your brain at the top where you do your thinking. You're left with a tiny slice of brain in this area. What would happen to you?

a) You'd be left with the brains of a half-witted stick insect.

b) You'd be as brainy as anyone else ... but only for five minutes a day. The rest of the time you'd blunder around like a zombie in a horror movie.

c) Your brain would work normally and you could be as brainy as your science teacher. (Yes, teachers are said to be intelligent.)

4 What would you feel if someone stuck a finger into your brain and waggled it about?

a) Unbearable agony – the worst pain in the world.

b) You'd feel hot and cold shivers all over your body.

c) Nothing because the brain cannot feel touch.

5 How much energy does your brain use in a science test?

a) Such a small amount that it can't be measured (especially if you don't know the answers).

b) Enough to light up the classroom. No wonder the test makes you light-headed, ha-ha.

c) Just enough to power a dim light bulb.

6 Why do you feel tired after the test?
a) All that mental effort strains the brain.
b) During the test your brain drew extra energy in the form of sugar in your blood. After the test your body feels tired because it lacks this vital blood sugar.
c) You were so tense your muscles bunched up and used up energy. And your muscles feel tired – not your brain.
7 How much of your brain is water?
a) About 5 per cent
b) 32 per cent
c) About 80 per cent

Answers:
All the answers are **c)**, so you can check them without taxing your brain too much. And here are a few more details to get you thinking.
1 A bump on the head can injure the brain (see pages 441-451 for the grisly details). Yet the brain can survive dreadful injuries. If one half of the brain is injured, the half that's left learns how to do the work of the damaged half.
2 This operation was performed in the 1960s on patients suffering from violent fits. The operation stopped the fits from spreading through the brain. But

afterwards the two sides of the brain acted like separate people. One woman tried to put on a different shirt with each hand. She ended up wearing two shirts.
3 People can be perfectly intelligent with very little cortex. This condition is caused by a disease called hydrocephalus (hi-dro-cef-al-us). This results in too much fluid sloshing around the skull, so there's less room for the brain.
4 Your nerves take signals from elsewhere in your body to your brain. This means you actually experience pain, touch, taste, smell, sound and vision in your brain. But oddly enough, there are no touch sensors on the brain itself. (You'll find the low-down on senses on pages 357-376.)
5 Yes, in light bulb terms we're all rather dim. Scientist Louis Sokoloff of the US National Institute of Mental Health has found the brain uses the same amount of energy gazing dreamily at a sunset as it does in a tough science test. So what would you rather do?
6 If the questions were really easy, and you managed to relax in the science test, you wouldn't feel so whacked.
7 That's why when you become a brain surgeon and get to touch a brain it'll feel like squidgy blancmange or a soft-boiled egg. The brain needs water for vital chemical reactions such as sending nerve signals. Without water, a brain begins to overheat and starts to see things that aren't there. Ultimately it will die.

Bulging brain secrets

Psst – wanna know a brain secret? There's more to your brain than water. For example, your brain's made up of millions of cells and each one is so small you need a microscope to see it. (No, these aren't cells that people get locked up in.) Read on, your brain might learn something...

Bulging brain cells

1 Your brain is bulging with 100,000,000,000 – that's 100 *billion* – nerve cells or neurons. These are special cells used for sending signals inside the brain. If you don't believe it, try counting them yourself.

2 Each cell is a living blob and some are so tiny that you can fit 25 on to this fullstop. (You'll need a steady hand for this.)

3 If you laid the cells from just one brain in a line they would stretch 1000km – a quarter of the way across the USA.

4 Unborn babies grow new brain cells at the rate of 2,000 every *second.* And all your brain cells were already in place when you were born. But after you get to 25, about 12,000 cells die each day (that's 4.4 million a year).

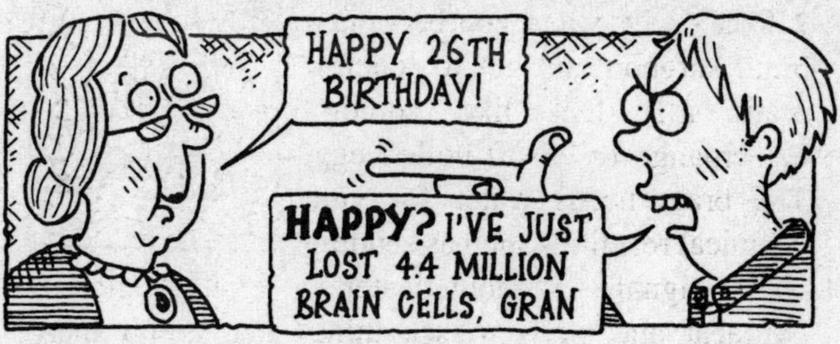

Don't worry! You can lose cells at this rate for a lifetime and still have 98 per cent of them left.

5 Your brain cells are desperate for oxygen. Starve a brain of blood for just seven seconds and it goes on strike and switches itself off. You might call this fainting. Scientists aren't quite sure how this fascinating process takes place.

Yep – even now scientists are baffled by the mysterious brain. But not quite as baffled as the people who first probed the brain's grisly secrets. Check out the next page and prepare to be baffled, bewildered, bemused and ... *horrified.*

BULGING BRAIN BOFFINS

The first brain surgeons had a problem. The bulging brain is mysterious because you get no clues to tell you what's going on inside it. I mean there's no helpful sign saying...

Unlike certain other parts of the body the brain doesn't do interesting things like digest food, burp or even fart. The brain just sits around all day squelching to itself.

So it's not so surprising that these early pioneers made some mind-boggling mistakes.

Mind-boggling mistakes

The ancient Egyptians and Greeks thought that the thinking part of the body was the heart. This seemed right because your heart beats faster when you're upset or excited. Is that why your teacher (who could be as old as the pyramids) makes you learn boring facts "by heart"? Well, anyway, the ancient Greeks and Egyptians were *wrong*.

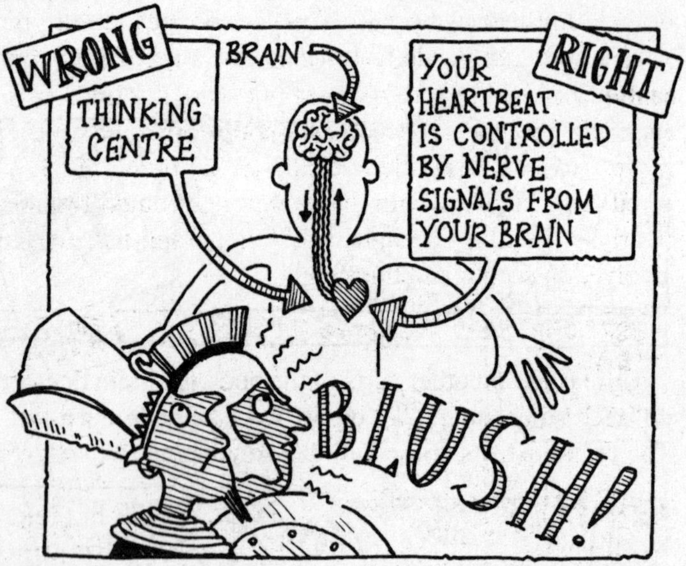

Brainy Greek philosopher Aristotle (384-322 BC) also thought the heart did the thinking. He reckoned the brain was simply a cooling system for the blood. According to Aristotle when you get a cold your cooling system overflows. (That's why snot dribbles out of your nose.)

But he was *wrong* too. Snot is made in the lining of the nose to catch germs and dust. Your nose is runny in a cold because your body is trying to flush out the germs that cause the illness.

Actually, Greek doctor Alcmaeon of Croton (6th century BC) had already figured out what the brain was up to. He cut up dead bodies and noticed that there were nerves running from the eyeballs to the brain. He also noted that patients with head injuries couldn't think clearly. "Clearly," thought Al, "the brain has to be involved in seeing and thinking."

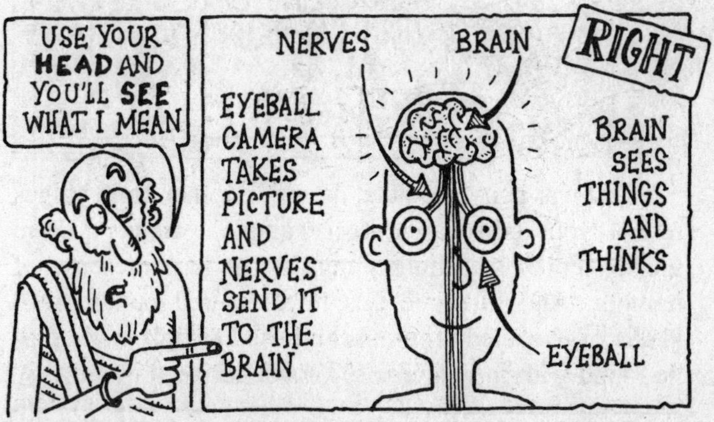

But for over a thousand years doctors remained puzzled. They weren't sure how the brain worked or what the different bits were for. There were theories, of course. One widely held view was that you did your thinking in the fluid-filled spaces inside the brain known as ventricles (ven-trick-als). The rest of the brain was a squelchy bubble- wrap to cushion the vital holes. But by the 18th century scientists were looking at the brain in a more scientific way. And making strange and grisly discoveries...

Bulging brain secrets: Franz Gall (1758-1828)

As a child Franz noticed that one of his school friends had bulging eyes. This boy was good at spelling and Franz wondered if everyone who is good at spelling has bulging eyes. After he became a doctor in Vienna he cut up dead bodies and came to the conclusion that the eyes bulged because the brain behind them was also bulging. Franz reckoned this bulging area dealt with spelling.

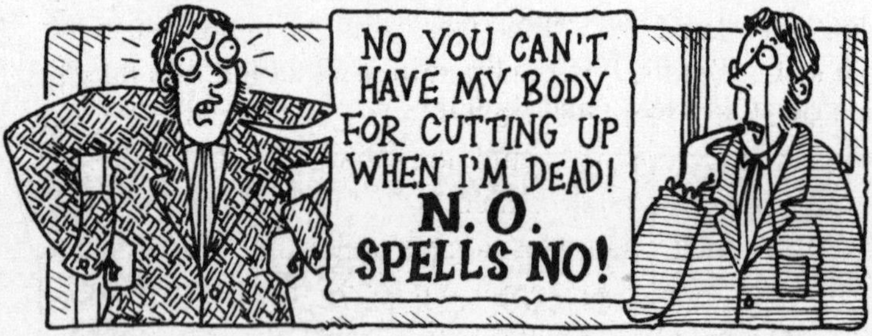

Franz was convinced that the size of other brain bulges reflect your personality, for example, whether you're greedy, enjoy smashing things up or have a sense of humour. And to prove this he measured hundreds of skulls of executed criminals and tried to link the bumps he found with the criminals' known personal traits.

Despite his many skulls, er, I mean skills, Franz was on the wrong track. There is no link between the shape of your brain and your personal qualities. But up to the 1850s many people believed Franz had found a way to measure personality. And when Franz's own brain was examined after his death it was found to be smaller than average. Now, I wonder what that could mean?

The talking brain: Paul Broca (1824-1880)

Paul was working as a surgeon in Paris when he met a patient named Tan. "Tan" was his nickname because the poor man had suffered a brain injury that left him unable to speak any word except "tan". Tan was already ill when he saw Broca. Broca could do nothing to help his patient and a few days later he died.

Tan's misfortune was a great opportunity for science. Broca cut open Tan's brain and found that the injury was in what's now imaginatively known as Broca's area (surely it ought to be called Tan's area?). Broca realized that this area of the brain helps you pronounce words properly.

This was a major discovery, but as far as speech goes it wasn't the last word – geddit? In 1874 German scientist **Carl Wernicke (1848-1905)** found another bit (now known – surprise, surprise – as Wernicke's area) which helps you *choose* the right words. People with brain damage in this area often talk utter drivel but with perfect grammar. (For more details see page 387.)

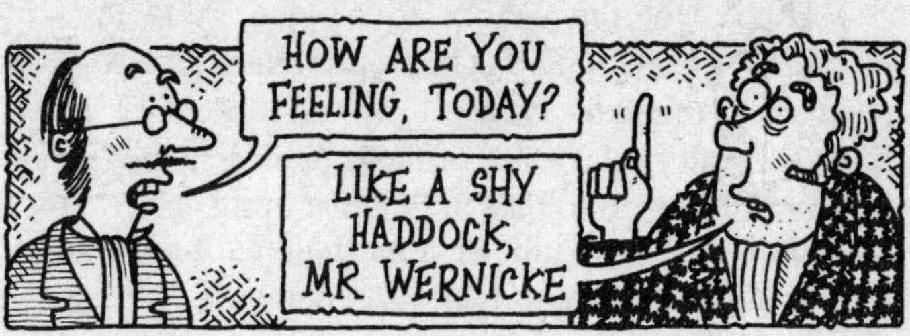

The twitching brain: Julius Eduard Hitzig (1838-1907)

If Mrs Hitzig had walked into the bedroom unexpectedly one day in 1870 she would have received a horrible shock. Her husband and his pal Gustav Fritsch were experimenting on a dog's brain using her dressing-table as a workbench.

At the time, Hitzig was working as a doctor in Switzerland but he didn't have a lab of his own. (By the way it's a bad idea to use your mum's dressing-table to practise your brain surgery. You could use the bathroom instead, but make sure you mop the floor afterwards.)

Actually, the dog was getting quite a shock too. An electric shock to the left side of its brain. Hitzig found that this made the dog's right legs twitch. This electrifying test proved that the left side of the brain controls the right side of the body and vice versa. Later in the year war broke out between Germany and France, and Hitzig got the chance to try the same tests on wounded soldiers with bits of their brains shot away. The results confirmed his theory.

As a result of the work of these pioneers, new groups of scientists began to take an interest in the brain. You'll be coming across some of them later on in this book. Here's a handy guide to help you spot them...

Spot the scientist

1. Neurophysiologist

(new-ro-fizzy-olo-gist)

INTERESTED IN: finding out how the brain and nerves work.

WHAT THEY DO: study bits of chopped-up brain and analyse chemicals from the brain.

WHERE THEY WORK: University laboratories or large hospital labs.

2. Neurologists (new-rol-lo-gists)

INTERESTED IN: Studying the brain and nerves, too, but they're especially keen on horrible but fascinating brain and nerve diseases.

WHAT THEY DO: Treat patients with diseases of the nerves and brain. Some of them are also neurosurgeons which is the posh term for brain surgeons.

WHERE THEY WORK: Hospitals.

3. Psychiatrists (si-ki-a-trists)

INTERESTED IN: Diseases of the mind. Psychiatrists are trained as doctors rather than purely scientists.

WHAT THEY DO: Talk to the patient and attempt to find the causes of their illness.

WHERE THEY WORK: general hospitals and psychiatric hospitals and clinics.

4. Psychologists (si-col-lo-gists)

INTERESTED IN: Studying the brain by looking at the way it makes people behave.

WHAT THEY DO: Set up experiments to find out how people react in certain situations. Some of these tests are a bit wacky. Some psychologists are interested in diseases of the mind, but unlike psychiatrists they are not trained as doctors.

WHERE THEY WORK: University labs and hospitals.

Peculiar psychologists

The psychologists take their lead from a very peculiar German scientist, and here's his story...

Horrible Science Hall of Fame

Gustav Fechner (1801-1887) Nationality: German

Fechner's brain was always bulging with ideas but his interest in the mind began with a horrible accident. The physics professor was studying light when he blinded himself by looking at the sun. (Something you should never do.) So you could say poor old Gus got blinded by science – geddit. He became so miserable that he went mad for two years.

But one day he was sitting in the garden and he felt a sudden impulse to tear off his bandages. Amazingly, he found he could see again! Incredible colours flooded his brain and he was so excited he imagined he could see brains inside flowers. (Yes, you did read that last bit correctly.) Gus wrote a peculiar book describing how plants have minds. (Believe this and you're a real cabbage-brain.)

Two years later Gus was enjoying a lie-in. Well, maybe "enjoying" is the wrong word. Gus was racking his brains. And not about whether he'd find a toy in his packet of breakfast cereal or how to make contact with a turnip. He was trying to think of a way to study the brain using scientific experiments rather than cutting it open on an operating table. Then he had a brainwave.

All you had to do was measure how the brain reacts to different sensations. For example, in one test Gus shone a light in a volunteer's eyes and slowly increased the brightness until they noticed the change. This allowed him to measure the brain's ability to notice changes in brightness.

Gus had launched a new branch of science called psychology – the study of human behaviour (although the name actually means "study of the mind" in Greek).

And this exciting new science owed its existence to the fact that the scientist fancied an extra snooze. (Tell your parents this story next time you want a lie-in, you never know they might even fall for it.)

Fechner's work was continued by German **Wilhelm Wundt (1832-1920)**, who set up the world's first psychology lab. Wundt never laughed or smiled or joked and spent his entire life working.

His books totalled 53,735 pages – that's equal to writing a 500 page book every year for 100 years. He wrote so much that critics complained that it was hard to discover what Wundt actually thought. American psychologist George A. Miller wrote...

Brilliant, eh? So if you want to baffle your teacher write a 500 page essay for your science homework. But this tactic didn't stop other psychologists disagreeing with Wundt's approach to psychology. Increasingly they were finding that the brain did a lot more than simply respond to sensations.

Another German psychologist **Max Wertheimer (1880-1943)** wondered if the brain plays tricks to help make sense of a film. A film is made up of thousands of pictures that you see very quickly – about 24 pictures a second. The brain can't keep up with this rapid change so it sees the pictures as a continuously moving scene. So your brain gets the whole picture – and you get the whole movie, including the exciting bits *and* the happy ending.

Max dreamt up this idea on a train in 1910. He was supposed to be on holiday but he excitedly leapt off the train (he waited for it to stop first – he wasn't that excited) and set up experiments to find out why.

Max proved the brain sees the whole scene first and then figures out how the moving objects relate to one another. And he worked out a new theory of psychology called Gestalt (ges-stal-t) based on these ideas. Gestalt actually means "whole" in German and the new theory underlined the importance of finding out how the brain makes sense of things like the film. This was a step forward from Wundt's work, which simply looked at how the brain responds to sensations.

Meanwhile American psychologists such as **John B. Watson (1878-1958)** and, later, **Burrhus Skinner (1904-1990)** were changing the behaviour of rats by training their brains. (You can read more about Watson and his wacky experiments on pages 398-401.)

Bulging brain expressions

Two brain surgeons are quarrelling...

Is the quarrel about gardening?

Answer: No. The amygdala (a-mig-dal-a) and putamen (putt-you-men) – almond and fruit stone in Greek – are odd names for areas of the brain.

Confused yet? Well, there are lots more bits and pieces you'll need to know about if you're going to be a brain surgeon. Maybe things would be clearer if you could get your hands on a real dripping brain. Fancy a squidge? Hope so, if not the next chapter's so nasty, it could drive you out of your mind.

Better sharpen that scalpel...

BULGING BRAIN BITS 'n' PIECES

As a brain surgeon you need to know all about the main bits and pieces in the brain. Fortunately we've got hold of a real genuine brain from a real genuinely dead person to help you. Go on, take a peek – it won't bite you.

Brain bits and pieces

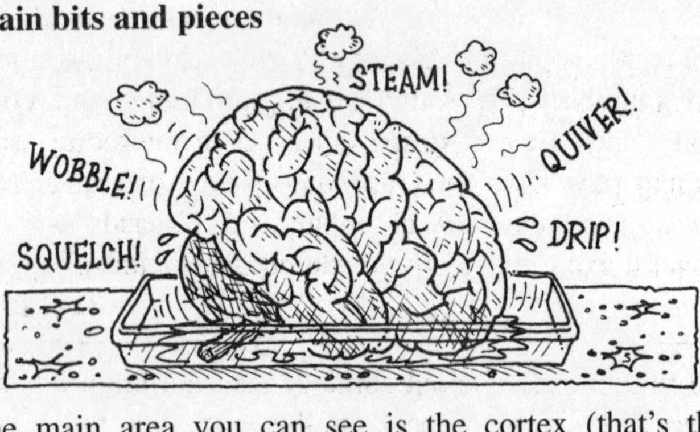

The main area you can see is the cortex (that's the wrinkly, thinking bit, remember?).

Dare you discover ... why the cortex is wrinkly?
Ever wondered why brains are wrinkly? Now's your chance to discover the *real* answer...

All you need is:
Two sheets of A4 paper. (Your school report might come in handy here.)

All you do is:
1 Screw one sheet of paper into a tight little ball.

2 Open it up but don't flatten it.
3 Place it over the second sheet of A4 paper.

What do you notice?
a) The screwed-up paper seems to have shrunk.
b) The screwed-up paper has got bigger.
c) Both sheets of paper are the same size.

Answer:
a) The wrinkles and bumps on the paper make it take up less space. The wrinkles on your cortex allow a larger area to squash between your ears. And that's very important because the cortex is very thin – no more than 3 mm (0.12 inches) thick. If your brain was flat it would be the size of a pillowcase and you'd need a huge head to contain it.

To find out more about some of the vital brain bits and pieces let's have a peek at this gory but fascinating medical textbook.

BRAIN SURGERY FOR BEGINNERS

Chapter 1: Brain bits and pieces

Cerebrum (ser-ree-brum)
This is the largest bit of the brain – it's so big it makes up 85 per cent of the brain. This area is REALLY important because its wrinkly surface is the cortex, where thinking takes place. The cerebrum is divided into two halves (no one knows the reason for the split). The halves are linked by a bridge at the base made of millions of nerves cells.

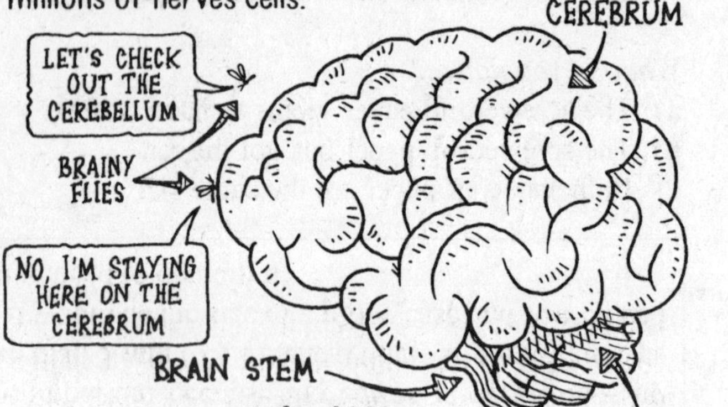

Cerebellum (ser-ra-bell-um)
The name means "little brain" in Latin – because it looks a bit like a little brain. This pear-sized blob has two halves – one for each side of the brain. Both sides help the brain balance and control its body's movements.

Bet you never knew!
When you learn a skill such as riding a bike you think about what you're doing. Well, hopefully – otherwise you'd fall off. But after a while you happily pedal around without thinking. Oh, so you knew that? Well, when you stop thinking about what you're doing your cerebellum takes over from your thinking cortex and tells your body what to do. Scientists have found that with the cerebellum in charge you can move faster and less clumsily. (For more details on what the cerebellum can do check out pages 386 and 412.)

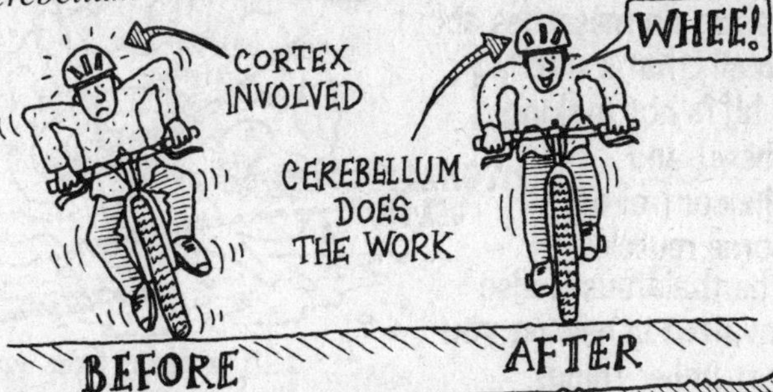

Spinal cord

This is a bundle of nerves 45 cm (18 inches) long and as thick as a thumb. Although it's not technically part of the brain, as a brain surgeon you need to know what it does. It actually takes signals to and from the brain.

Brain stem

This bit links the brain with the spinal cord. It's useful for helping the brain to go to sleep. And it's also useful for waking up the brain to danger or something interesting.

As a brain surgeon you'll need to know a bit more about the even smaller but still vital bits and pieces that lurk deep within the brain. We've cut some brains in half to help you . . .

Thalamus (thal-a-mus)
You've got two of these - one on either side of the brain. Each thalamus is full of nerve cells, and nerve signals reaching this area can be rerouted to other parts of the brain. What's more, each thalamus passes on messages about smell (that's sniffing whiffs not making them), and the control of some muscles. The thalamus is also involved in helping you remember things.

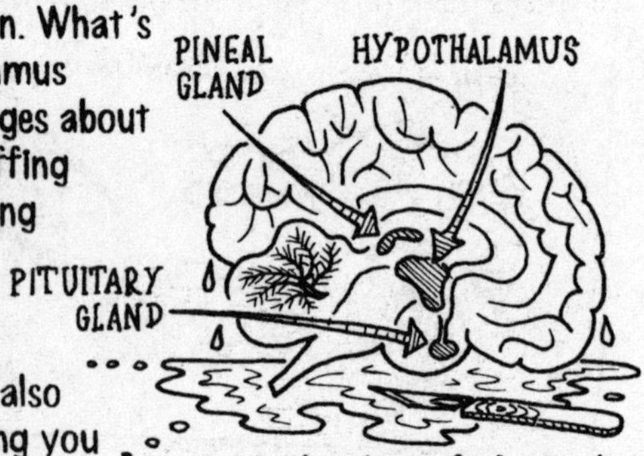

half a brain (side view)

Hypothalamus (hi-po-thal-a-mus)
A bossy little blob the size of one of your knuckles. It reckons *it's* the boss of the entire body. Controls the water content in the blood, its temperature, sweating, shivering, growing, when you sleep, etc.

The pituitary gland
Vital sidekick for the hypothalamus. Follows its orders and makes the chemicals that go round in the blood. These chemicals, or hormones as scientists call them, order the body to do what the hypothalamus wants.

The pineal (pi-nee-al) ***gland***
The name means "pine cone" because it looks a bit like a tiny one. It 's sensitive to the amount of light in the day – and this may make you feel tired in the evening and wake you up in the morning. There's a type of fish called a lamprey that has a pineal like an extra eye on top of its head. The extra eye gives it all-round vision. (Scientists have failed to prove the common belief that teachers have this eye in the back of their heads.)

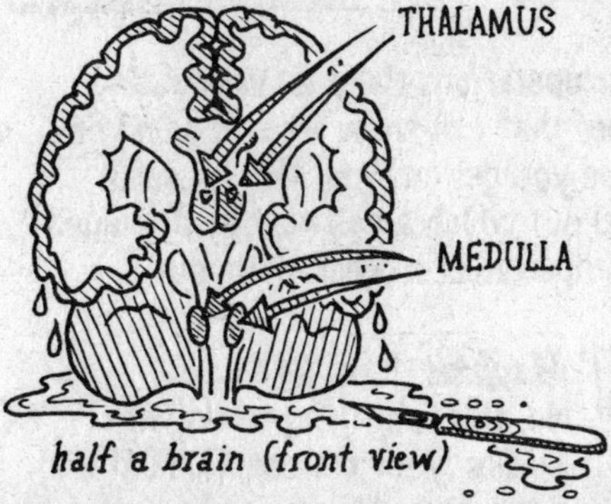

half a brain (front view)

Medulla
Looks after the digestive and breathing jobs. It does this work automatically – which is kind of handy. Just imagine if you had to think how to do these things. You might end up breathing in your supper and then you'd be choking on your food and making a mess on the table.

Limbic *(lim-bick)* ***system***
An odd mixture of bits and pieces including the amygdala (known in English as the "almond") deep in the brain. Shapes your feelings and is also involved in memory.

BRAIN SURGERY FOR BEGINNERS

Chapter 2: Vital brain tests

Of course, as a brain surgeon you'll be performing operations on living patients (hopefully they'll still be alive after the operation too).

To help you plan your operations there is an amazing collection of machines that can show what's going on inside the brain before you get cutting. This is useful because you can find out which areas may be damaged or not functioning properly. Let's check them out . . .

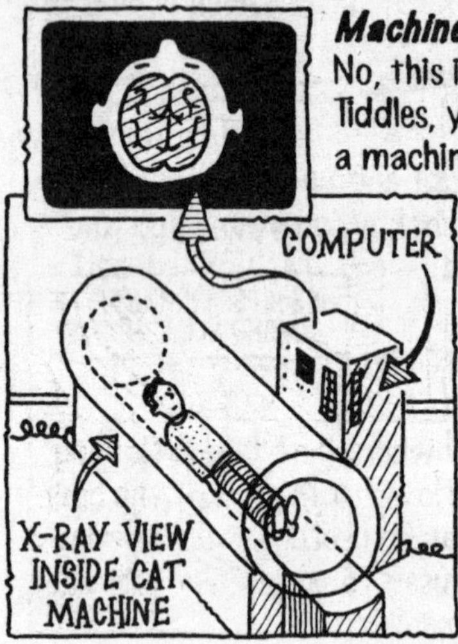

Machine 1: a CAT

No, this is nothing to do with Tiddles, your pet cat. This CAT is a machine. CAT stands for Computerized Axial Tomography (ax-e-al toe-mog-graf-ee). As a brain expert you should be able to spout this kind of jargon effortlessly. The machine sends weak X-rays through the brain and shows up the result on a computer screen.

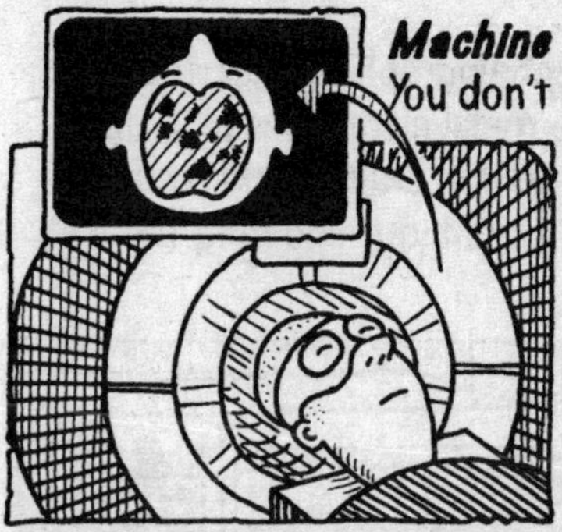

Machine 2: a PET

You don't need cat food for this PET either. It's a Positron Emission Tomography (poz-it-tron e-miss-e-on toe-mog-graf-ee) machine. Your poor old patient has to be injected with a radioactive chemical. The scanner detects what happens when the blood takes the chemical into their brain. The blood flows to the bits of the brain that are most active. So you can see what's going on and spot any areas that don't seem to be working properly.

Machine 3: an NMR

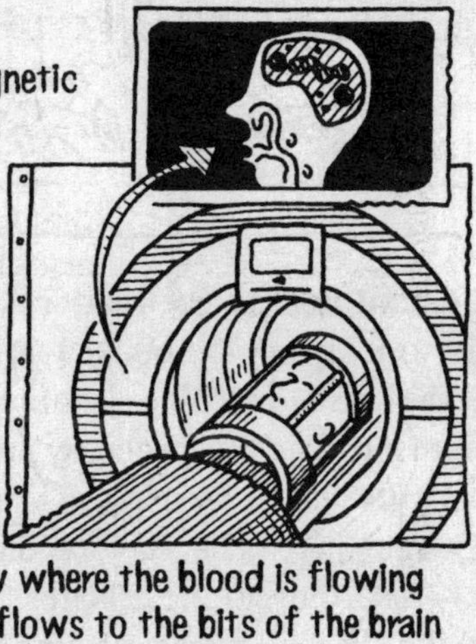

This stands for Nuclear Magnetic Resonance. This nifty device surrounds the brain with a magnetic force and bombards the blood in the brain with radio waves. The atoms (tiny bits that make up chemicals) in the blood bounce back a special type of radio wave that can be detected by the machine. The NMR scan can also show where the blood is flowing inside the brain. More blood flows to the bits of the brain that are thinking, and this can be useful for discovering which areas of the brain are used for particular jobs such as solving maths problems or talking.

Machine 4: an EEG

This stands for electroencephalograph (el-leck-tro-en-cef-falo-graf) machine. The metal electrodes pick up electrical signals given off as the brain thinks and the machine displays them as a print-out showing the signals as peaks.

Important note to the reader:

Sorry to interrupt the book. Just a quick message to say that the EEG machine is an ultra-sensitive piece of equipment. This was tested by an American doctor in the mid-1970s who wired up a lime-flavoured jelly to an EEG machine. (The flavour didn't actually affect the test.) According to the machine, the jelly was alive and thinking! In fact, it was reacting to people chatting in the next room. So make sure you read this book q-u-i-e-t-l-y.

Checking the print out

Here's what your EEG print out might show.

1 An alpha rhythm. This means the brain's thinking in a dreamy kind of way.

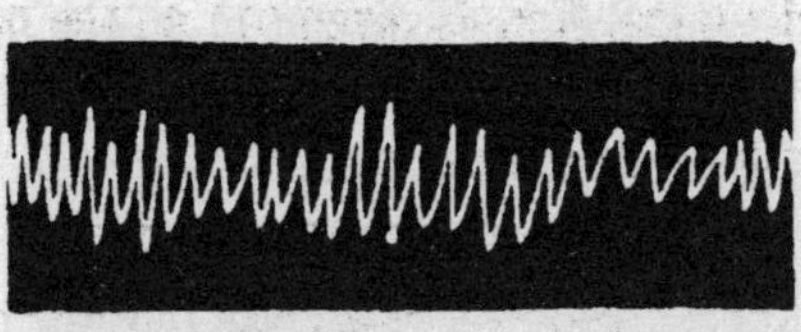

2 Beta rhythm (a bit faster). The brain is paying attention to what's going on.

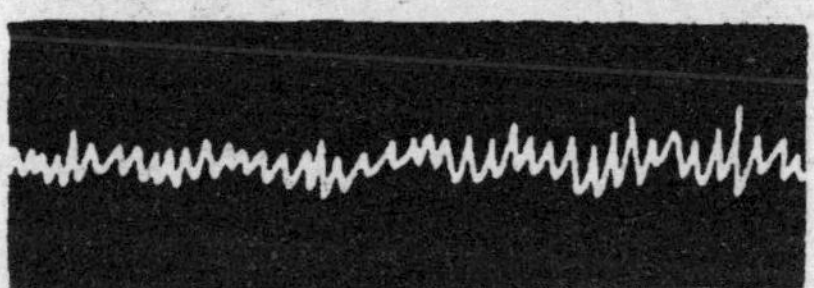

3 Theta rhythm (a bit slower). The brain is feeling sleepy.

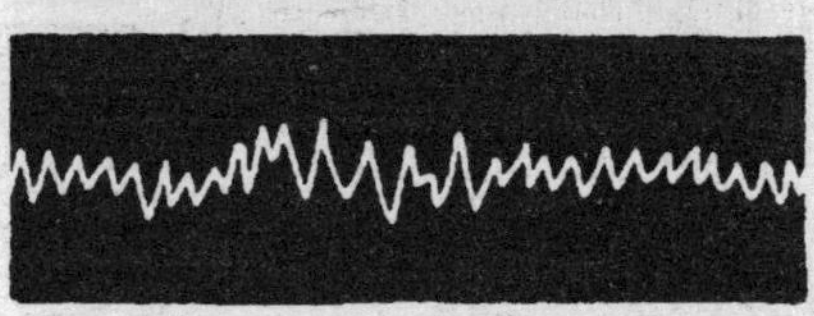

4 Delta rhythm (very slow). The brain has fallen into a deep sleep. (This has been found to be a common condition amongst children in science lessons.)

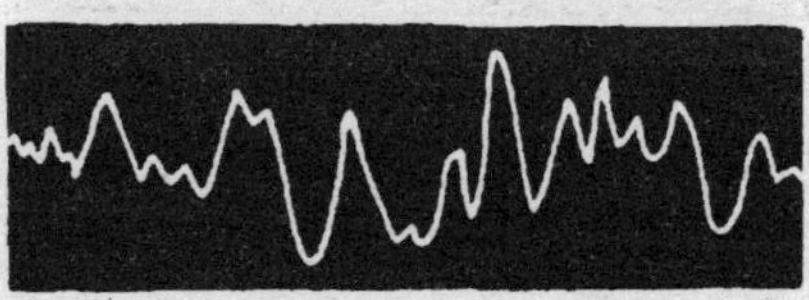

If the line is completely flat you should check that your patient is still alive. A flat line normally means the patient is dead!

Bet you never knew!

The EEG was invented by German Dr Hans Berger (1873-1941) who spent five years sticking electrodes on people's heads to measure brain activity. He even tested his invention on his children. Hans reckoned he would be able to show what his children and the other patients were thinking. He couldn't do this but he spent another five years writing up his experiments. And then ... no one took any notice.

It wasn't until British Scientist Edgar Adrian (1889-1977) showed that unusual wave patterns could be a sign of brain disease that EEG machines were used in hospitals.

BRAIN SURGERY FOR BEGINNERS

Chapter 3: Surgical tools

Congratulations, you're now almost ready for your first brain operation! First, though, you need to get familiar with a few brain surgeon's tools.

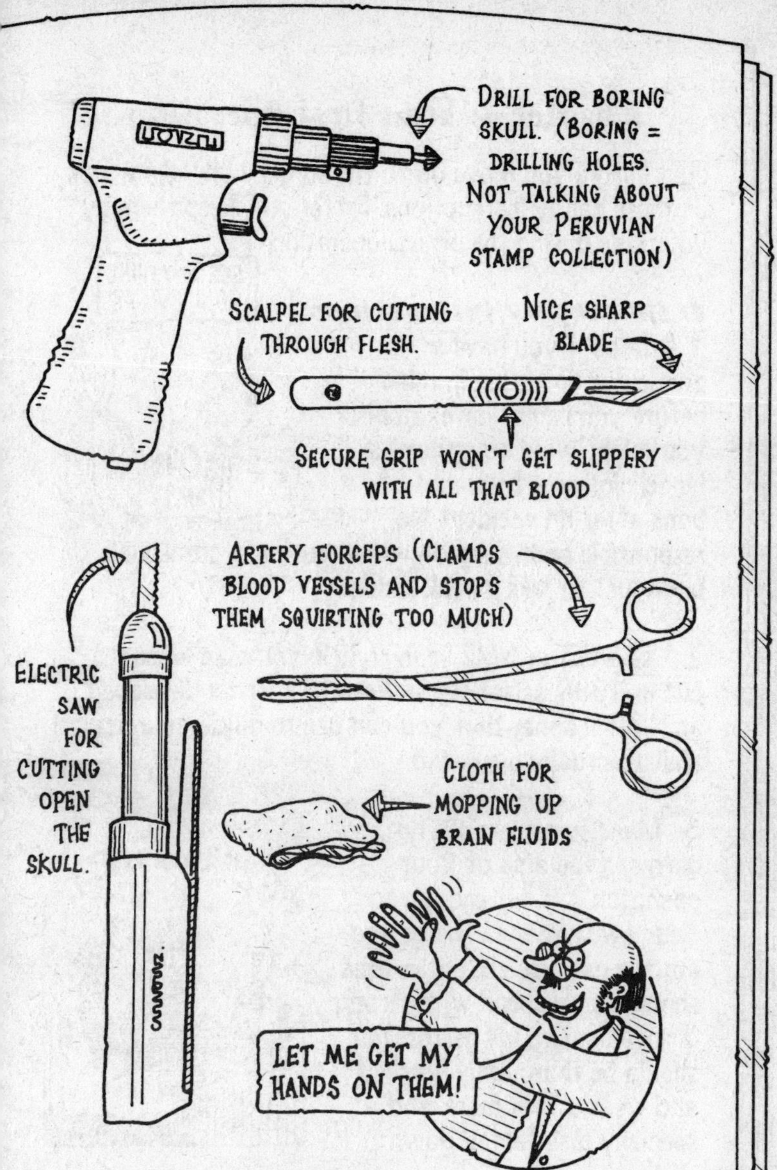
DRILL FOR BORING SKULL. (BORING = DRILLING HOLES. NOT TALKING ABOUT YOUR PERUVIAN STAMP COLLECTION)
SCALPEL FOR CUTTING THROUGH FLESH.
NICE SHARP BLADE
SECURE GRIP WON'T GET SLIPPERY WITH ALL THAT BLOOD
ARTERY FORCEPS (CLAMPS BLOOD VESSELS AND STOPS THEM SQUIRTING TOO MUCH)
ELECTRIC SAW FOR CUTTING OPEN THE SKULL.
CLOTH FOR MOPPING UP BRAIN FLUIDS
LET ME GET MY HANDS ON THEM!

Chapter 4: Your first operation

Just before you move on to the surgery bit, take a look at these handy instructions. Better still, keep them by your side during the actual operation.

Brain surgery instructions

1 It helps if you have a particular operation in mind before you begin. For example you might want to remove a blood clot or a fragment of bone after an accident. No responsible brain surgeon would cut open someone's brain just to take a peek inside.

2 Use a PET or NMR scan to help you plan where to cut. In 1998, scientists at Toronto Hospital developed an NMR scanner that you can use to guide your scalpel whilst actually operating.

3 Make sure there are no germs in the area of your operation. It's not enough to clear away the tea things and put the cat out. The entire area should be scrubbed with strong disinfectant to kill germs. You should be thoroughly washed and wear a face mask and a specially disinfected gown.

4 Draw a line on the patient's head to show where you intend to cut. Oops! Nearly forgot. The patient's head should be shaven to prevent bits of hair getting mixed in with their brain.

5 To get at the brain you need to remove a bit of skull. First drill some holes in the skull. (You'll have to concentrate. One slip and you might drill through the brain.)

6 Next, saw between the holes and lift up a flap of skull and meninges (men-in-gees) – the protective layers under the skull. As you lift the meninges you may hear a *sclurping* noise as the clear fluid that surrounds the brain bubbles out.

7 If everything goes according to plan the brain should be pulsing as the blood squirts through its blood vessels.

8 Now to begin your brilliant brain operation...

HORRIBLE HEALTH WARNING!

Stop! Don't do anything until you've read the next page!

Important and very urgent announcement:

In order to do brain surgery properly you have to study in medical school for at least seven years. You didn't really think you'd be allowed to do brain surgery at your age did you? Sorry to disappoint you. You'd better stick everything back together and be grateful. Why? Because practising brain surgery without proper training could land you in serious legal trouble and result in your pocket money being stopped for 33,000,000 years. Sorry!

Still, there's lots more fascinating things to find out about the brain. For example, there are the amazing ways in which it manages to find out what's going on around you. These are called "senses". So here's a challenge for your brain – has it got the sense to read the next chapter? Better find out!

STARTLING SENSES

Without senses life would be like sitting in a dark cupboard. Yep, even more boring than a science lesson. But thanks to your brain you are bombarded with startling sights and sounds and smells. It's lucky you've got strong nerves to cope with it all. After all, your senses won't work without nerves...

Bulging fact file

NAME: Nerves

BASIC FACTS: **1** A network of nerves spreads from your brain and your spinal cord to reach every nook and cranny of your body. Their job is to carry signals from your senses to your brain and orders from your brain to get those lazy muscles moving.

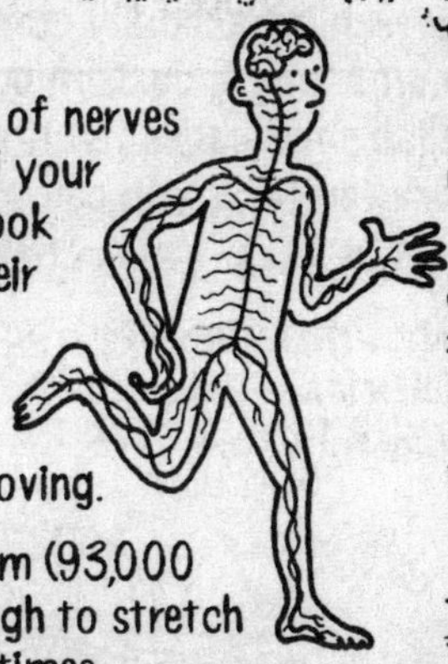

2 In all you have 150,000 km (93,000 miles) of nerves. That's enough to stretch round the Earth nearly four times.

3 An average-sized nerve is made up of thousands of neurons.

DISGUSTING DETAILS: **1** Your nerves are always keyed up and ready for action. In fact, when they send a signal they actually stop working! (See next page for details.)

2 So it's more relaxing for your nerves when you do something than when you laze around all day doing nothing!

Your nerves are a bit like an amazing telephone system that takes messages all around your body. Just imagine they were a phone system – the manual would make fascinating reading...

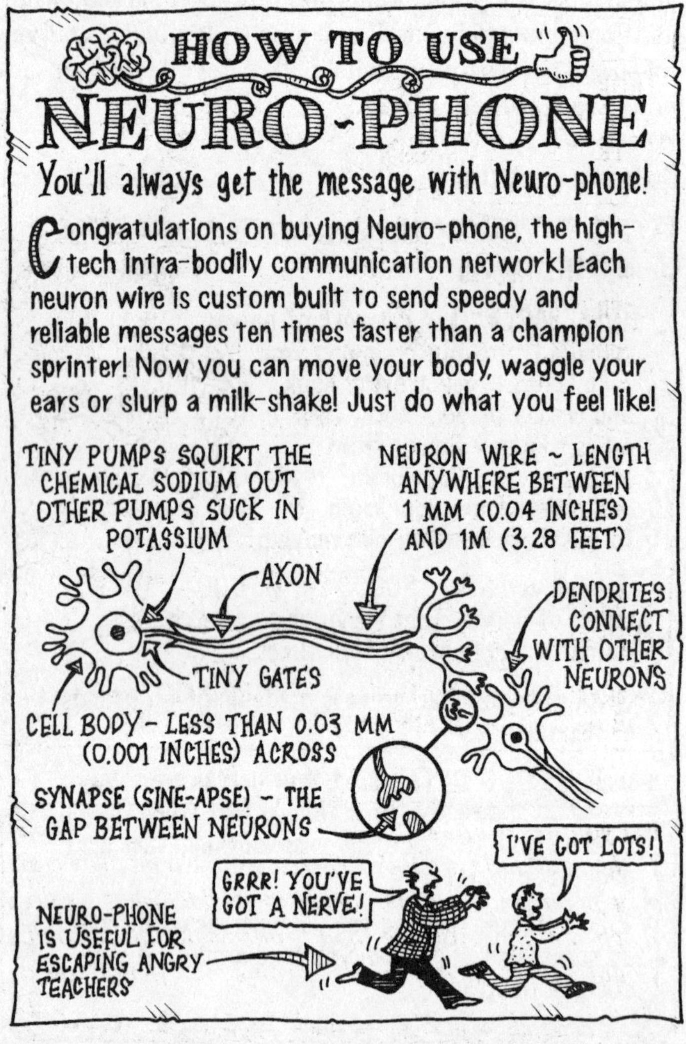

Bet you never knew!

1 Nerve signals are F-A-S-T. Tests show a monkey can spot a banana, use its cortex to decide what to do, reach out and grab the food – all inside one second. Could you move any faster if someone offered you a choccie?

2 Remember that a science test only produces enough electrical activity in your brain to light a dim light bulb? (See page 325 if you don't.) Well, what do you have to do to light up a Christmas tree? The answer is, even when you're doing nothing there's enough electrical nerve energy in your nervous little body for the job. After all there are no fewer than 100 billion neurons in your body.

Sensational senses

Thanks to your sensational senses you can appreciate the true beauty of the world. A lovely blue cloudless sky, the delicious aroma of new-baked pizza and the soft smooth touch of velvet...

Let's take a closer look at these marvellous abilities...

Bulging brain expressions

Some psychologists are chatting over dinner...

Are these weird types of food?

Answer: No. These are problems caused by blows on the head.
Anosmia = you can't smell anything.
Parosmia = all food tastes disgusting. Of course the scientists might have been eating a school dinner. Then their food would have tasted *really* horrible!

Bet you never knew!
The sense of taste gets weaker as we grow older. At present scientists don't understand why this happens, but you can observe the effects any lunchtime. Many children can't stand the vile flavour of school dinners but elderly teachers happily relish the revolting recipes.

Dare you discover ... a touch of the ridiculous?

All you need is:
Your body
Clothes (don't forget to put some on your body)

All you do is:
1 Nothing. If only all science experiments were this easy!
2 Concentrate on trying to feel the clothes you are wearing against your skin. (Don't touch them with your hands.)

What do you notice?
a) I can't feel anything except my itchy socks.
b) I can feel the material against my skin. Funny I never noticed it before.
c) This experiment has given me a headache.

Answer: b) If your nerves feel a constant sensation like your clothes they get used to it and stop firing. That's why you don't feel your clothes and you may forget you're wearing any. Hopefully, you should notice if you're not wearing any.

If **c)** stop concentrating so hard and if **a)** consider the possibility that you're only wearing your socks. This could be a sight for sore eyes, and talking about vision...

Seeing is believing

You might think that you see with your eyes. But your eyeballs simply act like cameras and pick up light patterns from the outside world. It's the brain that makes sense of this information. Sounds complicated? Well, fortunately, the Neuro-phone people have logged the neuron calls involved so you can make sense of it all.

Take a look at this...

You see through your eyeballs. An image of the scene falls on the retina and the one million neurons in your optic nerve take the image in the form of nerve pulses to your brain. Now read on...

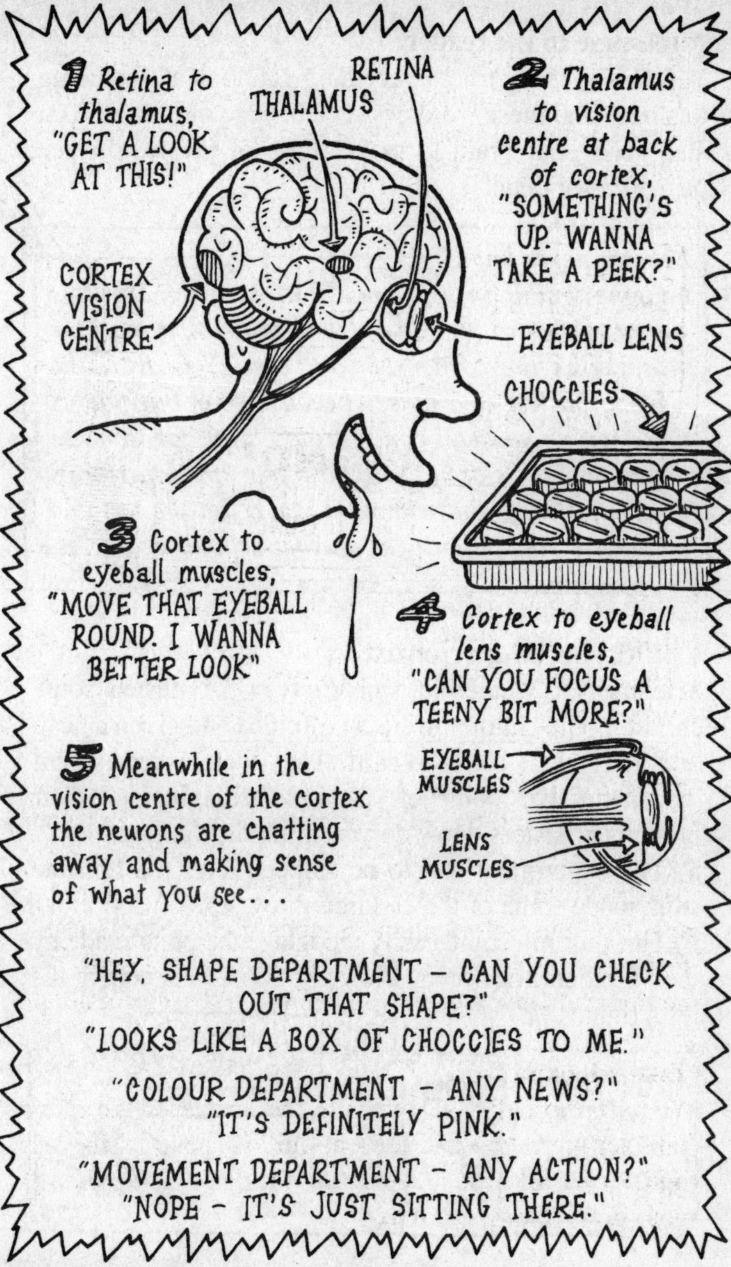
1 Retina to thalamus, "GET A LOOK AT THIS!"
RETINA
THALAMUS
2 Thalamus to vision centre at back of cortex, "SOMETHING'S UP. WANNA TAKE A PEEK?"
CORTEX VISION CENTRE
EYEBALL LENS
CHOCCIES
3 Cortex to eyeball muscles, "MOVE THAT EYEBALL ROUND. I WANNA BETTER LOOK"
4 Cortex to eyeball lens muscles, "CAN YOU FOCUS A TEENY BIT MORE?"
5 Meanwhile in the vision centre of the cortex the neurons are chatting away and making sense of what you see...
EYEBALL MUSCLES
LENS MUSCLES
"HEY, SHAPE DEPARTMENT – CAN YOU CHECK OUT THAT SHAPE?"
"LOOKS LIKE A BOX OF CHOCCIES TO ME."
"COLOUR DEPARTMENT – ANY NEWS?"
"IT'S DEFINITELY PINK."
"MOVEMENT DEPARTMENT – ANY ACTION?"
"NOPE – IT'S JUST SITTING THERE."

A message to the reader:
Yep, this is really true. Everything you look at, including this page and these words, is seen *inside* your brain. You also need your brain to make sense of the words (see page 393 for details).

Bet you never knew!
Imagine you're in a science test. At times like this you're concentrating so hard your brain blots out your vision from the corner of your eyes. You also stop hearing background noises because your brain blots these out so you can concentrate on the job you are doing. Scientists aren't sure how your brain performs this useful trick. But without it you'd fail the test and there'd be a terrible BLOT on your school record.

Could you be a scientist?

Scientists at Vanderbilt University, USA, tested some children. The children were blindfolded and given a heap of smelly old T-shirts to sniff. They were asked to spot the distinctive pong of T-shirts belonging to their brothers or sisters. How do you think they got on?

a) The experiment had to be stopped after the horrible stink made some of the children throw up.

b) The children could easily recognize the pong made by their brothers and sisters. They got over 75 per cent of the tests right.

c) The children found it impossible to identify the smell made by their brothers and sisters.

Answer: b) And in tests 16 out of 18 parents could identify their children by their smell. Your sense of smell is better than you may imagine. If you lie on the floor you can actually detect the cheesy pong where someone in a dirty sock walked on the floorboards.

(No need to test this remarkable skill just now.) And you can identify over 10,000 different whiffs and stinks. (Heaven nose how you do it.)

Bringing it all together

Of course in everyday life your brain uses all your senses together to build up a picture of what's going on outside your head. Maybe you'd like to discover how it all slots together. Your mission, should you choose to accept it is to ... (BIG ROLL OF DRUMS HERE) ... eat a chocolate.

(Yep, but it's not as simple it sounds.) Before we start let's listen into those Neuro-phone messages and get an idea of what's involved.

Just a bite

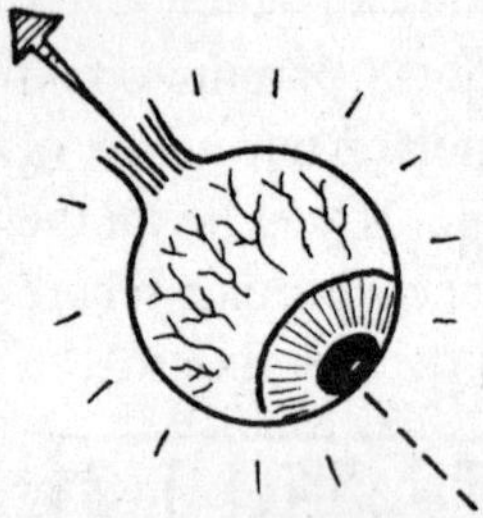

Retina to vision centre and brain stem, "I CAN'T TAKE MY EYES OFF THOSE CHOCOLATES."

Brain stem to cortex, "THERE'S SOMETHING INTERESTING AHEAD. WANNA CHECK IT OUT?"

Cortex to fingers and arms, "EXTEND FINGERS AND PICK UP A CHOCOLATE. HOW DOES IT FEEL?"

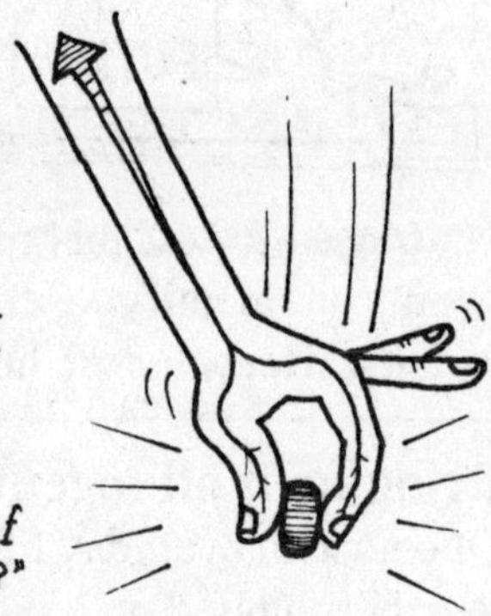

Finger-touch receptors to thalamus, "TELL THE CORTEX IT'S LOVELY AND COOL AND SMOOTH AND VELVETY."

Thalamus to sensory area of cortex, "YOU GOT ALL THAT?"

Ears to medulla, "HEY, LISTEN TO THAT LOVELY RUSTLE IN THE BOX."

Medulla to thalamus, "PSST! TELL THE CORTEX TO GET A LOAD OF THIS."

Nose to thalamus, "WOW! WHAT A LOVELY CHOCOLATEY WHIFF – TELL THE CORTEX TO GET A SNIFF OF THIS."

Tongue to cortex, "I'M READY TO SWALLOW. THERE'S LOADS OF SPIT DOWN HERE!"

A note to the reader:
Drooling spit at the sight of a choccie is a reflex (see page 372), triggered by nerves leading from the brain to your gooey saliva glands. Are you starting to drool too? If so, try not to dribble on the nice clean page.

Another note to the reader:
So do you fancy trying this mission for yourself? Chances are you've already had quite a bit of practice.

But if you feel like checking whether your brain can handle all these senses it's worth asking your parents for chocolates. You could explain that you need an extra large box in order to get this vital science experiment absolutely right. And if your parents fall for that, you might as well ask for a day out at a theme park, too.

So how did you get on...?

a) I ate the chocolate so fast I didn't have a chance to follow the instructions.

b) I got muddled up with the instructions and bit my tongue by mistake. Ouch!

c) It was great and all my senses and brain bits worked perfectly.

(If you ticked **a**): oh dear, that's tough, better practise on another choccie. If **b**): you might as well go on to the next section. Because it's a bit of a PAIN too.)

Putting up with pain

Pain is the worst thing you can sense. But you know all about pain already...

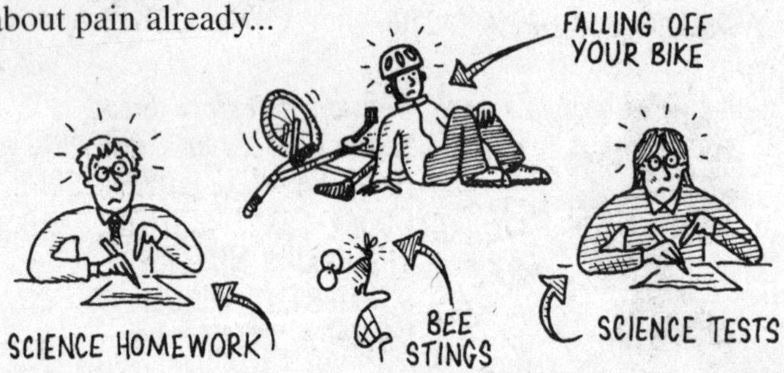

Dare you discover ... how to put up with pain?

Note to the reader:

This experiment has been banned on the grounds that it's far too cruel. Here are a few facts instead.

A few painful facts

1 Pain is a big trick played by your bulging brain on the rest of your body. Imagine you stub your toe on a stone or even the cat.

You might think you feel the resulting pain in your big toe. But you actually experience the pain in your brain because that's where the nerve signal goes.

2 Your body is crowded with countless thousands of pain receptors. Obviously any damage to the body is red-hot urgent news for the brain – there may be more damage just about to occur so the pain receptors try to let the brain know what's going on NOW.

3 The crushed pain receptors let in a chemical released from the injured areas. This kick starts a nerve signal that blasts up to your brain.

4 The deeper the pain receptors the less sensitive they are – that's why a really bad injury can hurt less than a little scratch. Pain deep in the body often feels like a dull miserable ache.

5 Different pain signals move at different speeds. A sharp prick on your skin hits your brain at 29.9 metres (98 feet) a second. A longer pulse like a burning or aching pain moves through the neurons at a slightly more leisurely 1.98 metres (6.5 feet) a second.

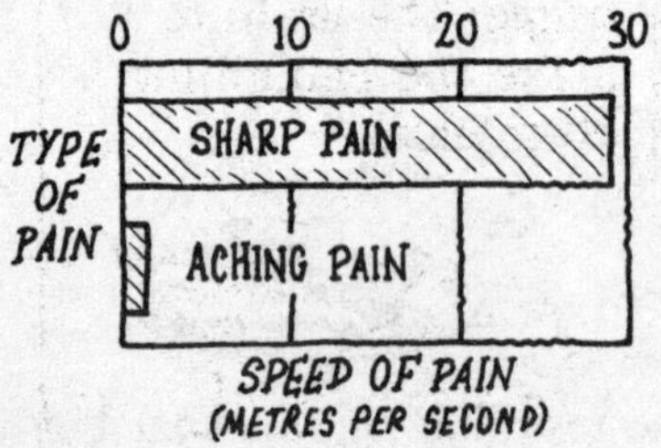

But there's much more to pain than just a horrible feeling in the brain. Here, for a change, is a bit of good news...

THE DAILY BRAIN

The paper that makes you think! Issue 3,752 . 1975

What a relief!

Scientists at Aberdeen University, Scotland, claim brains help deaden pain. Brain researchers John Hughes and Hans Kosterlitz were following a lead from neurophysiologists in Baltimore, USA. Now they reckon they've found what they were after. Previously unknown chemicals called enkephalins (en-kefa-lins) that block pain signals. Well we at *The Daily Brain* salute this great new discovery.

If we didn't have these chemicals we're sure they'd be *sorely* missed.

Daily Brain Science Correspondent Dr Alan de Mind writes..

The newly discovered chemicals may explain why taking exercise or other distractions such as a white knuckle ride or an exciting film takes your mind off pain. Presumably doing these things can trigger the brain to make the painkilling chemicals.

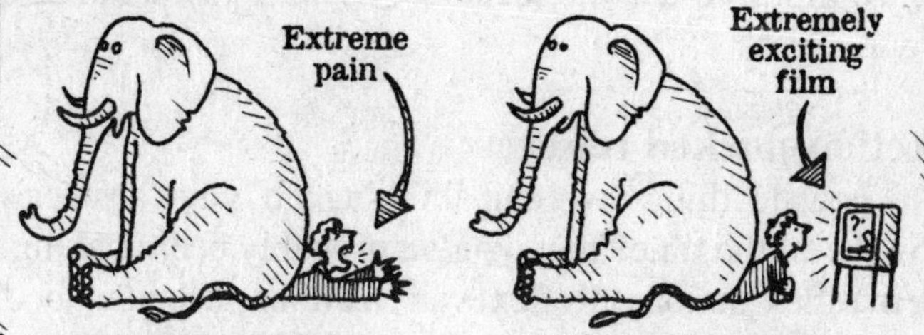

SUPPORTING WEIGHT OF ELEPHANT WITHOUT ENKEPHALINS

SUPPORTING WEIGHT OF ELEPHANT WITH ENKEPHALINS

Bet you never knew!
Another way to deaden pain is to confuse your nerves by getting them to send other signals. So if you bang your shin you could try rubbing it with your hand or a lump of ice. This gets the nerves sending more signals that swamp the pain signals.

The painful truth

Afterwards it's hard to remember exactly what pain is like. Your cruel heartless brain wants every pain you feel to seem really awful and unexpected. That way you'll do something about it. The painful truth is that pain is there so your brain can teach you a painful lesson.

You might think it would be lovely to live in a world without pain. Life would be brilliant, wouldn't it? You could wander around endlessly bumping into things, and not worrying about how much it was going to hurt. Until one day you noticed that your fingers had dropped off. Of course, if you'd felt pain in the first place you'd have got away with a nasty cut rather than no fingers on one hand. By the way, if the thought of all that blood makes you feel like throwing up at this point feel free – being sick, or vomiting to use the technical term, is just another of your...

Action-packed reflexes

Do you do things without thinking? If your answer is "yeah, all the time" then you've probably been making a few reflex actions. Reflexes are actions that your body does in response to startling signals from your senses. These are things like sneezing and coughing and dribbling that you can't stop once they start. (For this reason farting or burping are not reflexes and you've got no excuse for doing them during mealtimes.)

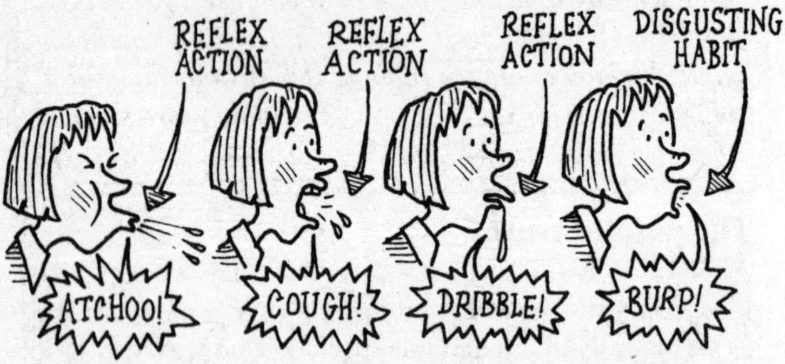

A few more facts you ought to know about reflexes

1 Your brain isn't involved in reflexes. The signals go to your spinal cord and out again in nerves that control your muscles. This saves time and means that you can whip your hand away from the hot plate of the cooker in 0.03 seconds instead of up to 0.8 seconds if your brain was consulted.

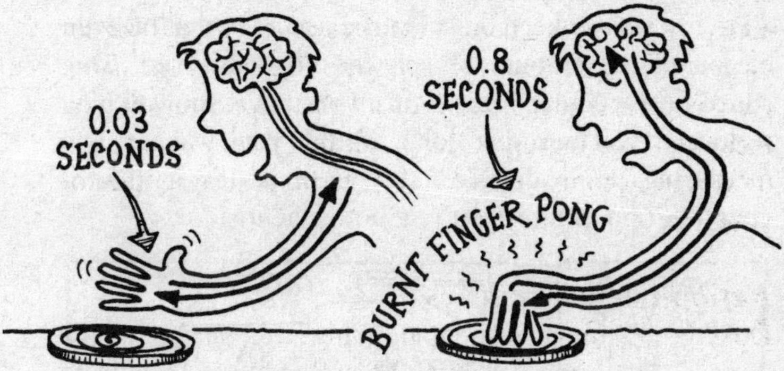

2 Some of the most important work about reflexes was carried out by Russian Ivan Pavlov (1849-1936). Pavlov was a cold unfriendly man who flew into terrible rages if anyone dared criticize him. And no, he wasn't a teacher, he was a scientist.

3 His most famous experiment was to show that you could train dogs to make reflex actions. Dogs dribble when they see food. Pavlov rang a bell every time the dogs were fed. After a while he stopped feeding the dogs but they still dribbled when he rang the bell.

4 Pavlov was so keen on scientific accuracy that he even measured the amount of spit the dogs dribbled. This added no particular value to his work but it showed how seriously he took his job. Would you want a job measuring dog's dribble? If you think it's a mouth-watering opportunity you're a born scientist.

Dare you discover ... a reflex action?

All you need is:

One dog (count first to make sure it's got four legs)

All you do is:

1 Rub the dog's back until the dog reacts.

2 Note what happens next.

What happens next?

a) The dog falls over.

b) The dog scratches its back with its hind legs. (It probably thinks your hand is an extra large flea.)

c) The dog wags its tail and sticks its tongue out and dribbles everywhere.

Answer: b) The dog often scratches its back without thinking in a reflex action – much like you sneezing. The nerves involved in the dog's reflex were discovered by British scientist Sir Charles Sherrington (1857–1952) who won the Nobel Prize for this breakthrough. I expect he was itching to tell his pals about it – ha-ha. If **a)** your dog is probably missing a leg or two.

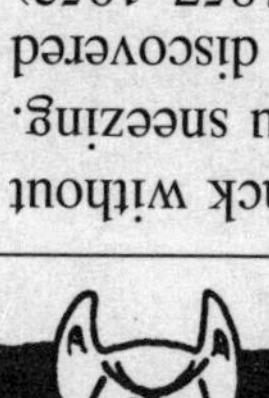

HORRIBLE HEALTH WARNING!

Don't try the above experiment with the neighbour's Rottweiler or you may never tie your own shoelaces again.

CONGRATULATIONS! You've successfully read this chapter. Now for the bad news. So far you've been looking at the easy-peasy stuff your brain gets up to. You might find the next chapter rather more mind-bending.

Yep – it's time to put your bulging brain to work.

BULGING BRAIN-WORK

Sometimes you need your bulging brain for something more intelligent than scoffing a choccie. Jobs like listening to music, and thinking and talking and reading. Oh, so you don't think they sound too difficult? Well, they are. But don't worry, by the time you've read this chapter you'll have boosted your bulging brainpower. Well, maybe – just a bit.

First sort your left from your right

Your cortex (that's the wrinkly, thinking bit of the brain, remember) is split into two halves. To understand how you use your brain you first need to know how the two halves work together. Bear in mind that one side of the cortex is stronger than the other and takes over most of the work. But which side is that? Well, the diagram below will help you sort that out. But don't forget that the left side of the cortex looks after the right side of the body and vice versa. Got all that?

Anyway, here's the diagram...

(If the teacher was left-handed these arrangements would be reversed.)

Are you ambidextrous?

Ambidextrous means that you're able to write or draw or hold a tennis racquet or play the guitar or pluck a chicken equally well with both hands.

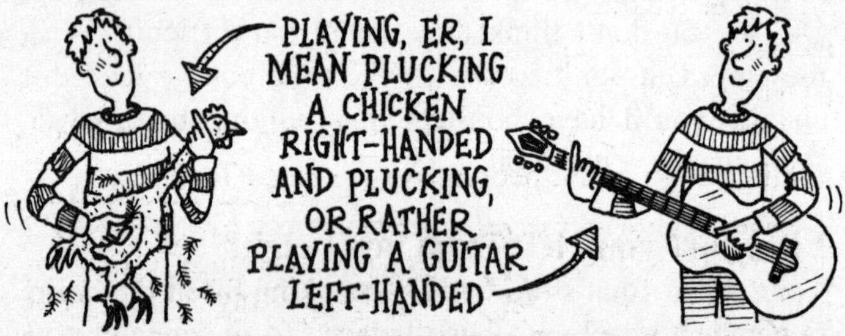

This is because neither side of the cortex is stronger than the other. Famous ambidextrous people include English artist Sir Edwin Landseer (1802-1873) who often drew a horse with his right hand and a stag with his left hand at the same time. Try it for yourself – it's much harder than it sounds.

Test your teacher

Is your teacher left-handed, right-handed or ambidextrous? Well, this teacher teasing test will certainly keep her brain fully occupied until the end of the class. By the way, if you're feeling kind you can give your teacher one clue before you start the test: all the answers are for right-handed people.

1 Are babies always...

a) Left-handed?

b) Right-handed?

c) Ambidextrous?

2 Which side of your brain do you use for working out hard maths questions?

a) The left.
b) The right.
c) Neither, I use a calculator.
3 Which side of your brain do you use for having a chat with your friends?
a) The left.
b) The right.
c) The left for chatting with friends but the right when talking to important people like the Head Teacher.

4 Which part of your brain do you use for painting a watercolour?
a) The left.
b) The right.
c) Neither, it's the cerebellum that does the work.

5 How do Japanese people differ from the usual right–left division of work within the brain?
a) They use both sides of their brains for talking.
b) Annoying insect sounds trigger brain activity on the left side of their brains instead of the right for everyone else.
c) They can talk aloud without their brains showing unusual activity.

Answers:

1 c) In babies, both halves of the cortex are equally strong. One side doesn't take over until the child is about two.

2 a) If you're right-handed you read, write and work out sums mostly using the left part of your brain. (If you're left-handed you are more likely to use the right side of your brain for these tasks.)

3 a) The left side also deals with talking aloud. The poor old right side has to spend its life listening to the left side nattering.

4 b) At least the right side of the brain gets to deal with all the enjoyable artistic jobs like making a collage or drawing.

5 b) This finding was reported by Japanese scientist Tsunoda Tadanobu. Some Japanese words sound like insect or water sounds. So the scientist suggested Japanese people listen to these sounds with the left side of their brains that normally deals with language. (Award your teacher an extra mark if they managed to explain this theory.)

Bet you never knew!

For reasons that scientists don't quite understand... You see things at the back of your cortex (not at the front, which is where your eyes are). You see things to the left in the right side of your brain.

Things to the right get seen in the left side.

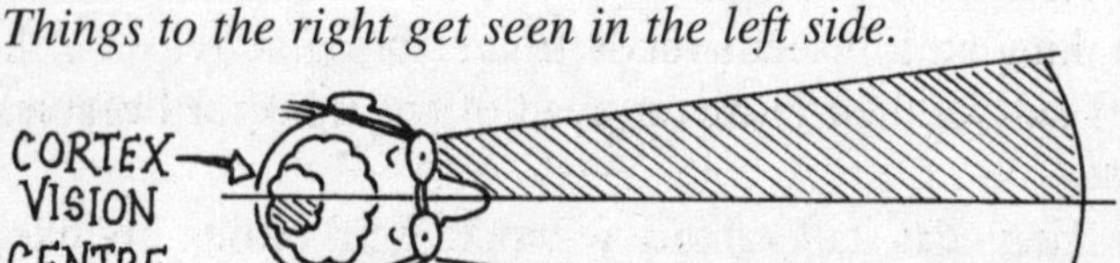

Dare you discover ... if you're left- or right-eyed?

Your left eye is controlled by the right side of your brain and vice-versa. But which side of your brain is stronger? Here's how to find out...

All you need is:

A finger (preferably one of your own)
Two eyes (these should definitely be your own)
A stationary object 1 metre away (it doesn't matter what this object is. It could be a picture, the wallpaper or even a dead wombat)
A ruler

All you do is:

1 Stick your finger 12 cm (5 inches) in front of your nose.
2 Focus your eyes on the stationary object. The finger should appear out of focus. Note the position of the finger.
3 Now wink each of your eyes in turn.

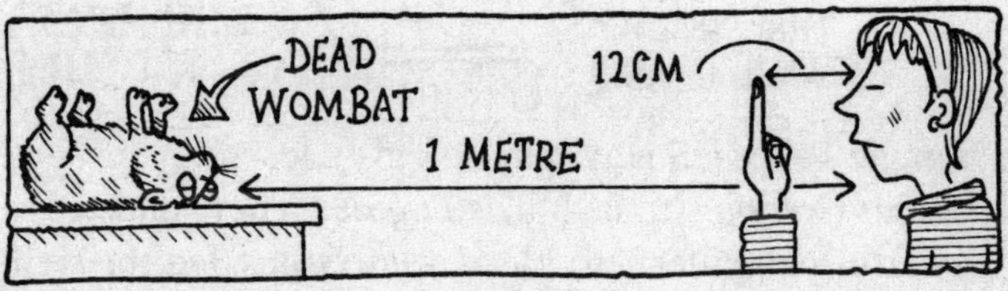

What do you notice?

a) Nothing and people started asking me whom I was winking at. It was all very embarrassing.
b) Each time I winked an eye the finger seemed to jump sideways.
c) The finger seemed to stay where it was when I winked one eye and jump sideways when I winked the other.

Answer: c) The finger didn't appear to move when you looked at it through your dominant eye. This is because with both eyes open you see mostly through that eye. Right-handed people usually have a dominant right eye and so they do most of their seeing in the left-hand side of their brains. OK, got all that? Here's a chance to rest your eyes for a bit and listen to some music.

Could you be a scientist?

When you listen to music the following areas of your brain are involved...

In the 1970s US neurophysiologists Joseph Bogen and Harold Gordon studied these areas. They injected a powerful painkiller into blood vessels that fed the right side of their patients' brains. This put the right side of the brains to sleep for a while. When the patients tried to sing using only the left sides of their brain what did they sound like?

a) They sang beautifully, like trained opera singers.
b) They could open their mouths but no sound came out.
c) They sounded like a calf bellowing.

Answer: c) Without the help of the right side of their cortex the singers couldn't produce a tune. Mind you, some people seem to have this problem with both sides of their brain in working order.

Teacher's tea-break teaser

A note to the reader:

You try this teaser at your own risk, OK? Don't blame me if you get expelled. To do it all you have to do is sing loudly outside the staff room...

Answer: Words are controlled by the left side of your brain and tunes by the right. When you sing it's hard for your cortex to cope with two sets of information at the same time. I mean – just think, you have to access your memory centres to remember what the words and notes actually sound like. Very musical people actually grow extra neurons in the areas of the right cortex that deal with sound and hearing. OK, got all that? No? Why not ask your brain to chew it over...

Think for yourself (it's not that easy)

1 Thinking is the way that your brain makes sense of the world and organizes the information it gets from your senses. Scientists believe that thinking is a wave of brain activity that spreads as neurons fire signals at each other. Does that get you thinking?

2 The brain has different areas for different jobs like talking or sniffing things, remember. But neurons all over the cortex are involved in thinking and the active areas vary according to what you're doing. Your level of concentration or even your feelings can affect the pattern of brain activity.

3 Brain neurons fire most of the time and scientists think that this could mean your brain is vaguely mulling over past memories. The increased activity caused by thinking might be due to your brain drawing on memories to build up a particular thought.

4 When you do two different things at once (see page 386) each half of your brain has separate thoughts. Is that a good thing? Well, maybe you're in two minds about it.

Bet you never knew!

There is no limit to the number of thoughts you can have. So you don't believe me? Well, read on. Your brain has billions of nerve cells, remember that bit? If you look at a neuron magnified 10,000 times it appears like a tiny tree with over 5,000 branches.

Scientists think there are more than 100,000,000,000 that's ONE HUNDRED BILLION brain synapses. (These are the gaps between neurons, remember.) And scientists believe a thought can travel through these synapses in ANY order. So there may be more possible routes for a thought than atoms in the entire universe. And that means that there's NO LIMIT to the thinking power of your brain.

WOW! That really was something to think about. But oddly enough, although your brain is unbelievably powerful it finds doing several things at once a bit of a strain...

Could you be a scientist?

Some psychologists gave two students a brain-teasing task.

How do you think the students got on?

a) They were useless. The brain simply can't manage to read, talk, listen and write all at the same time.

b) The students found themselves writing the story and repeating out loud the lists the scientists were reading to them.

c) Although the students started off slowly and made mistakes they soon learnt how to do the tasks at the same time.

Answer: c) The brain can be trained to do different things at once. The part that helps you to do this is the cerebellum. And this explains how your hairdresser can cut your hair and chat at the same time without snipping your ears off.

And speaking of talking or talking about speaking the next bit of this chapter will really get your tongue wagging.

Speak for yourself

Try listening to yourself talking and you'll realize that speech is full of hesitation – er ... (sorry, bit of a hesitation there), repetition and mistakes. Yep – speaking is one of the hardest things your brain gets up to. In order to talk properly you've got to...

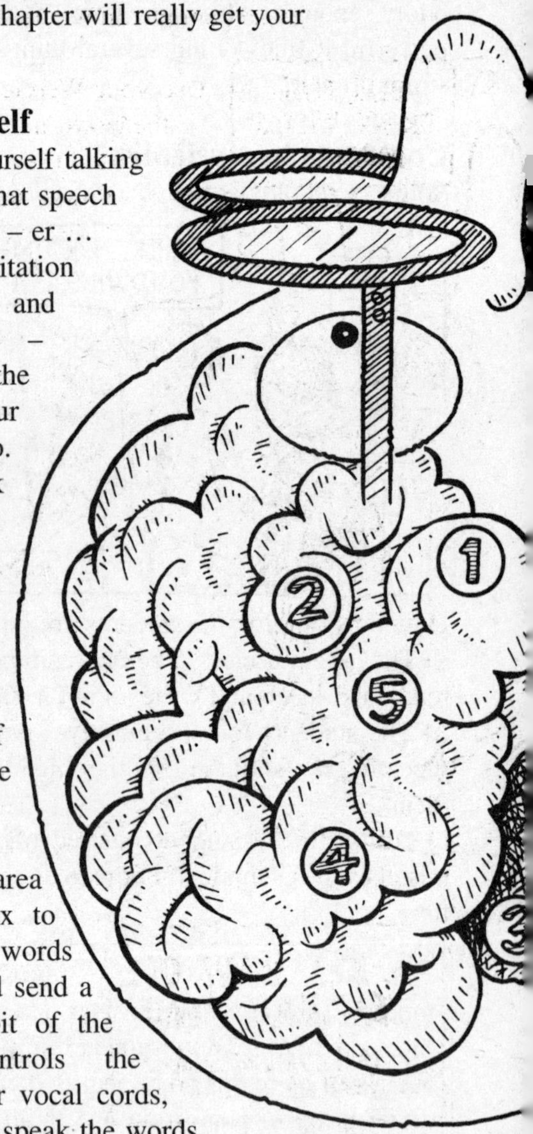

Access your memory (**1**) for the correct words and your memory of how to pronounce them.

Use the Broca's area (**2**) of your cortex to pronounce the words correctly. It should send a message to the bit of the cortex that controls the movement of your vocal cords, tongue and lips to speak the words.

You will need your cerebellum (**3**) to co-ordinate all these complex movements.

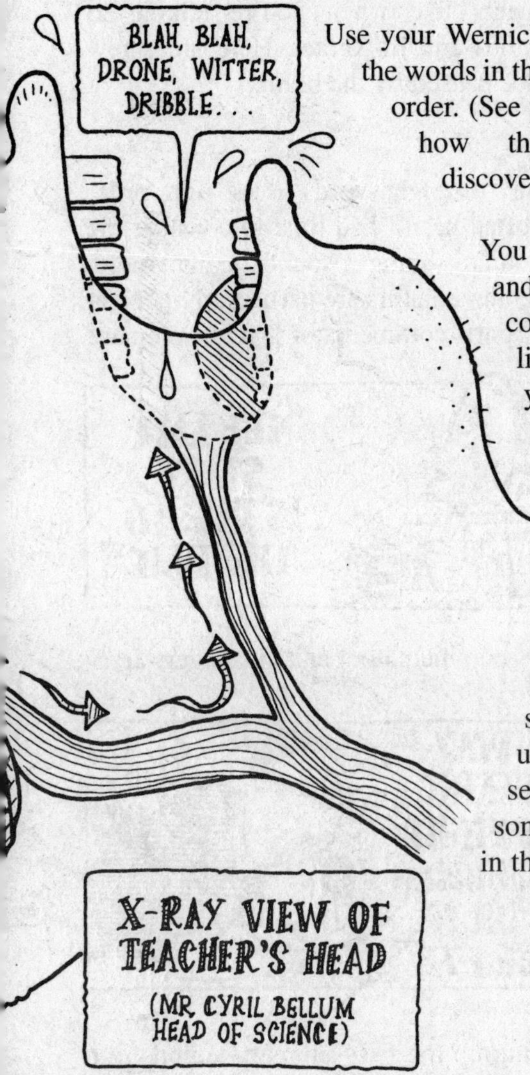

Use your Wernicke's area (**4**) to put the words in the right grammatical order. (See page 21 for info on how these areas were discovered.)

You will need your ears and the part of the cortex that deals with listen-ing (**5**) to hear your words and the rest of your cortex to check they make sense.

It's (not) that easy! Yet amazingly scientists have found that a good speaker can speak up to three words a second even when someone is mumbling in their ear.

Unspeakable speech problems

But, of course, things can still go wrong. Usually at embarrassing moments like when you're talking to someone really famous and important. Here are a few problems that may be caused by the brain...

1 Stupid sayings

This is when you say the right words in the right order but because your cortex hasn't had time to consider the meaning of what you are saying it sounds really stupid. Fast talking sports commentators are particularly good at this. Here's British sports commentator David Coleman:

And US baseball commentator and manager Jerry Coleman:

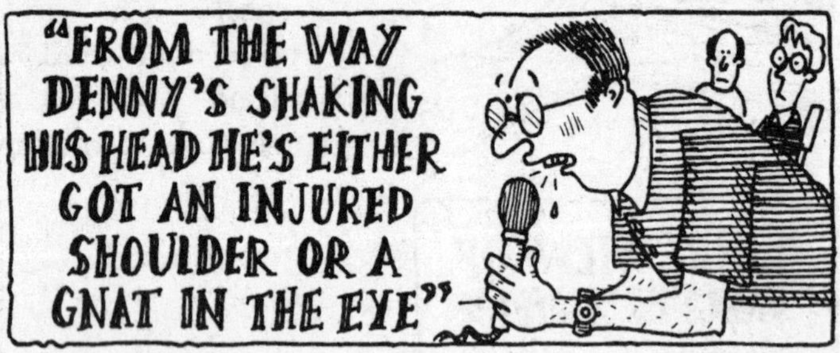

2 Spoonerisms

This means muddling up the first letters or sounds in a series of words. For example, instead of saying, "I have a half-formed wish in my mind," you might accidentally say, "

Usually you wouldn't realize you had made a mistake. It's most likely caused by a fault in the Broca's area (that's the bit of the cortex that deals with speaking words, remember?). Spoonerisms are named after British clergyman Dean William Spooner (1844-1930) who made rather a lot of them.

Bet you never knew!

1 *About one in a hundred children suffer from stammering. Stammering is jerky, hesitant speech in which the first sounds of some words are often repeated. Sufferers report that they know what they want to say but they can't say it.*

2 *Scientists aren't quite sure what causes stammering but it seems to affect boys more than girls and it seems* *to be made worse by worry. It's probably linked to a problem in the Broca's area.*

3 *In the Middle Ages the problem was thought to be due to the tongue not working properly and useless cures were tried such as burning the tongue with a hot iron.*

4 *Nowadays stammering can be overcome by helping the sufferer to feel more relaxed when talking. Techniques used include learning to speak more slowly and to begin words with a more gentle movement of the lips and tongue.*

Bulging brain expressions

Two psychologists are chatting...

Maybe you could ask this LAD to help with your homework?

Answer: Possibly. Some psychologists believe part of the brain can grasp grammar without being taught. They call this area a Language Acquisition Device or LAD for short. So who knows – maybe your LAD is already helping you, and without it learning new words or even a new language would be much harder.

A whole new language

Sometime in your school career you will have to learn a foreign language. There are about 5,000 languages in the world and they use a huge range of sounds.

For example, some languages in Southern Africa such as Xhosa and Zulu include unusual clicking sounds. Well, whatever languages you learn, once you've learnt to speak the words you then have to learn how to read them. And by some eerie coincidence that's what you're doing right now.

Read all about it

OK, so how are you getting on reading this book? Finding it easy or having a bit of bother with some of the incomprehensible inapprehensible numinous words...

Go on, have a go at remembering them – they're numinous words for bamboozling science teachers.

Scientists reckon that children learn about ten new words a day at school – but that's not such a bad thing because everywhere you look there are written words.

A grown-up who reads a daily paper might get through about 100,000 words every week. This includes all the words they might read in an office job, road signs and even the back of cornflakes packets.

Riveting reading

Reading is great. You can settle down with a good book and forget about the rest of the world. But you won't even reach the end of this sentence without the help of your brain. Here's your chance to discover what your brain is up to when you read. Simply listen in to some more of those fascinating Neuro-phone calls...

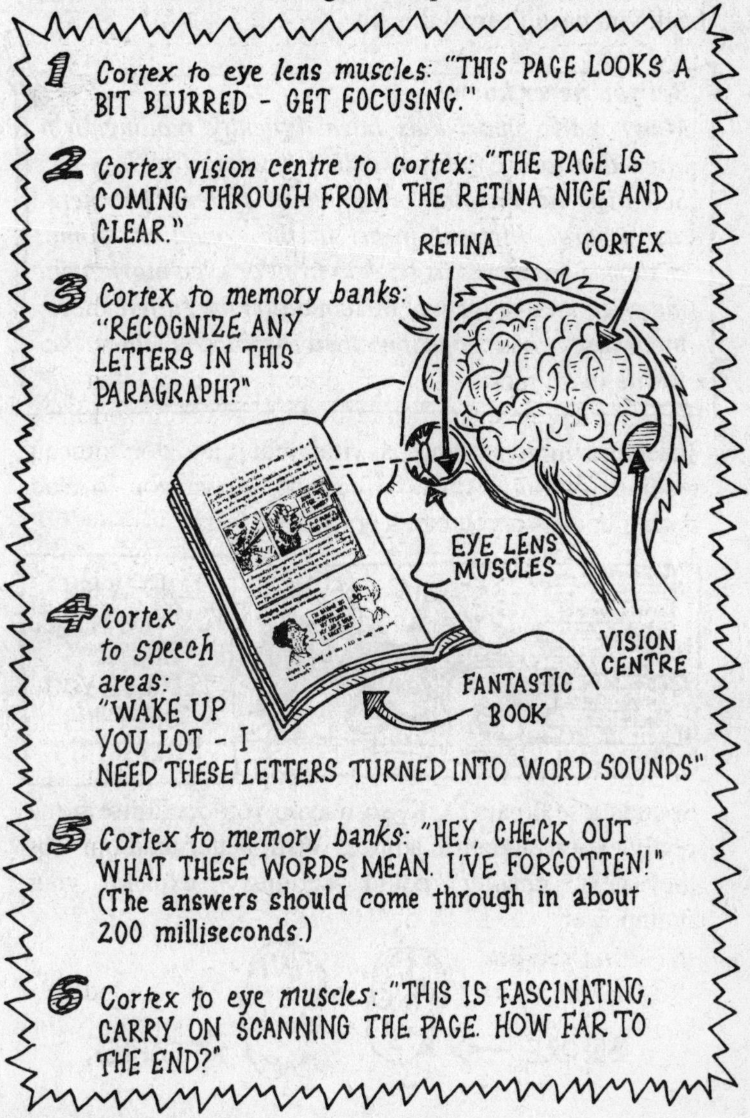

A note to the reader:
Now ask your brain to move your eyes to the next chunk of text. This should take 30 milliseconds. Hey! Come back you haven't read this bit...

Bet you never knew!
Many really smart kids have difficulty reading. It's often due to a condition called dyslexia (dis-lexy-a). Scientists can't explain what causes dyslexia but there are several different forms of the condition. Some dyslexics see words as back to front or even moving on the page. In one form of the condition the sufferer sees the words on a page but their brain can't turn the words into sounds.

Teachers think reading is vital, but they don't mean reading for fun – oh no. Teachers expect you to read boring books so you can learn lots of facts.

Sounds a real pain? OK, so maybe you could use some really expert scientific advice? Well, better read on, 'cos the next chapter could seriously expand your brainpower...

LOATHSOME LEARNING

Do you find learning fun? Do you tumble out of bed shouting…

Or do you crawl out of bed thinking...

Well, cheer up! Learning is one of the most vital tasks of your bulging brain and it CAN be fun – but only if you've got something interesting to learn. Like now – so read on.

NAME: Learning

BASIC FACTS: Here's how you learn . . .

1 Someone tells you something.

2 You remember it.

3 You use this information to help you in whatever you are doing.

DISGUSTING DETAILS: Some psychologists believe that learning gets harder over the age of 25. This could be because the memory starts to weaken. But other scientists claim that learning gets easier as you get older. So why don't they send grown-ups back to school?

A few facts to learn (and make sure you do)

1 You learn things all the time – not just in school. You learn whenever you notice anything new or try out a new skill.

2 Learning can be nice or nasty:

NICE THINGS TO LEARN: CHOCOLATE ICE-CREAM TASTES YUMMY.

NASTY THING TO LEARN: EAT TOO MUCH AND YOU'LL WANT TO THROW UP.

3 Most people learn by trial and error. Remember learning to ride a bike. But once you've learnt something you can do it effortlessly and without thinking. Like riding that bike.

Teacher's tea-break teaser

Put a fly in your teacher's morning cuppa with this tricky teaser. And remember, if your teacher doesn't believe you – this fact is TRUE. Tap gently on the staffroom door. When it opens, smile brightly and enquire...

Answer: Yes, in the 1960s US psychologist Burrhus F. Skinner invented a teaching machine called a didak. The machine showed a sentence and you had to complete it. If you got the answer right you got a chance to answer harder questions. Oh goodee! THE GOOD NEWS: The machine never told you off. THE BAD NEWS: It couldn't answer your questions and didn't know how to chat.

Bet you never knew!

It doesn't matter whether they have real teachers or machines to help them – some kids have trouble learning. There are loads of possible reasons for this. Sometimes the difficulties are caused by dyslexia or an eye problem so the child can't read easily. More often the child isn't interested in the lessons. Or perhaps the lessons require skills such as speaking or writing that the child isn't good at. Oddly enough one psychologist who studied how the brain learns suffered learning difficulties as a lad...

Horrible Science Hall of Fame

John B. Watson (1878-1958) Nationality: American

As a boy John B. Watson had a problem with learning. Maybe that's why he was for ever getting into trouble, starting fights and terrorizing his home town in South Carolina, USA.

As he grew older John got mixed up in crime. But when he turned 16 he had a sudden change of heart and started to study really hard at home. He had to study really hard because he had decided to go to university and become a scientist.

But at university John continued to find learning difficult. He couldn't understand his teachers and their boring lectures (sound familiar?).

But he did become fascinated by how rats learn things. Here's what Watson's notebook may have looked like...

The Great Rat Experiment

Today's the BIG day!!! I'm planning to find out if rats can learn from a nasty experience. I've been working hard all week building a three metre long alley for the tests – I call it the "rat-run".

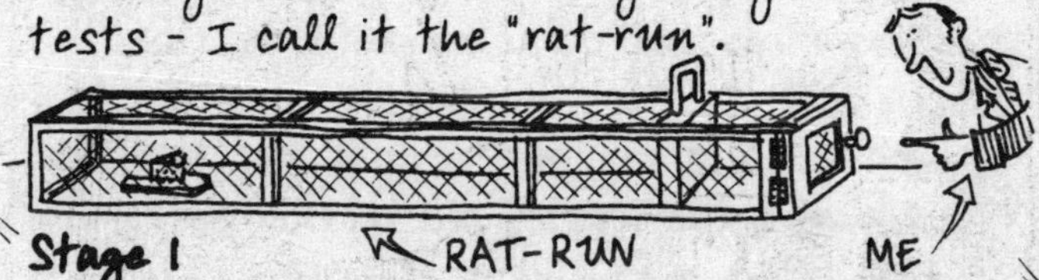

Stage 1

Now to try it out. Will the rat do the obvious and go and grab the food? YES! YES! YES! ...

The rat runs down the rat-run and grabs the food. Atta boy! This proves that learning happens when you give a rat something new – like the food. This changes the rat's behaviour. Now to test my idea a bit further.

NEXT DAY Stage 2

I've blocked off the rat-run with a thick glass barrier. Will the rat still go down it? Here goes...

Yes – like a streak of lightning and bumped his little nosy on the barrier. Oh dear, poor old ratty. If I'm right the new information about the barrier will change the rat's behaviour – let me see...

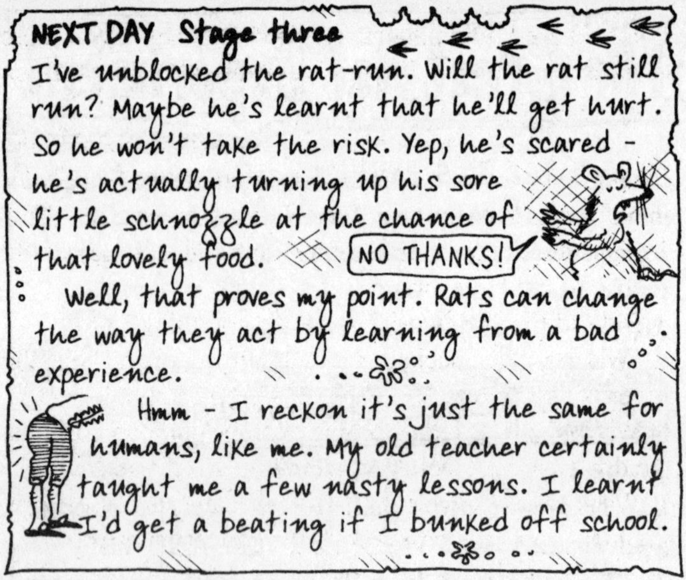

Watson's experiments inspired a whole new movement of psychologists called behaviourists who believed that you could help rats – or humans – learn with rewards or punishments. But although Watson was certain that you could learn about human behaviour from studying rats there were squeaks of protest from other scientists when he compared humans to rats...

Eventually Watson resigned his university job to go into advertising. Here he put his ideas on learning into practice by selling baby powder. Watson reckoned:

1 Rats chased down the rat-run because they learnt there was food at the end. So by giving the rats a reward you could change their behaviour.
2 You could use advertising to give people the impression that by buying your brand of baby powder they would feel happier and be better parents. This feeling would be a kind of reward. So people would choose to buy your brand.

But did the plan work? What do you think?

a) Watson was sacked after featuring a rat on the advertising posters.
b) Watson's plan failed. People can't be compared to rats. We don't have to feel good when we go shopping.
c) Watson's plan worked and he became a millionaire. His ideas form the basis of modern advertising.

Answer: c) If advertising teaches you that buying a product will improve your life, then you'll probably feel like buying it.

Are you intelligent?

Are you good at learning things? If so, you may be intelligent. But you might be surprised to know that psychologists don't agree what intelligence is all about. Many, though, believe that intelligence means an ability to solve new problems. Anyway, whatever you call it –

intelligence, being clever, smart or brainy – here's a quick intelligence test to put you through your paces.

True or false?

1 People with small heads aren't as intelligent as people with big heads. This is because people with big heads have bigger brains. TRUE/FALSE

2 As you learn, you develop extra connections between the neurons in their cortex. TRUE/FALSE

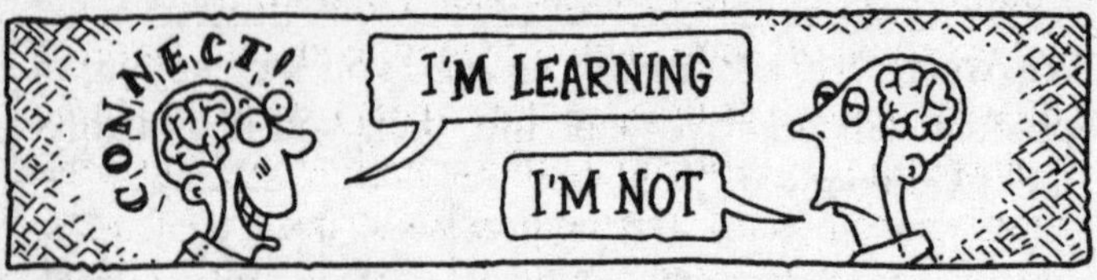

3 Playing lots of computer games can make you more intelligent. TRUE/FALSE

4 Eating fish is good for your brain. TRUE/FALSE

Answers: 1 FALSE. Your brain size is nothing to do with intelligence. For example at 8 kg (17.6 lb) an elephant's brain is more than five times heavier than ours, but no one fancies an elephant to win this year's Nobel Prize. **2** TRUE. Being clever is more to do with building up lots of neuron connections in the cortex. If you've got the vital connections you can learn things faster and people think you're really brainy. **3** FALSE. But scientists think that children who play lots of computer games develop extra connections in the area of the cortex that controls delicate hand movements. This helps them play the games faster and win more often. **4** TRUE. Eating fish really can boost your brainpower. Sea fish are rich in a chemical called iodine. This makes your body cells burn energy faster and your brain think faster. Also, fish and white meat and egg whites are rich in chemicals called amino acids that your brain uses to make neuron chemicals such as noradrenaline. As a result your brain feels more alert and clear-thinking. It can learn faster and become more intelligent.

Bulging brain development

Did you know that you learnt half of everything you know in your first five years?

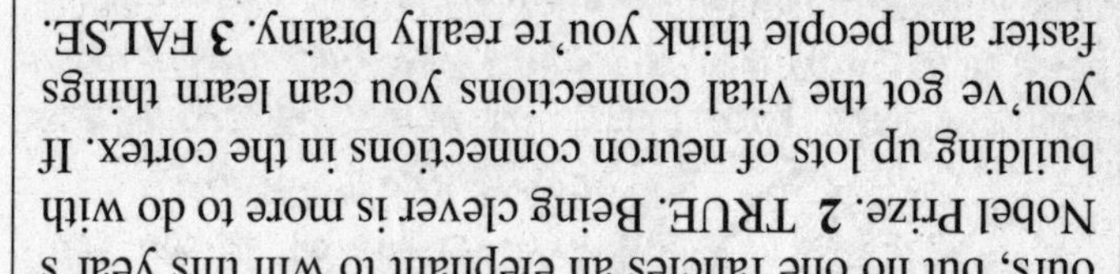

In some countries that's before children even start school! Oh, so you don't remember this vital learning period? Well, here's a quick reminder...

The first five years...

0 to six months

When you were born you could breath, suck, swallow and then throw up, dribble, cry, sneeze, cough and stretch. And that's about all because your brain wasn't developed.

Six months

Your brain had doubled in size. The neurons were growing and branching and forming millions of synapses. You could roll over and smile. You could also copy the expressions on grown-up faces. (Don't try this now – you'll only get told off.)

One year

You had learnt how to pick things up with your hands and you had just spoken your first word. Before then grown-ups probably spoke to you in baby talk and you tried to make the same sounds back. But you hadn't got the hang of the tongue and lip movements so it came out as baby noises. You were just beginning to learn to walk, and falling over quite a lot.

Two years ...

You could walk run and speak about 274 words. Two vital words you learnt were "wee" and "poo". You were able to recognize the feeling when you had to go and now you could even tell people about it. Soon afterwards you learnt how to use a potty without making an embarrassing mess. And if things went wrong you could take off your underwear without help.

Three years

You could speak up to a 1,000 words in short sentences and feed yourself (but not at the same time). You were also learning to draw. Sometimes you were so wrapped up in your drawing or games you might poo or wee in your underwear. (Hopefully this no longer happens.)

Four years

Your brain was four times bigger than when you were born. You were asking loads of questions using about 1,500 words, and going to the toilet all by yourself.

Five years ...

You could tell stories and hop and skip and you knew about 2,000 words. And round about this time you started school. ....

The next few years...
After you turned six, things in your brain got a bit less hectic but the neuron links in your cortex carried on forming. Some time between the ages of six and ten most children learn the following skills:

Tick here
☐ How to play ball games really well.

☐ Reading and joined-up writing.

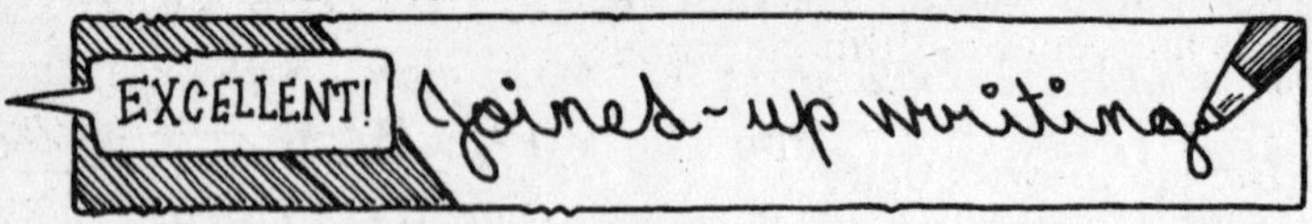

☐ Writing and telling stories.

☐ Drawing, painting and making models.

☐ Simple cooking and cleaning and even washing up. Oh yes – this is part of growing up, I'm afraid.

☐ Loads of facts and new words at school.
So how far have you got?

Of course not all kids develop at the same speed. Some are late-developers. That doesn't make them stupid – scientific mega-genius Albert Einstein didn't learn to talk until he was four. And girls' and boys' brains develop to different time-tables anyway. For example, for reasons scientists can't quite explain, the parts of the cortex that deal with speech develop earlier in girls than boys. So girls often learn to talk earlier. And boys' and girls' brains go on developing in different ways at different times.

Boys v. girls

Not surprisingly psychologists have found that boys and girls are better at different things...

Bet you never knew!

For example, girls may be better at talking than boys. Oh so you knew this already? Brain scans performed at Yale University School of Medicine, USA, show that men only use the left side of their brains to talk but women use both sides. But who comes out top overall – the battling boys or the gutsy girls?

Read on and find out in...

The battle of the sexes

Scientists have found that boys and girls tend to be better at different things. Of course, you might be different and scientists always argue about the results...

1 One study showed that boys are often quicker at solving tricky maths problems in their heads. Very gifted boys use the right sides of their brains to concentrate on the problem. But girls tend to use both sides and waste time putting their thoughts into words.

2 When boys and girls are given 3-D puzzles to assemble, the boys are better at imagining what the finished puzzle will look like. Once again girls tend to waste time explaining to themselves in words how they will solve the puzzle.

3 But girls' brains are better at controlling their finger movements for delicate fiddly tasks. So the girls might well be quicker at putting the puzzle together.

4 Boys tend to have a good sense of direction. They are very good at building up a clear idea of a route in the right side of their brains.

5 But they're not so good at remembering landmarks. Girls with their better memory for words can remember the landmarks even if they're sometimes less sure about the direction.

Important note: In conclusion, every scientific study has found that boys and girls have differing abilities in some areas and use their brains in different ways. But, and here's the important bit, OVERALL, THEY ARE EQUALLY CLEVER. So shut it, OK?

And there you have it. Learning is a vital function of your bulging brain. Now, have you learnt everything in this chapter? Well, one thing's for certain – you won't have learnt anything without a memory. Luckily, the next mind-expanding chapter can help you. And you'll soon find those memories flooding back...

MIXED-UP MEMORY

Welcome to this unforgettable chapter. It's about memory. Just what is this mysterious ability? And how does it work? And will you remember anything after you've read this book? Er … now what was I talking about?

Bulging fact file

NAME: Memory

BASIC FACTS: Memory works like this . . .

1 You sense something.

2 You put it in your memory.

3 You can recall the memory when something reminds you of it. The reminder might be a word, an event or even a smell.

DISGUSTING DETAILS: You've got not one but *three* memories.

1 Short term memory. Useful for phone numbers, etc. You forget these memories in 30 seconds. Some kids store their science knowledge in here.

2 Long term memory. This is stuff you remember for years. It's where Grandpa stores all those boring old yarns of life when he was a lad. These first two memory systems are based in your cortex.

3 A special memory for skills like riding a bike that you can use without being aware of having to remember them. This memory seems to be based in your cerebellum.

Mysterious long-term memory-makers

Two areas deep in the cortex, the thalamus and the hippocampus (hippo-camp-us), help create longer-term memory. People with injuries to the thalamus have difficulty in remembering the injury. And in 1953 an American man had the hippocampus on both sides of his brain removed. This was intended to stop fits caused by uncontrollable neuron firing. The fits stopped. But although the man can recall old memories from before the operation, he can't remember anything that's happened since then.

Bet you never knew!

Older people also suffer from this problem. And this, too, seems to be linked to damage to the hippocampus. From the age of about 30 the neurons in this region begin to die off and by the time a person reaches extreme old age they've lost about 30 per cent. Although scientists aren't too sure why this process takes place, the effects on the memory are fairly obvious. Perhaps some of your more mature teachers are already suffering from the effects.

Hopefully your memory is much better? Well, let's pick up the Neuro-phone and check out how it works...

A memorable joke

The brain is about to try and remember a joke...

(OK, I didn't say the joke was any good.)

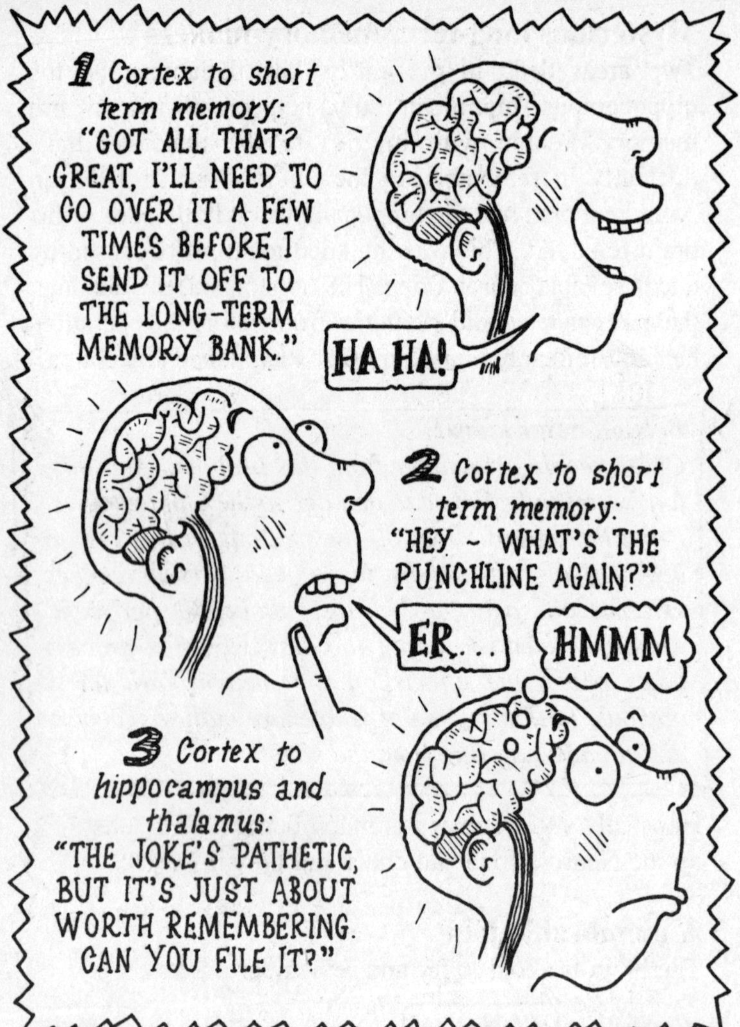

Scientific note

Scientists aren't quite sure how this happens. It seems to involve a change in neuron chemistry. This makes it easier to send a message along a particular route through the maze of neurons in your cortex. (Each neuron pathway is storing a particular part of a memory. Some store colours and others can store shapes.) The memory of the joke should remain in your brain even if you can't recall it. People call this "sub-conscious memory".

A few weeks later...

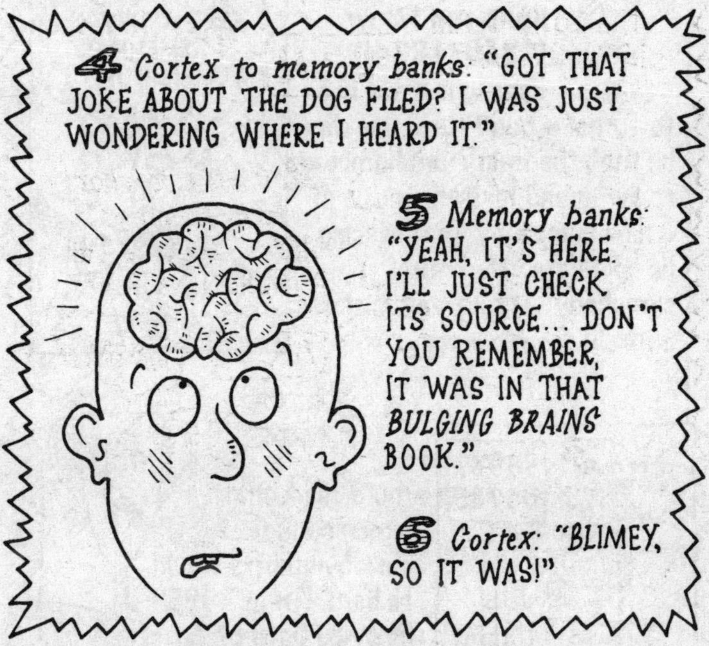

No doubt you'll be pleased to hear there's room in your memory for lots more jokes (and other stuff). Remember all those billions of neurons and synapses in your cortex? Well, scientists reckon you can squeeze facts in your memory to fill 20,000 encyclopaedias. Do that and your brain really would be bulging. You might even win a memory competition...

The Horrible Science memory competition

This competition is unforgettable. All the prize winners have shown powers of recollection that will live long in our memories.

Fourth Prize

German conductor Hans von Bülow (1830–1894)

Hans was never one to forget a good tune. One day he took the train from Hamburg to Berlin and read the music of a new symphony. That evening he conducted the entire symphony without any mistakes *entirely from memory*.

Third Prize

You'd think that remembering boring numbers would be hard. But in 1995 **Hiroyuki Goto of Japan** recited the mathematical number pi to 42,195 places with no mistakes. The performance took over 17 hours including breaks to go to the toilet. At the end I expect he was flushed with success.

Second Prize

Devout **Mehmed Ali Halici of Turkey** recited 6,666 verses of religious text in 1967. Could you do that in your school assembly? Come to think of it would you fancy an assembly that was 18 hours long?

First Prize

Goes to **Russian Solomon Veniaminoff.** Solomon wanted to be a violinist but an ear disease slightly damaged his hearing. In the 1930s he decided to become a journalist. Later he worked as a stage entertainer where he wowed the crowds with his unforgettable talent for remembering incredibly long numbers or lists of words. From time to time he also helped psychologist Alexander Luria (1902–1977) with his work on memory. Here's Solomon's story. Of course, we can't remember the exact details but this story is based on the real facts. . .

The man who never forgot

Moscow, May 1928

The slender young man was clearly on edge. "My name is Solomon," he stammered. "My editor sent me to see you because of my memory."

"What's wrong with it?" asked Alexander Luria curiously as he leaned back in his rocking-chair. Solomon nervously swept his black hair from his eyes.

"People say that I have an exceptional memory. The fact is I can remember every single thing that has happened to me since I was one year old."

"Fascinating but unlikely," smiled Luria. There was an uncomfortable silence broken only by the ticking of the large old clock on the mantelpiece. Then Luria sighed.

"Oh well, I suppose we'd better test you. I'd like you to try to remember this sequence of numbers."

The scientist quickly jotted down a series of 30 numbers and then read them out to the young man.

Solomon looked even more worried and gazed briefly into nothing. His dark, dreamy eyes seemed fixed on a distant object that Luria couldn't see.

Then he repeated the numbers perfectly.

The scientist's mouth dropped open. "But that's astounding!" he gasped.

"I could say them backwards if you like," said Solomon quietly. And he gave a shy, fleeting smile.

1958

Thirty years later Alexander Luria sat in the warm sunshine gazing vacantly at his garden. He was lost in thought and as usual he felt rather tired. In front of him lay a pile of old papers covered in his spidery handwriting. The paper was crinkled and yellow with age.

"So how do I turn all this into a book?" he mused to himself. "Where to begin, that's the first problem."

"Why not begin at the beginning?" said a voice. Luria looked up in surprise at the man sitting quietly in the corner. The visitor's hair was grey with age and his figure was stooped and thick-set.

"Oh, Solomon I'm so sorry, I quite forgot you were here. Now what were we saying?"

"We were discussing the book you were going to write about memory and our 30 years of working together. That's why you invited me here at 4.24 p.m. yesterday."

"Has it really been that long?" asked the scientist wearily.

"Well, on and off, when I wasn't working on the stage."

"I think I'll begin my book on that day in June, when

was it? 1929 when you first came to see me."

"It was 1928," said Solomon firmly, "and the month was May. I remember you in your grey suit sitting in your rocking-chair. And that old-fashioned clock you had. And then those 30 numbers ... what were they now? 62, 30, 19, 41..."

Luria gazed in growing shock at the first page of his yellowing notes. Yes, there in his own handwriting was the exact sequence of numbers repeated with eerie accuracy over a gap of 30 years.

"But that's astounding!" he wheezed breathlessly.

"That's what you said at the time," said Solomon with his familiar shy smile.

"But you must have remembered millions of pieces of information since then. You're a lucky man Solomon, I do admire this gift of yours."

"It's no gift!" exclaimed Solomon bitterly. "As I told you in 1929 it's a curse. I often wished I could forget things. Sometimes all these facts and numbers and lists jostle in my mind like a huge crowd – like words in poetry or sparks in a fireworks display. They drive me crazy! The greatest gift is to forget things. But that's one gift I will never possess. Forgetting is a wonderful thing."

And his eyes sparkled with tears.

Solomon's secret

After years of patient study Luria figured out the secret of Solomon Veniaminoff's astonishing memory. It was due to the way his mind worked. Solomon suffered from a disease called synaesthesia (sin-ees-thees-ia). Incredible though it sounds this rare brain disease made Solomon experience sounds as colours. He told one psychologist...

By remembering the colours he saw when hearing things and by imagining numbers as people he found it easy to remember tons of information. But the only way he could ever forget something was to imagine it was written on paper and he was burning it.

Boost your memory

Would you want a memory like Solomon's? Probably not – but with a more powerful memory you could get top marks in your science tests every time and even remember your dad's birthday. The good news is you don't need a special brain to develop an excellent memory.

Bet you never knew!

One painful way to improve your memory is to stick electrodes into your brain. Experiments in the 1900s by surgeon Wilder Penfield in Canada found this gives you vivid flashbacks from your past. I expect some of them proved a bit shocking.

Picture this...
But don't worry, there are many less painful methods of improving your memory. Here's one of them. Supposing tomorrow you have a science test and you need to remember to feed the goldfish and take your sandwiches to school.

1 *Try* to remember to do these things. This should store the information in your short-term memory.

2 For reasons that scientists don't quite understand you can remember pictures better than facts. It might be because you can link pictures with other memories more easily and in some way this makes them easier to recall. So make up a mental picture to help you remember. For example, you could imagine your teacher eating a goldfish in a sandwich.

3 When you get up the next morning and get ready for school, the thought of facing your teacher again will immediately make you remember the image of her eating a goldfish sandwich. So you use your teacher as a memory cue – that's a kind of clue to help you remember the goldfish, the sandwiches and the test, stupid.

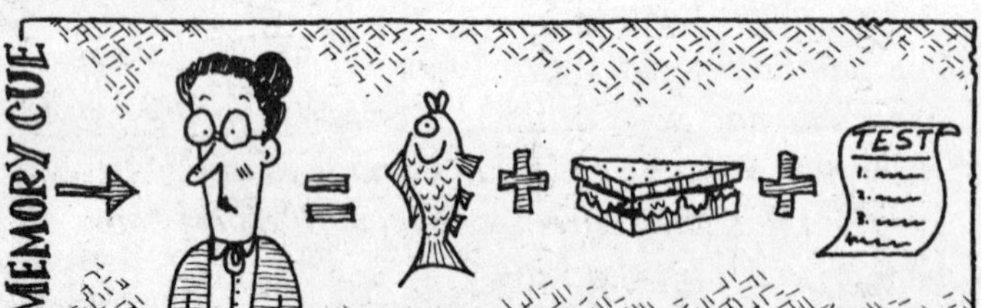

Terror in the air

Your memory can be affected by your feelings. In the 1950s Mitchell Berkun, a scientist working for the US Army, dreamt up this horrible experiment.

Of course, the whole incident including the fire engines on the ground had been set up by Berkun. The terrible test showed that the recruits could only remember half the instructions when they were scared out of their wits.

And talking about feelings ... the next chapter's all about them – the highs, the lows, the excitement and the horror. So, do you feel like reading a bit further?

FORCEFUL FEELINGS

Are you a touchy-feely person who is always laughing or weeping? Do you pride yourself on being the strong, silent type? Well, whatever you're like on the surface, your brain is bulging with powerful feelings.

Feeling the force

Scientists claim there are six types of emotion that people feel all over the world. Huh – what do they know? When was the last time you saw an emotional scientist? Well, we've managed to find one and photograph the full range of his six emotions.

Of course, feelings can get horribly mixed up. That's why people cry when they're happy or sometimes feel a bit down after some good news.

Scientists have scarcely begun to explain why our emotions get so tangled. However, as you're about to discover, emotions can be triggered by several different chemicals. With so many of these chemicals sloshing about at the same time it wouldn't be surprising if your brain got some mixed messages.

Complicated feelings

Feeling emotion is actually more complicated than you might think. For one thing you need to co-ordinate three areas of your brain. And that really gets the Neuro-phone lines buzzing. Just listen to this: Your teacher is telling you off...

Scientific note:
Dopamine (dope-a-mean) is a chemical that seems to make your neurons more active and fire more signals. Obviously the emotion you feel depends on what's going on. It could be terror or joy or anything in between.

Bulging brain expressions
One neurologist says to another...

Is that some kind of stove?

Answer: No. The reticular (ret-tick-u-lar) activating system or RAS for short is the area in the brain stem that makes the dopamine. By the way, you might be interested to know that in small kids the RAS is easily switched on and that's why they get so easily scared. As you grow up the RAS quietens down because your cortex learns when there's a real monster and when it's just a curtain blowing in a darkened room.

Dizzy dopamine v. serious serotonin

So dopamine shakes up your limbic system and you feel emotion. But you don't always do what you feel like doing. That's because of another brain chemical called serotonin (seer-ro-tone-in). This is squirted by neurons linking the limbic system and the cortex. Serotonin tends to calm the neurons down and makes you feel more sensible. (It can also make you feel happy and relaxed.)

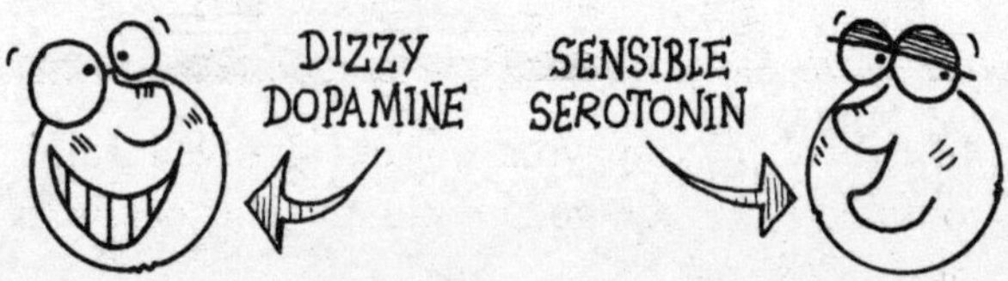

Imagine you've guzzled some lovely cream buns and you're greedily eyeing up the rest.

In other words serotonin tells you *not* to do things. It's like having a sensible teacher stuck between your ears. (Now that *is* a scary thought!)

By now you might be wondering why your cortex needs to get involved in feelings. After all, you feel things in the limbic system and you've got dizzy dopamine to get you all worked up and serious serotonin to calm you down. Well, the cortex is there to think things over and make the ultimate decision...

And of course, getting your cortex involved helps you stop to think when you get emotional. This can help you control your temper.

Bet you never knew!
Scientists believe that people with low levels of serotonin can become bad-tempered or even violent. That's because they find it harder to control their feelings. And talking about uncontrollable feelings...

HORRIBLE SCIENCE HEALTH WARNING
There's a feeling of TERROR lurking just over the page.

Fear and fury

Although feelings are controlled and felt in your brain, your body also joins in and helps you to feel emotions. Sometimes in a horrible way. Just imagine you haven't done your homework for the third time running: your teacher is seething. Never mind, here's your chance to make interesting scientific observations on the effect of anger and fear...

An angry teacher

Did someone mention scientific observations? Well, maybe you're not in the mood. Inside you might be feeling a bit wobbly, petrified even. Maybe a bit like this...

A scared child

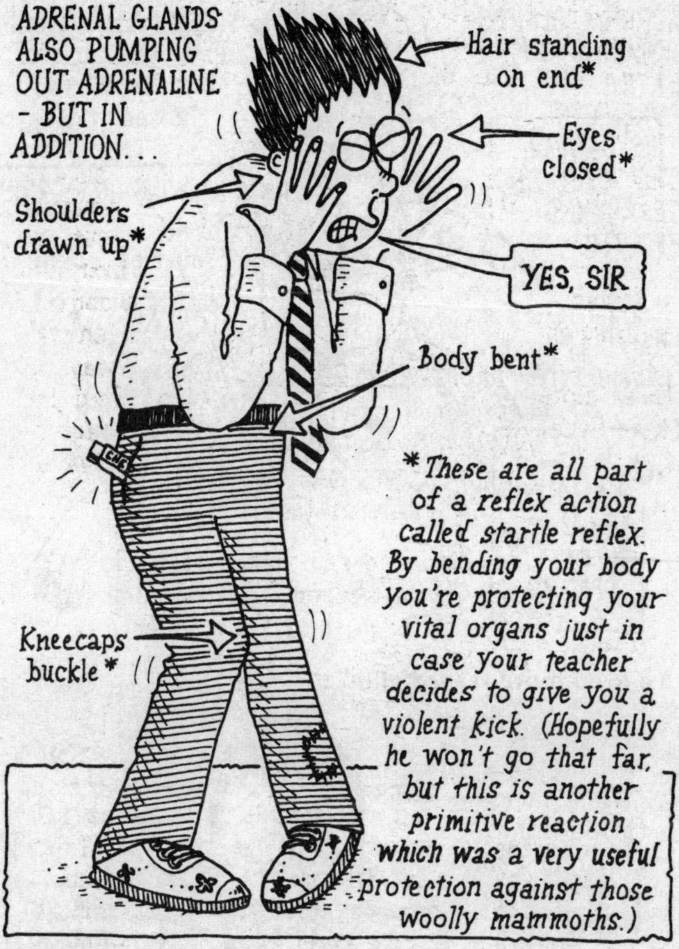

Important note:

Oh no! Your teacher's figured out it was you who absent-mindedly left chewing gum on his chair. Oh-er, you're going to cop it now. TAKE COVER! YOUR TEACHER IS ABOUT TO GO BALLISTIC...

A teacher who is just about to explode

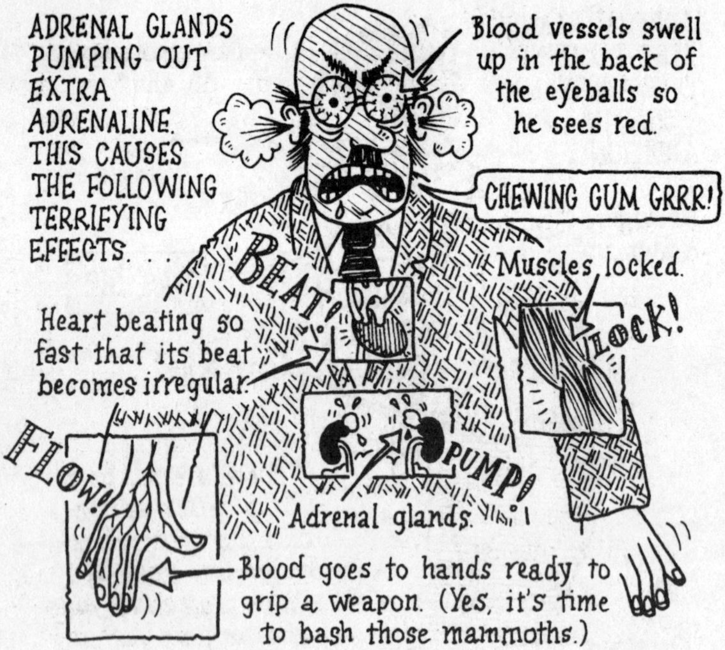

An even more scared child

The long, long, long wait outside the head teacher's room

So you've been sent for a little chat with the head teacher? Oh dear, this could prove painful. Here are a few things to think about whilst you're waiting for the axe to fall...

Four fearful feelings facts

1 You feel stress. This is the fear you feel when you're scared but you can't run away. Well, you can but they'll only catch you and then you'll really catch it. Some kids feel stress when they start a new school and some feel it every day they go to school.

2 Chewing your fingernails yet? Masticating keratin* is a common response to stress.

*(Mas-tic-kate-ing) = posh term for chewing. (Ker-rat-in) = the substance your nails are made of.

Scientists think that people feel more cheerful when they chew things. It's healthier to chew gum (sugar-free, of course) but that's what got you into this mess. By the way, when you're stressed-out your sense of taste stops working. So the gum would taste like someone's already chewed it.

3 Your adrenal glands are squirting a hormone called cortisone (cor-ti-zone). The aim of this chemical is to prepare your muscles for action later on. Sugar pours into your blood, your brain feels more alert because it's getting more sugar and the nerves are firing like crazy. But you feel rotten – all nervy and jittery. Yikes!

4 You'd better apologize to the head teacher – you might even be let off without a punishment. But there's one feeling that's even worse than being stressed. It's worse because it makes you feel really miserable, really sad. It can spoil your whole life...

Bet you never knew!

Depression is a brain condition that makes you so miserable you want to go to bed and cry and stay there for ever. Scientists think it may be the result of a shortage of brain chemicals such as serotonin. If you ever feel this way try taking a deep breath. Let it out slowly and relax. Yep, that's it: for some reason relaxing actually helps you feel better. Remember this rotten scary fearful miserable feeling is caused by a few chemicals in your bulging brain.

The secret of happiness

For hundreds of years people have searched for this elusive secret and got very uptight and miserable because they couldn't find it. But it's here, here in this very book! Ahem, wait for it... This next bit is based on research by US psychologists Paul Costa and Robert McRae. In the 1970s, Costa and McRae interviewed large numbers of different people and tried to discover what it was in their personalities that made them happy or sad. Here's what they found: to be happy it helps if you enjoy meeting new people.

Don't expect too much from life. That way good things come as a pleasant surprise.

But always look for the bright side of every situation.

And if you can't find happiness by using these simple techniques then don't worry. Science has found ways of making you cheer up whether you like it or not...

Bet you never knew!

1 *In the 1950s it was common to treat diseases of the mind by cutting the nerves to the front part of the cortex. This made the patient less emotional (maybe that's because it's hard to be emotional when you've got a thumping headache).*

2 *US surgeon Walter Freeman invented his own version of this horrible treatment. Walt stuck an ice-pick through a patient's eye-socket into the brain and cut the nerves that way. I expect he only wanted to pick their brains, ha-ha. Hardened doctors were known to swoon at this revolting spectacle. The patients also felt sick and confused afterwards.*

3 *In 1963 scientist RG Heath tried a new technique to control feelings. He stuck electrodes in the brain of a man with a brain disease that caused uncontrollable rages. By pressing buttons the man gave electric shocks to different areas of his brain.*

But you don't have to drill holes in your skull or wield ice-picks or even suffer electric shocks to feel emotional. Try tuning into your favourite music. Yep, why not enjoy the feel-good factor with our exclusive relaxation tapes...?

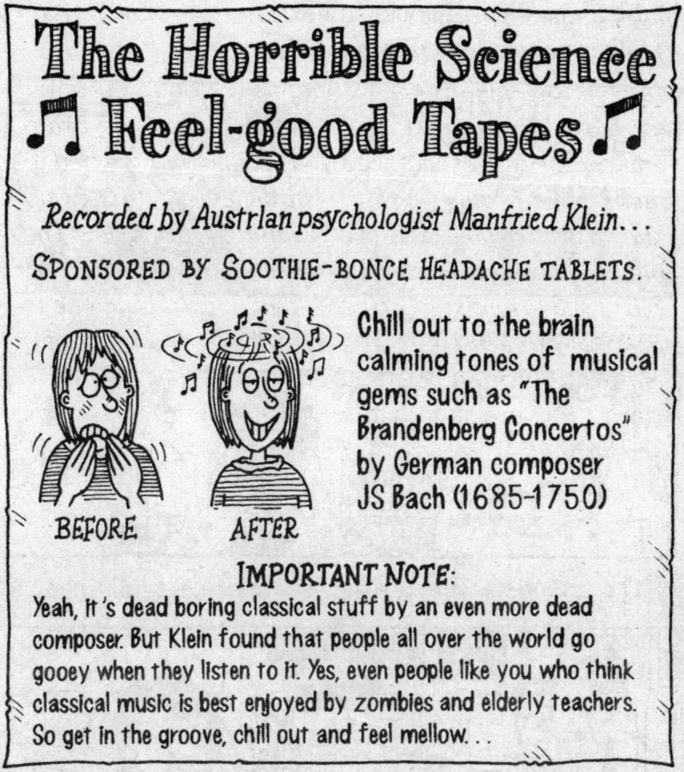

Could you be a scientist?

The situation you're in and the reactions of other people can affect the way you feel. Sounds common sense, doesn't it? But psychologists have tried to find out precisely how important these factors are. And they've dreamt up a few brain-boggling experiments...

1 In the late 1960s two psychologists from New York University, USA, played frisbee in the waiting-room of Grand Central station. They laughed and joked and got in the way. After a while they threw the frisbee to a third scientist who was pretending to be a stranger. She joined in the game. What happened next?

a) Other people joined in the game.

b) Everyone ignored the frisbee players.

c) The scientists were arrested for causing a nuisance.

2 The same team put three people in a room and gave them forms to fill in. Then they wafted smoke through vents to make it look like the room was on fire. Two of the people were actually psychologists in disguise and they ignored the smoke. What did the third person do?

a) Ran about shouting…

b) Ignored the smoke.

c) Got a fire extinguisher and squirted the scientists with foam from head to foot.

3 US psychologist Philip Zimbardo set up a tasteless experiment. A nice, friendly scientist was given the job of persuading complete strangers to eat fried grasshoppers.

Next, another scientist rudely ordered people to eat the insects. What did the results show?

a) People were more likely to eat the grasshoppers when they were asked nicely.

b) The test was scrapped when someone threw up. This is odd because grasshoppers are a delicacy in parts of Africa such as Morocco. They have a lovely crunchy texture and taste like dried shrimp.

c) People ate the grasshoppers on both occasions. But they said they felt different when they were ordered to eat them.

Answers: All the experiments show how your view of the situation can shape your feelings.

1 a) When one person joined the game everyone else felt good enough to want to take part. The scientists actually had trouble halting it. In another experiment the "stranger" pretended to be grumpy and no one else got involved.

2 b) If everyone else ignores an event – even a dangerous fire – it's hard to feel excited about it.

3 c) When people were asked nicely, they said they ate the grasshoppers because they didn't want to upset the nice scientist. When the people were ordered to eat, they said they felt like trying the grasshoppers anyway.

Mind you, there's one situation where you'd feel nothing. It's when you get knocked out cold by a bash on the head. And if you want to find out what it does to your brain take a look at the next chapter. It's a real knockout.

As you've probably realized by now, the brain is an intricate and delicate bit of equipment. So, not surprisingly, a bash on the head can damage the brain in all sorts of horrible and unexpected ways. Luckily, you do have a bit of natural protection.

Bulging brain protection

Your bulging brain is naturally well protected. Let's take a look at this CAT scan.

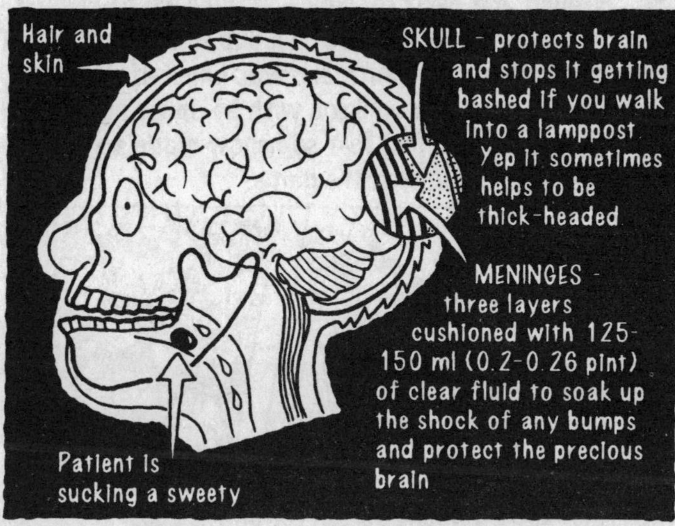

A nasty blow

Despite these elaborate defences a bash on the bonce can make you lose your memory – or cause amnesia to use the scientific term. In this state you can't remember what hit you, or even that you've been hit. And you may lose consciousness. And consciousness is actually the most incredible thing your bulging brain gets up to...

Bulging fact file

NAME: Consciousness

BASIC FACTS: It means being aware of your thoughts and feelings. Scientists aren't too sure how this happens. The whole of your cortex seems to be involved in making you aware of your thoughts and what they mean.

DISGUSTING DETAILS: It's possible to run around and perform simple actions whilst unconscious. In the 1956 FA Cup Final goalkeeper Bert Trautmann was knocked unconscious in a collision with an opposing player. But battling Bert somehow made a vital save and completed the game.

His team, Manchester City, won the cup.

Bulging brain bumps

Here are some vital facts to bump up your knowledge.

1 When you get up in the morning your brain gets a rude awakening. As you lift your head up your brain slops forward and bangs against the front part of your skull.

Luckily your meninges and the fluid around the brain stop it getting too battered.

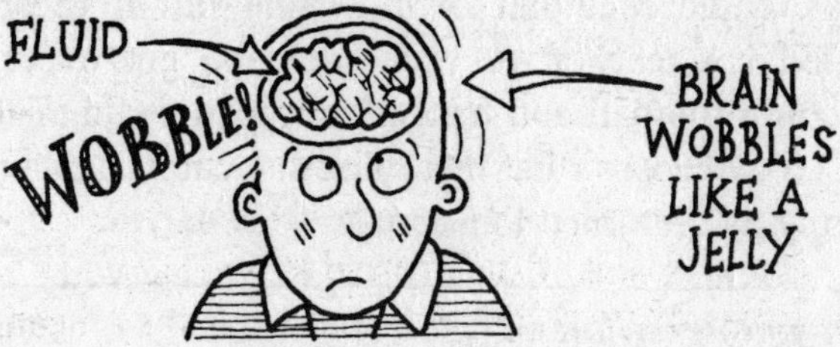

2 Some neurologists think the shock makes some people feel bad-tempered in the morning. (It's either that or the sour milk in their tea.)

3 In car crashes the effect of the brain being thrown forwards is far more damaging than a blow on the head. The shock is more likely to tear blood vessels and the brain itself, leaving wounds that cannot easily be treated because they're inside the skull.

4 The effects of an injury can depend on which part of the cortex gets damaged. It can lead to problems reading, smelling or tasting, or amnesia – that's loss of memory, remember?

5 In 1997 Vicky, a ten-year-old British girl, banged her head and started writing backwards and upside-down. Vicky could read her own writing but it must have baffled her teacher. A year later she got overexcited watching football and banged her head again. The next day, for reasons that neurologists can't explain, her writing had returned to normal.

Bet you never knew!

In 1998 a retired Scottish footballer said that his memory loss was due to heading the ball too much. His wife said that he often chatted to his grandchildren and then forgot whom he was talking to. Before the 1950s, footballs were made of heavy leather and when it rained they sucked in water and got heavier. If they hit you on the head they could knock you out.

HORRIBLE HEALTH WARNING!

So let that be a warning. Don't go bashing your head against hard solid objects such as brick walls, floors or teachers. It's horribly unhealthy.

Bulging fact file

NAME: Headache

BASIC FACTS: A headache is a brain-pain. But wait a minute – didn't someone say the brain can't feel pain? This is true, but when you're under stress more blood squirts into your brain.

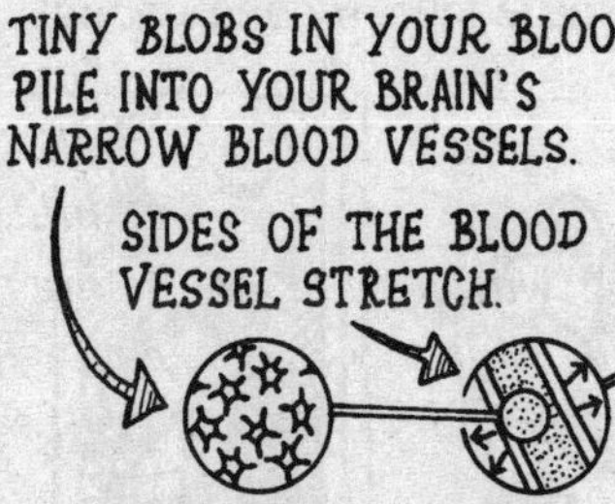

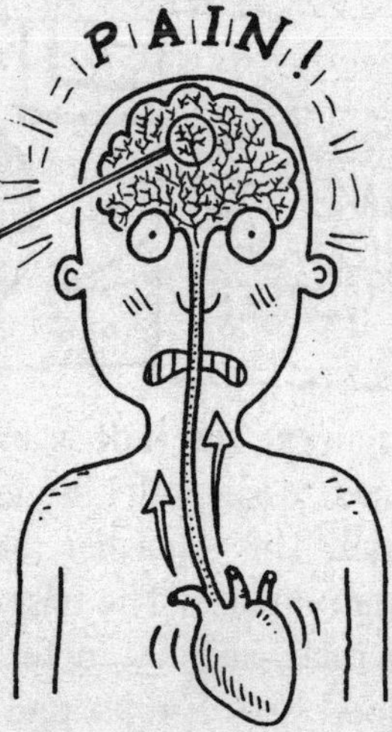

DISGUSTING DETAILS: A headache can be caused by eating ice-cream. If the ice-cream touches the roof of your mouth it shocks the nerves that lead to your brain.

The best thing to do is to touch the roof of your mouth with your nice warm tongue. This relaxes the nerves.

Alternatively, you could let the ice-cream melt a bit before stuffing your little face.

Teacher's tea-break teaser

To succeed in this teaser you need split-second timing, oodles of charm and skin like a rhinoceros. All you do is choose a morning when your teacher has been teaching an extra-difficult class. He'll probably have a headache and will be gulping down a few painkillers with his tea.

Tap quietly on the staff-room door (remember teachers have feelings too). When the door opens your teacher will be looking grim. So smile sweetly and enquire...

Answer: Yes, it does and here's why. By frowning you squeeze several kilometres of blood vessels in your head. This squashes the platelets and makes the pain more intense. The best thing to do with a headache is to relax and try to feel happy. When you smile the blood vessels relax and your headache should ease.

Ahh, that's better!

Horrible headache cures

And that's a lot better than the ancient Roman treatment for a headache. Roman doctor Scribonius Largus recommended whacking the patient on the head with an electric fish. This fishy shock treatment was supposed to cure the ache. It didn't. Mind you, if you lived in the Stone Age there weren't any of those nice painkillers or even an electric fish around.

Stone age brain surgery

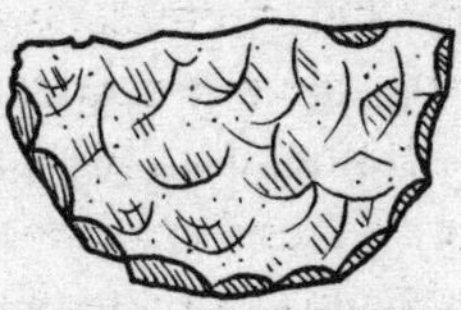

1 Take a sharp bit of flint.

2 Scrape the hair and skin off the patient's head.

3 Ignore any screams from the victim, sorry patient.

4 Carry on until a hole appears in the skull.

No one is sure why this operation was carried out in the Stone Age but it was used in ancient Greece to tackle persistent headaches. Although it didn't do much good the victims often survived with their brains bulging out of the gory hole. Stone Age skulls have been found in which the skull had started to heal.

Actually this treatment – known today as trepanning (trep-panning) – is still performed by surgeons. You'll be relieved to know they use modern instruments rather than lumps of rock. It's done in an emergency to relieve a build-up of blood pressure in the brain caused by a blood clot. And, as you now know, people can survive with a hole in the bonce. A person can even survive with a hole made by an accident.

Groaning Gage

Everyone liked Phineas Gage of Vermont, USA. The young railway foreman was a lively and happy-go-lucky chap. Until one day in 1848...

Phin was blasting a path for a new railway. He was trying to push some dynamite down a hole using an iron bar. When disaster struck...

The dynamite blew up and the iron bar shot straight through Phin's head. The bar was found a few metres away spattered with bits of poor Phin's brains.

Phin was knocked out by the blow but quickly came

round and even managed to walk to the doctor's. The hole was big enough for the doctor to put his fingers inside Phin's skull...

Amazingly, Phin lived – although he was ill for a few weeks. But as a result of his injuries he was a changed man. He was moody, foul-mouthed, rude and often drunk.

He lost jobs frequently, but his wits remained sharp. He made money by exhibiting himself in fairs with the iron bar stuck through his head.

Scientists were eager to study Phin's battered bonce. So he sold his body to *several* medical schools for cash up front.

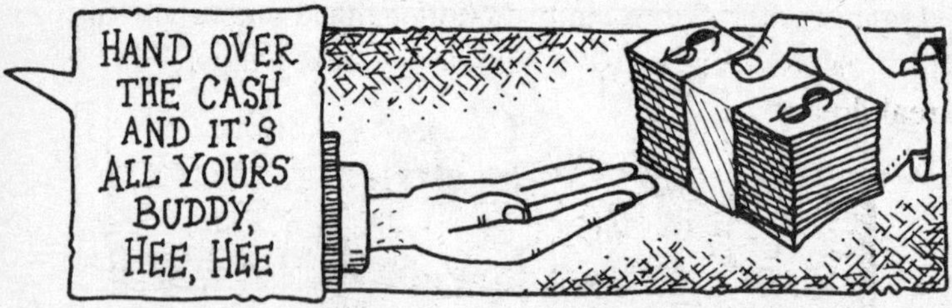

After Phin's death the medical schools argued over who owned the body and, of course, the brain. The doctors were keen to remove Phin's brain and look at the damage.

The doctors found that Phin's brain hadn't been able to repair the damage it suffered. The damaged front cortex area wasn't vital for life but it had clearly shaped Phin's personality.

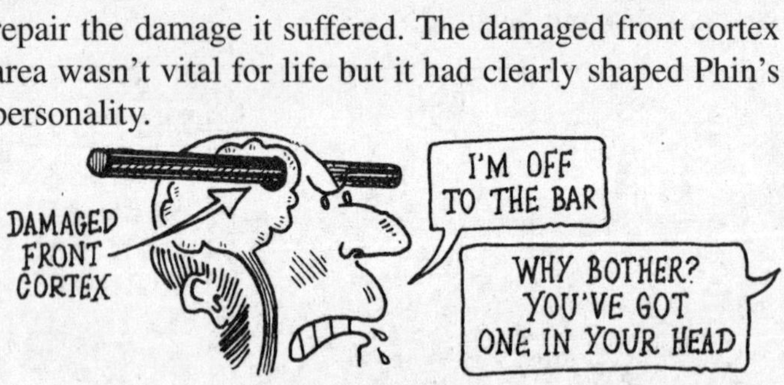

The famous iron bar ended up in the museum at Harvard Medical College. Hope they cleaned it up first.

But you don't need a near-fatal brain injury to lose consciousness. No, in fact you do it far less painfully every night when you curl up your tootsies and snuggle down in your nice warm bed. And if that's where you are right now why not take a peek at the next chapter? It's a real dream.

Or is it a nightmare?

NASTY NIGHTMARES

This chapter is about sleep. It's about dreams and it's about nightmares...

Warning to sensitive readers: Are you easily scared and reading this chapter in bed? Well, if you must scream, scream quietly.

But, try not to be too petrified – nightmares and dreams are fascinating effects made by your bulging brain in the middle of sleep. Here are a few more facts to sleep on...

Bulging fact file

NAME: Sleep

BASIC FACTS: When you go to sleep you lose consciousness. Your sleeping brain produces delta brainwaves (see page 351) and you're unaware of your surroundings. Oh, so you knew that already? Well try and stay awake for the next bit.

DISGUSTING DETAILS: Staying awake for two weeks can kill you. Scientists believe that the body needs a period of rest each day. Without it, the body gets more and more exhausted and vital functions like heartbeat begin to falter.

So sleep is good for you. And whilst you're lying in bed you can always listen in to those chattering Neuro-phone wires as your brain tries to help you to nod off...

Sleepy signals

Cortex to all brain areas: "I'M REALLY WIDE AWAKE. DO I HAVE TO GO TO SLEEP?"

Pineal gland to cortex: "NIGHT-NIGHT, CORTEX. SOME OF THIS NICE MELATONIN WILL CALM YOU DOWN"

SCIENTIFIC NOTE
Melatonin (mel-a tone-in) damps down the activity in the cortex. The pineal gland pumps out melatonin every night on a 24-hour cycle.

Cortex: "YAWN, I'M FEELING REALLY SLEEPY."

RAS to cortex:* "COME ON, CORTEX, TIME YOU WERE TUCKED UP. HERE'S SOME NICE SEROTONIN** TO HELP YOU SLEEP."

SCIENTIFIC NOTE
At this point your brain should lose consciousness. But you won't notice that bit. Why? Because you'll be asleep, too, stupid.

Cortex: "Zzzz."

* That's the reticular activating system in your brain stem, remember.

** That's the "sensible" chemical that damps down your feelings. The serotonin should calm your cortex down even more.

Bulging brain expressions

Two psychologists are chatting.

Is this dangerous?

Answer: No, but it's annoying for everyone else. Somniloquy (som-nil-o-kwee) means talking in your sleep. Somnambulism (som-nam-bew-lis-m) means walking in your sleep. So the psychologist walks and talks in his sleep. Well, could be worse: in 1993 a British businessman had to be rescued by fire-fighters after falling into a rubbish chute. He had fallen in whilst sleepwalking in the nude.

Spot the sleepwalker

One in twenty children walk in their sleep and some adults do this when they're feeling stressed. Does your mum/dad/brother/sister/hamster sleepwalk? Here are a few signs to look out for.

Mind you, some teachers act this way on a Monday morning when they are supposedly awake.

Bet you never knew!

It's quite harmless to wake a sleepwalker but it's a good idea to do it gently. After all, it's a bit confusing for someone to wake up suddenly and find themselves out of bed. On waking up, the sleepwalking person can't remember where they've been. So break the news gently, OK?

A bit of an eye-opener

Any sleep, even with a bit of sleepwalking thrown in, is better than no sleep at all. In the 1960s scientists kept volunteers awake to measure the effects of lack of sleep on their brains and bodies. What you are about to read is a story based on real events that happened in these tests. So try to keep awake for the next few minutes...

HORRIBLE HEALTH WARNING!

Don't try this experiment at home. You might keep parents awake and this can have a magical shrinking effect on pocket money. And, as you are about to find out, losing too much sleep is very unhealthy. For this reason scientists are no longer keen to perform this experiment.

SLEEP DEPRIVATION EXPERIMENT DIARY

by **Arthur Sleep** (volunteer)

Notes by **Dr Irma Wake** *(day-shift) &*

Dr Hugh Kant-Dropoff *(night-shift)*

Monday night

I'm wide awake and feel like I could stay awake for ever! I drink coffee to keep me going. The only problem is that Dr Kant-Dropoff insists on coming to the toilet with me to check I don't doze off in there.

4a.m. Tuesday morning. Feeling a bit sleepy: I could do with some shut-eye. I fight the feeling off and play some snooker.

TUESDAY MORNING
Dr Kant-Dropoff writes. . .

Arthur is fine. His heartbeat and reflexes are normal. I wired him up to an EEG machine and his brainwaves are normal. I'm a bit sleepy now myself – could do with a bit of kip. Oh well, off to bed – I'm handing over to Dr Wake who will monitor Arthur during the day.

Tuesday night – I nearly dropped off tonight but Dr Kant-Dropoff rudely shook me and shouted "wakey-wakey" in my ear. I feel really cross with him.

Dr Kant-Dropoff writes. . .

Arthur seems more tired and irritable tonight. Shouted at me at 3 a.m. after I stopped him from falling asleep.

WEDNESDAY
Dr Wake writes. . .

Arthur is slurring his words today. He keeps repeating things and he moves about slowly. He can still play chess, though, and even beat me in a game. Obviously the areas of his brain dealing with thinking are still functioning normally.

Wednesday night – I'm not talking to Dr Kant-Dropoff after last night's row. Played loud music to keep awake. I could see Dr Kant-Dropoff didn't like it – ha-ha!

I'm really tired all the time now. If I close my eyes I could fall asleep. Got to keep going.

Dr Kant-Dropoff writes. . .

Arthur has been extremely quiet tonight.

Thursday

I don't like the way Dr Wake shouts "rise and shine" each morning. Why does she have to be so cheerful? I mean it's not as if I've been asleep. I bet she gets a good night's sleep, though...she must have something against me. Yes, that's it: *she's getting at me.*

Dr Wake writes. . .

Arthur is clearly exhausted and his pulse rate keeps going faster and then slower.

Thursday night - My beans on toast tasted funny tonight: I feel sure Dr Kant-Dropoff put some drug in my food. But why? WHY? Maybe he's getting back at me for playing loud music. I'll show him. . .

Dr Kant-Dropoff writes. . .

Arthur seems to be suffering from strange ideas. This is typical of people who lose too much sleep. We'll have to monitor the situation closely.

Friday – Refused to finish my cornflakes this morning – the milk tasted odd. Dr Wake gave them to me so she must be in on the plot with Dr Kant-Dropoff. Ha-ha! They think I don't suspect they tamper with my food.

4.15 p.m. When I stood up the floor was heaving like the sea. I must have been poisoned!

Dr Wake writes. . .

Arthur appears to be seeing things. I must contact Dr Kant-Dropoff and discuss ending the experiment.

FRIDAY NIGHT
Dr Kant-Dropoff writes. . .

Arthur has locked himself in the toilet. He keeps shouting for me to keep away and stop poisoning him. I will monitor the situation from the outside. I'm afraid he will use violence.

I'll be safe here. All quiet – I think Dr K-D's gone away. Phew, I can relax! Just close my eyes now for a minute. . . Zzzzzzzzzz

SATURDAY MORNING
Dr Kant-Dropoff and Dr Wake. . .

We broke into the toilet and found Arthur fast asleep. He didn't stir when we moved him to a bed.

Sunday evening – I've just woken up. I still feel really sleepy but all my tiredness has gone. The last few days seem like a nightmare. Did I really imagine the doctors were trying to poison me? And here they are now, all smiles with some tea and biscuits. They wouldn't harm a fly. That's the last time I miss a night's sleep.

CONCLUSION BY
Dr Wake and Dr Kant-Dropoff

Arthur seems fully recovered. His pulse, heart-rate and brainwaves are normal. The experiment proves lack of sleep can cause mistaken thoughts and cause other problems such as disorders to the pulse and heartbeat. It appears these can be put right by a longer than usual period of sleep.

Bet you never knew!

Although scientists no longer keep people awake, in one experiment volunteers were woken up as soon as they started to dream. The scientists wanted to find out how the brain would act if it couldn't dream. The poor volunteers ended up getting woken over 30 times a night as their brains tried harder to make them dream.

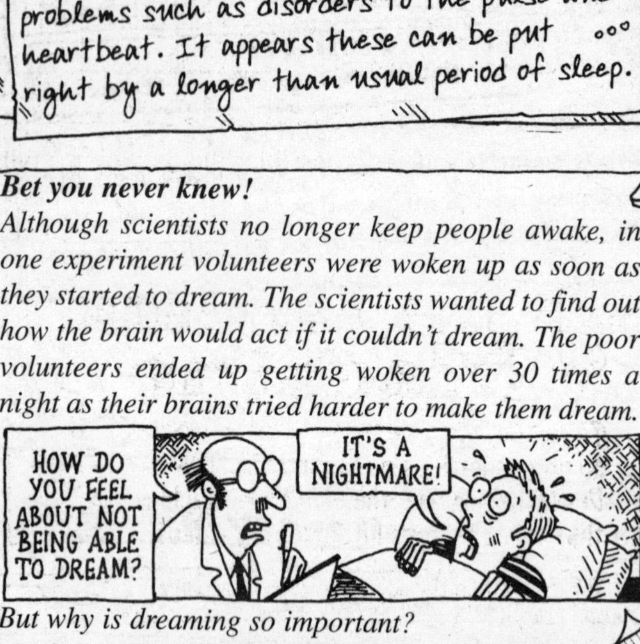

But why is dreaming so important?

Bulging fact file

NAME: Dreams

BASIC FACTS: Dreams are mixed-up memories that pass through your mind when you are asleep. Your cortex often puts them together to make a story.

DISGUSTING DETAILS: Scientists think that in the future a special kind of video camera could be invented to pick up signals in the neurons of your brain and turn them into pictures. So you could watch reruns of your happiest dreams and even your scariest nightmares – if you're brave enough.

Let's imagine it's already possible: this is how it might happen...

1 To set up the machine, plug it into your video. Strap the brainwave detecting hat to your head.

2 Go to sleep. Nothing will happen for at least 45 minutes as your body drifts from light to deeper sleep. As you relax your mouth might drop open and start to dribble – this is entirely normal.

3 After you have been to sleep for about 45 minutes your eyes will start moving under your eyelids. This is also perfectly normal. It is known as rapid eye movement (REM) sleep and it accompanies dreaming.

4 As you dream, your brainwaves will speed up and become irregular. This triggers the dream machine to start recording your dreams.

5 You will not be able to move your body whilst dreaming. Your brain squirts a chemical into the brain stem that blocks nerve messages to your muscles. This is a sensible precaution to stop you sleepwalking.

6 Relax and enjoy your dream show. Your brain will be going into REM mode about six more times during the night. And the following morning you can replay your video and entertain the whole family with your amazing dreams!

So what do you think of this invention? It sounds really good, doesn't it? Well, here's something else that will really get your little grey cells buzzing...

EPILOGUE: SOMETHING TO THINK ABOUT

With its billions of neurons and synapses your bulging brain is the most complicated object in the known universe. So it's no wonder that people find it hard to get their heads round the science of the brain. Even the experts can't make up their minds.

Bishop Nemesius of Emesia (4th century AD) reckoned...

These are the fluid-filled spaces inside the brain, remember. One thousand years later Italian scientist Mondino de Luzzi (14th century) was convinced...

Yuck! He must have had worms on the brain.

And even modern-day scientists can have misleading ideas on the brain. For example, until the 1980s many scientists believed you could decode what the brain is thinking by looking at the pattern of neuron signals. But it's now known that this pattern varies according to your mood and your level of concentration (see page 423). This means that you can have exactly the same thought and yet each time produce a different pattern of neuron signals.

At present much of what we still don't know about the brain boils down to one awkward little word: why? Why do we have emotions? Why do we sleep?

Or, even over two hundred years after Franz Gall started wondering about it...

Question, questions, questions. What do you think?

Thanks to the brilliance of the human brain, people have walked on the moon and explored the depths of the oceans. But at present we still know more about the surface of the moon or the ocean floor than the workings of our own brains. No wonder some people think we'll never find out the whole truth about our brains. They would say...

(This does make sense – just you try thinking about it!)

But, on the other hand, it's the mystery that surrounds the brain that makes brain science so exciting. And although bulging brains in tanks or dream machines are still a few years off, scientists regularly make new discoveries. They might find a new brain chemical such as serotonin that affects mood. Or perhaps a new job for an area of the brain.

For example, in 1998 scientists at the University of Iowa carried out a remarkable experiment. Healthy volunteers and people with damaged amygdalas were shown photos of faces. The volunteers thought that some faces looked untrustworthy but the brain-damaged people couldn't make these judgements. The scientists believe that in addition to shaping feelings of fear and anger the amygdala makes us distrust others. (The amygdala is part of your limbic system – see page 347 if you don't remember.) So what do you think? Would you *trust* the scientists to get it right?

Well, one thing's for sure. Scientists will never cease to search for answers to the questions posed by the brain. And it's the ability to ask questions and to seek out answers that makes us human and our brains so unique.

That really *is* something to think about.

HORRIBLE SCIENCE

Science with the squishy bits left in!

Also available:

Ugly Bugs

The insect world goes under the magnifying glass. Observe some foul families of bugs, discover the secrets of strange scientists and test the theories of insect disguise. It's swarming with info!

Nasty Nature

Have a whale of a time finding out about the animal world! Grapple with some very ferocious creatures, meet some nosey naturalists and learn how to get on with a gorilla. You'll be howling for more!

Chemical Chaos

Put chaotic chemistry to the test! Uncover the facts about experiments that went horribly wrong, discover the secrets of strange scientists and try your hand at quirky chemistry in your own kitchen.

Fatal Forces

Can you resist the urge to discover why your *ears* stop you falling off your bike? You'll also find out what keeps the moon in the sky, how quickly your fingernails grow ... and what happens when an apple smacks a scientist on the bonce!

Sounds Dreadful

Lift the lid on noise and find out how sound waves make your ear drums tremble, how a microphone turns your voice into electrical pulses ... and why you might get a nose bleed listening to church bells. It's a real scream!

HORRIBLE SCIENCE

Evolve or Die
Why are we still here when other creatures have been turned to stone, for ever? Go back millions of years to see insects as big as birds, fish with teeth and why chimps could be related to *you*.

Vicious Veg
Get stuck into a feast of info. and discover which plants eat dead insects for breakfast, why stinging nettles grow on old skeletons and which fungi can make your toes drop off. It's bloomin' amazing!

Frightening Light
Discover what stops your eyeballs from falling out, why dead bodies can make ghostly glowing lights and how a laser beam can sizzle human flesh. It's blazing with info!

Suffering Scientists Special
Read the painful potted history of scientists and their discoveries, from the first Greek brainboxes to modern-day geniuses.

Deadly Diseases
From the common cold to shocking smallpox, find out what happens when your body comes under attack from germs. You'll meet some seriously dangerous diseases.

The Awfully Big Quiz Book
Do you have what it takes to challenge a chemist or fool a physicist? The Awfully Big Quiz Book is packed with hundreds of astounding science questions for testing your friends, your teachers ... and yourself.

HORRIBLE SCIENCE

Look out for:

Microscopic Monsters

Find out how toilet germs helped catch a thief, which creature lays eggs between your *toes,* why your toothbrush is covered in germs and what makes your guts the perfect home for bacteria. This is the tiny world of science!

Explosive Experiments Special

A collection of experiments that will blow your mind! Find out how famous scientists made some of their most important discoveries and how you can test a few theories at home!

Science has never been so horrible!

Horrible Geography

Geography with the gritty bits left in!

Have you seen:

Odious Oceans

Read our roving reporter's guide to the seabed, uncover the dreadful details of the *Titanic*'s last day and see if you're nautical enough to join the Navy.

Violent Volcanoes

Find out about volcano survivors, get clued-up with the spotter's guide to eruptions and plan an explosive holiday with our very own volcano vacation guide.

Raging Rivers

Join our heroic hydrologists on a turbulent river tour from ice cap to ocean, read the secret diary of a brave river explorer and get to know your watery wildlife with our spotter's guide.

Desperate Deserts

Visit the desert where it *snows*, find out how to make a tasty pudding from camel milk and why cactus juice could be a deadly drink. Have *you* got what it takes to survive?

Look out for:

Earth-shattering Earthquakes

With Syd the seismologist as your guide, take a tour round some of the world's most dangerous places as we see what it takes to make the earth shake, and what you should do if you're caught in an earthquake.

Freaky Peaks

Follow the adventures of mountain explorers, as they climb some of the world's highest mountains. You'll see the animals that live there, the plants that survive up mountains ... and whether or not the yeti really exists.